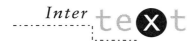
Inter

Working with Texts

'An ideal choice for foundation courses in language studies ... it is informative, challenging, engaging and entertaining. ... Major topics are explored via a wonderful range of texts and snippets, taken from truly contemporary English and popular culture in all its energetic and competitive diversity.'

Professor Michael Toolan, *University of Birmingham*

'New directions for understanding language are opened up here, for exactly those readers who have been denied access for so many years to a well-thought-out, well-designed and accessible introduction to the way in which language works.'

Professor David Birch, Foundation Professor of Communication and Media Studies, *Central Queensland University, Australia*

Working with Texts: A core book for language analysis provides a basic foundation for understanding aspects of English language crucial in the analysis of texts. The major topics covered include the sound system of spoken English, vocabulary, sentence grammar and discourse construction.

This accessible textbook, written by an outstanding team of authors, experienced in language and literature teaching, curriculum development, examining and writing, provides ideas and activities arising from experience and practice. It has multi-disciplinary appeal, but will be particularly useful to A-Level students and teachers and to under-graduates of English language, linguistics or English literature. It will also be of interest to teachers and students of EFL and ESL courses.

Ronald Carter is Professor of Modern English Language in the Department of English Studies, University of Nottingham, and the editor of the Routledge INTERFACE series in Language and Literary Studies. **Angela Goddard** is Senior Lecturer in Language at the Centre for Human Communication, Manchester Metropolitan University. **Danuta Reah** is the Principal Moderator, **Keith Sanger** a Team Leader, and **Maggie Bowring** a Moderator for NEAB English Language A-Level Investigation.

The Intertext series

◎ **Why does the phrase 'spinning a yarn' refer both to using language and making cloth?**

◎ **What might a piece of literary writing have in common with an advert or a note from the milkman?**

◎ **What aspects of language are important to understand when analysing texts?**

The Routledge INTERTEXT series will develop readers' understanding of how texts work. It does this by showing some of the designs and patterns in the language from which they are made, by placing texts within the contexts in which they occur, and by exploring relationships between them.

The series consists of a foundation text, *Working with Texts: A core book for language analysis*, which looks at language aspects essential for the analysis of texts, and a range of satellite texts. These apply aspects of language to a particular topic area in more detail. They complement the core text and can also be used alone, providing the user has the foundation skills furnished by the core text.

Benefits of using this series:

◎ **Unique** – written by a team of respected teachers and practitioners whose ideas and activities have also been trialled independently

◎ **Multi-disciplinary** – provides a foundation for the analysis of texts, supporting students who want to achieve a detailed focus on language

◎ **Accessible** – no previous knowledge of language analysis is assumed, just an interest in language use

◎ **Comprehensive** – wide coverage of different genres: literary texts, notes, memos, signs, advertisements, leaflets, speeches, conversation

◎ **Student-friendly** – contains suggestions for further reading; activities relating to texts studied; commentaries after activities; key terms highlighted and an index of terms

The series editors:

Ronald Carter is Professor of Modern English Language in the Department of English Studies at the University of Nottingham and is the editor of the Routledge INTERFACE series in Language and Literary Studies. He is also co-author of *The Routledge History of Literature in English*. From 1989 to 1992 he was seconded as National Director for the Language in the National Curriculum (LINC) project, directing a £21.4 million in-service teacher education programme.

Angela Goddard is Senior Lecturer in Language at the Centre for Human Communication, Manchester Metropolitan University, and was Chief Moderator for the Project element of English Language A-Level for the Northern Examination and Assessment Board (NEAB) from 1983 to 1995. Her publications include *The Language Awareness Project: Language and Gender*, vols I and II, 1988, and *Researching Language*, 1993 (Framework Press).

First series title:

Working with Texts: A core book for language analysis
Ronald Carter, Angela Goddard, Danuta Reah, Keith Sanger, Maggie Bowring

Satellite titles to come:

The Language of Fiction
Keith Sanger

The Language of Newspapers
Danuta Reah

The Language of Advertising: Written Texts
Angela Goddard

The Language of Poetry
John McRae

The Language of Sport
Adrian Beard

Related titles:

INTERFACE series:

Language through Literature
Paul Simpson

English in Speech and Writing
Rebecca Hughes

Variety in Written English
Tony Bex

Textual Intervention
Rob Pope

Twentieth-century Fiction
edited by Peter Verdonk and Jean Jaques Weber

Feminist Stylistics
Sara Mills

Language in Popular Fiction
Walter Nash

The Language of Jokes
Delia Chiaro

Language, Ideology and Point of View
Paul Simpson

Language, Literature and Critical Practice
David Birch

Language, Text and Context
edited by Michael Toolan

A Linguistic History of English Poetry
Richard Bradford

Working with Texts

A core book for language analysis

- Ronald Carter
- Angela Goddard
- Danuta Reah
- Keith Sanger
- Maggie Bowring

LONDON AND NEW YORK

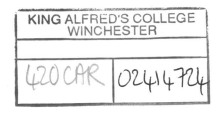
First published 1997
by Routledge
11 New Fetter Lane, London EC4P 4EE

Simultaneously published in the USA and
Canada
by Routledge
29 West 35th Street, New York, NY 10001

© 1997 Ronald Carter, Angela Goddard,
Danuta Reah, Keith Sanger, Maggie
Bowring

Typeset in Stone Sans/Stone Serif by
Solidus (Bristol) Limited

Printed and bound in Great Britain by
Butler & Tanner Ltd, Frome and London

*British Library Cataloguing in Publication
Data*

A catalogue record for this book is
available from the British Library

*Library of Congress Cataloguing in Publication
Data*

Working with texts: a core book for
language analysis/Ronald Carter . . .
[et al.].
– (Intertext)
1. English language – Discourse analysis
– Problems, exercises, etc.
2. English language – Written English
– Problems, exercises, etc.
3. Written communication
– Problems, exercises, etc.
I. Carter, Ronald
II. Series: Intertext (London, England)
PE1422.W67 1997
420'.141–dc20   96-43097
                                              CIP
                                              AC

ISBN 0–415–14596–1 (hbk)
ISBN 0–415–14597–X (pbk)

contents

Maggie Bowring is an English Language A-level Moderator for the Northern Examination and Assessment Board (NEAB), who has taught the syllabus in further education colleges for ten years. She currently teaches on A-level and degree courses at Barnsley College in South Yorkshire. She is co-author of *Something(s) to do with English Language*, 1990, and *Somemorething(s) to do with English Language*, 1994 (Pavic Publications, Sheffield Hallam University).

Ronald Carter has taught English in secondary schools and in further and higher education. From 1989 to 1992 he was National Director of the Language in the National Curriculum (LINC) project. He is currently Professor of Modern English Language in the Department of English Studies at the University of Nottingham. He is editor of the Routledge INTERFACE series in Language in Literary Studies.

Angela Goddard has taught English in primary and secondary schools, and in further and higher education. She co-ordinated the LINC Project for the Manchester area 1990–92, and was NEAB's Chief Moderator for A-Level English Language Projects from 1983 to 1995. Her previous publications include *Researching Language* (Framework Press, 1993). Currently, she works in the Centre for Human Communication at Manchester Metropolitan University.

Danuta Reah has taught English in further and higher education. She is involved in curriculum development work, writing courses for the open college network, and working as the Principal Moderator for NEAB English Language Investigation. Her previous publications include *Something(s) to do with English Language*, 1990, and *Somemorething(s) to do with English Language*, 1994 (Pavic Publications, Sheffield Hallam University). She is currently developing language and linguistic courses for students and teachers.

Keith Sanger has taught English at secondary school and sixth-form college level. He currently teaches English Literature, English Language and Theatre Studies at New College, Pontefract. He has an MA in Modern English Language from Leeds University, and has worked for many years as a team leader for NEAB's English Language A-level coursework.

acknowledgements

The following illustrations and texts have been reprinted by courtesy of their copyright holders:

1   *Ladder of Years* by Anne Tyler: Copyright © 1995 by ATM, Inc. Reprinted by permission of Alfred Knopf Inc.
2   'Why we read' and 'Why do we/adults write?': Angela Richardson and Veronica Kaiserman, LINC Primary Advisory Teachers, Tameside, Stockport and Manchester Consortium
3   Tampax advert: Abbott Mead BBDO Ltd
4   Hine advert: Thomas Hine & Co., London
5   Graphic novel *The Doll's House* by Neil Gaiman: Copyright 1990 DC Comics. All rights reserved. Used with permission.
6   Steve Bell cartoons: Steve Bell
7   England v. Spain: *Guardian*
8   Amnesty International advert: Amnesty International
9   Extract from *K is for Killer* by Sue Grafton: Molly Friedrich for Sue Grafton; Macmillan publishers
10 'Coco Chanel first introduced . . .' by Karl Plewka: *Observer*
11 'Off Course' by Edwin Morgan: Carcanet Press
12 Material from Oxfam Appeal envelope reproduced with permission of Oxfam Publishing, 274 Banbury Road, Oxford
13 Severn Trent Water advert: Severn Trent Water
14 'This is a Photograph of Me' by Margaret Atwood: © Margaret Atwood; Stoddart Publishing Co. Limited, Don Mills, Ontario
15 Friends of the Earth leaflet, 'It's Time you Joined Us': Friends of the Earth, Luton
16 'Man Critical After Pit Bull Attack': *Guardian*
17 'Gloire de Dijon' by D. H. Lawrence, from *The Complete Poems of D.H. Lawrence* by D.H. Lawrence, edited by V. de Sola Pinto and F.W. Roberts: Copyright © 1964, 1971 by Angelo Ravagli and C.M. Weekley, Executors of the Estate of Frieda Lawrence Ravagli. Used by permission of Laurence Pollinger Ltd; also Viking Penguin, a division of Penguin Books, USA Inc.
18 Sting CT advert: Monsanto PLC
19 VW advert: VW Group UK
20 Manchester City Planning material: David Kaiserman, Head of

xi

Planning and Environmental Health, Manchester City
Council

21 'Not Waving But Drowning' by Stevie Smith: Virago
Press, Little, Brown & Co.

22 Kellogg's advert: Kellogg Company of Great Britain
Ltd

23 Quaker advert: Quaker Trading Ltd

24 Ovaltine advert: Sandoz Nutrition Limited

25 Macallan advert: The Macallan Distillers Limited

26 Subaru advert: Subaru UK

27 Conservation areas advert: High Peak Borough Council

28 Extract from a speech by Michael Portillo: Michael Portillo

29 Extract from Nunan and Lockwood, 1990, *The Australian English
Course*: Cambridge University Press

30 Extract from *Lucky Sods* by John Godber: the proprietor

31 Pub sign of *The Quiet Woman*: the proprietor

32 Patwa and Standard English material: Judy Craven and Frances
Jackson, *Versions: Writing in Creole and Standard English*, Manchester
Education Committee, 1985

33 'The Fat Black Woman Goes Shopping' by Grace Nichols: Virago
Press, Little, Brown & Co., London

34 InterCity advert: Saatchi & Saatchi

Artwork for the Raleigh, BT and Leatherland adverts has been redrawn.

The publishers have made every effort to contact copyright holders
although this has not been possible in some cases. Outstanding
permissions will be remedied in future editions. Please contact Moira
Taylor at Routledge.

introduction

The contributors

The authors of this book are practitioners, with much experience of language teaching, curriculum development work, in-service training, examining and writing. The ideas and activities here have arisen from our own practice; they have also been trialled independently.

Aim of this book

The aim of this book is to provide a foundation for the analysis of texts, in order to support students in any discipline who want to achieve a detailed focus on language. No previous knowledge of language analysis is assumed; what is assumed is an interest in language use and a desire to account for the choices made by language users.

How this book is structured

The book is divided into five units which, taken together, cover the main aspects of language that it will be important to consider in any rigorous textual description:

> *Unit 1: Signs and sounds* explores some aspects of meaning in written sign systems and in the sounds that constitute the basic ingredients of spoken language;
> *Unit 2: Words and things* examines the nature of the lexical system;
> *Unit 3: Sentences and structures* considers the effects of various types of grammatical patterning;
> *Unit 4: Text and context: written discourse* focuses on the cohesive devices that tie texts together across sentence boundaries;
> *Unit 5: Text and context: spoken discourse* looks at some important aspects of spoken varieties, both in naturally occurring and in mediated texts.

Although the units represent distinct areas of language, these areas are not independent of each other in practice, when language is actually being used: for example, written symbols are combined to form words, and lexical patterning is an important aspect of written discourse. But in order to study language rather than simply use it, some systematic ways of paying attention to its various components are necessary. When working through this book, it is obviously important to understand each of the language areas being considered in the units; but it is equally important not to lose sight of language as a whole system while thinking about its parts. Practical reminders about the holistic nature of language occur in this book in a number of ways: in cross-references between the units, where some features of language are considered more than once, but from different perspectives; in analytical activities, where questions and commentaries on texts will focus on certain salient features, but will also suggest the larger picture to which these features contribute; in the developmental structure of the book, where later units will enable earlier skills to be re-applied and further enhanced.

The intention, then, is that the book should build a composite picture which enables students to appreciate the nature of texts as a whole while being able to discuss meaningfully the contributions made by different aspects of language.

Ways of working

Wherever possible, the features of language referred to are shown in operation, within texts. This means the book is not intended to be a passive reading exercise but, rather, a set of active learning materials: instead of simply being told about features, readers are asked to consider how they work within texts and in particular contexts. The wide range of different genres covered is intentional, to show that skills in analysing language can be successfully applied whatever the text, and to break down the idea that only high-status texts such as literary forms are worthy of scrutiny: literary texts are considered here, but there is equivalent, if not more, discussion of such texts as notes, memos, signs, advertisements, informative leaflets, speeches and spontaneous conversation. For students of literature, comparative studies across a range of textual types can enable interesting questions to be asked about the nature of literary language.

Commentaries are provided after many of the activities. These commentaries, which highlight and discuss some of the main points of language use, are not intended to be model answers or definitive accounts: rather, they are a way to compare readers' perceptions with those of the authors. It is hoped that readers will use these commentaries in the way that best supports their own learning.

While this book may form the basis for work in groups, it can also be used by individuals working alone. When readers work alone, the feedback that can often come via other group members is not available; the commentaries can, at least in part, make up for that.

At the end of some activities, suggestions are given for extension work. It is a common feature of many A-Level and undergraduate courses that students undertake their own language investigations. The ideas within the 'Extension' sections have this type of work in mind. As a core text, this book can only offer brief suggestions and pointers; the satellite titles that form part of the INTERTEXT series as a whole are designed to pursue many of these topics in considerably more detail.

Terminology and further reading

Because no previous knowledge of language analysis is assumed, the first usage of what is considered to be a technical term is emboldened in the text. Some of these terms are explained in context, but a brief explanation of most of these terms can be found in the 'Index of terms' at the back of this book. Suggestions for further reading are also provided.

New directions

It is an interesting time for language study. Recent projects in schools, such as LINC, and new courses in the post-16 sector, such as English Language A-Levels and new types of A-Level English Literature, have been matched in higher education programmes and research by fresh collaborations across academic disciplines that put studies of discourse at the centre. Linguistics itself, long constrained by the boundaries of the sentence, has developed a bigger vision and larger ambitions: to account for language use in a way that reflects its social purposes and its nature as a creative human resource. We hope that this book contributes to that process.

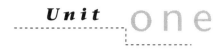

Unit one

Signs and sounds

1

Who's in the picture?

This brief section looks at signs and symbols involving human subjects.

Sounds

In this more extensive section you begin to analyse the sounds of English and how they are produced.

Texts used

- ◎ Signs and logos
- ◎ The use of birds to connote particular services or companies
- ◎ Shape poems
- ◎ Alphabets
- ◎ Early writing by young children
- ◎ Jokes, riddles and written symbols
- ◎ Extracts from novels
- ◎ Poetry and poems
- ◎ Cartoons which use signs and symbols
- ◎ Advertisements
- ◎ Visual shapes and sound patterns in texts
- ◎ Word repetitions and contrasts

Signs

WHAT IS A SIGN?

Language is sometimes referred to as a **semiotic** system.

This means that it is thought to be a system where the individual elements – 'signs' – take their overall meaning from how they are combined with other elements. The analogy that is often used to illustrate this principle is the system of road traffic lights: the red, amber and green lights work as a system, and the whole system has meaning which is not carried by any one of the lights alone, but by the lights in a certain combination and sequence. In the same way, written letters of a language are signs that have to be in a certain order to make sense to the reader, and the sounds of a language are signs that only have meaning to a hearer when they occur in predictable groups. To take this idea to its logical conclusion, it is clearly possible for the elements mentioned to occur in unpredictable ways – such as for a red and green light to occur simultaneously in a set of traffic lights, or for an invented word to have an odd spelling, such as 'mldh'; but, in these cases, we still make sense of what is happening – by explaining away these occurrences as 'breakdowns' or 'mistakes'. We are still therefore referring back to a system of rules, in defining such phenomena as deviating from what we expect.

Cultural analysts would go beyond language to look at all aspects of society as systems of signs: for example, films are a system where different signs are combined in patterned ways; dress codes embody rules where different elements can occur in many varied combinations; the area of food contains many rules about what can be combined with what, and when different foods can be eaten. In all such aspects of culture, conventions are highly culture-bound – in other words, different cultures have different semiotic systems.

Activity

This activity will focus on signs in the most traditional sense – road signs – and will explore the idea of how we read them. Look at the signs in Text: Road signs (1). These are all from an edition of the Highway Code published in the 1930s.

The originator of the idea of semiotics – the Swiss linguist, Ferdinand de Saussure – suggested that there were at least two types of sign in cases such as these: **iconic** and **symbolic**. An iconic sign tries to be a direct picture of what it refers to (although this may consist of a generalised line drawing rather than a picture in the photographic, literal sense). A symbolic sign is not a picture of what is being referred to (**referent**), but a picture of something that we associate with the referent.

◎   Which of these signs are iconic, and which symbolic?
◎   Where a sign is symbolic, how does it work – what are the associations (**connotations**) that are called up in the reader's mind?

Text: Road signs (1)

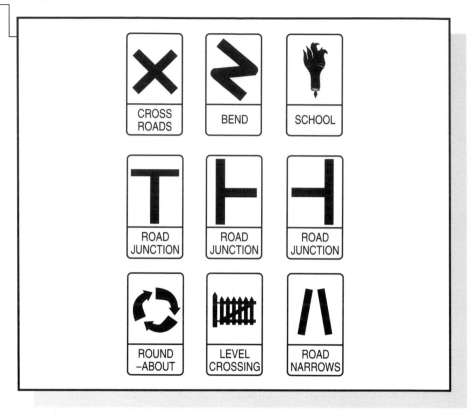

Commentary

All the signs are iconic apart from the sign for 'school'.

The 'school' sign, rather than picturing a school, symbolises a school by using a torch. This type of torch is often used on public statues, and carries classical references to such ideas as 'shedding the light of knowledge on dark areas', 'lighting up a path towards progress and civilisation' – ideas which are represented by the torch still used to mark the Olympic games. This same idea is in the word 'enlightenment', which is often used to describe a particular period in history when people looked towards classical civilisation (Ancient Greece and Rome) as ideal states.

Although all the other signs are iconic, the sign for 'crossroads' is slightly different from the rest in that it doesn't necessarily suggest the actual shape of roads coming up: instead, it takes the idea of the cross as a written symbol, and bases itself on that shape. Note that, outside the context of road signs, this shape can have other, highly symbolic, meanings – such as a 'kiss' on a personal letter, 'wrong' when written on an answer, or 'multiply' in mathematics.

Extension

Extension

Collect some examples of symbolic signs.

You might start by looking for more examples of the torch: for example, the contemporary Prudential Insurance logo; the Statue of Liberty; the logo of the Conservative Party.

Also look at a modern version of the Highway Code: how have the roads signs above changed? Do modern road signs work mainly in an iconic or symbolic way?

Activity

The fact that certain symbols call up powerful associations in the minds of readers is not lost on advertisers. The old adage 'a picture paints a thousand words' is demonstrated daily in the texts that advertising agencies produce.

In Text: Bird images are seven logos taken from texts advertising goods and services. Although each one is a picture of a bird, in each case the advertiser was using the bird image for its associations or connotations.

For each logo, write down the connotations that come to mind when you see it. Don't try to guess which product or service was being advertised, but rather concentrate on the image itself.

Text: Bird images

Commentary

The products/services and possible connotations are as follows:

1   Owl: from a small ads/services page in a local paper. The column headed by the owl logo was advertising children's reading clubs. We have connotations of the 'wise kindly old owl'; perhaps the fact that the owl has large, forward-facing eyes makes us associate the bird with reading and therefore acquiring knowledge. Or it could be that we associate reading with night-time activity, a time when the nocturnal bird is alert.

2   Sparrow: the logo of a local paper, placed in the top right hand corner of the front page, just below the title of the paper, which was *The Enquirer*. Sparrows are thought to be bold, inquisitive birds – qualities which the newspaper would presumably like to be associated with.

3   Seagull: from a holiday company. We associate seagulls with the seaside, and therefore leisure-time activities. The picture shows the seagull flying across the sun: to see the bird at this angle, we would have to be lying on our backs – presumably basking in the warmth and sunshine of a summer's day.

4   Swallow: from a futon company. Associations we have for this type of bird are likely to include grace, elegance, freedom – soaring high in the air, swooping and diving. These birds also often feature in oriental art, and the futon itself is Japanese.

5   Pelican and chicks: from an insurance company. The adult pelican is known to peck out its own feathers in order to line the nest for its chicks. Whether all readers would bring this idea to the image is doubtful, but even so the image of an adult bird with its chicks calls up associations for us of protection and security.

6   Swallow: from an airline company. The idea of 'flying high' would be something any airline would like to suggest. The design of the picture is very stylised and mechanistic, so in contrast to the futon company's 'natural' image, this picture suggests power and man-made speed, calling up the shape of an aircraft with its engines creating a slipstream of air.

7   Eagle: a bank. The eagle suggests power and strength. It has been used to symbolise the power of nation-states, as in the famous American bald eagle. It therefore calls up ideas of large, powerful institutions with extensive resources at their disposal.

There is nothing natural about the associations we have for these images: for example, the owl is, in fact, blind at night; and it would be absurd to suggest that a swallow felt 'freer' than a sparrow, that a sparrow thought of itself as cheeky, or that a seagull knew what a seaside resort was. These ideas are imposed on members of the animal kingdom by humans – a process so well recognised that we have a name for it – **anthropomorphism** (from Greek 'anthropos', human, and 'morph', shape). Further examples of this would be the 'cuddly' bear, the 'cunning' fox, the 'evil' snake. They are not universal ideas, but are culture-specific, and different cultures may well have very different connotations for the same animal.

As well as cultural associations, individuals of course bring their own experiences and feelings to images: a cuddly bear may not seem so cuddly if you've been attacked by one.

Signs such as the ones you have just been studying are powerful rhetorical devices, for a number of reasons: they call up strong associations in the mind of the reader; they are economic, using no verbal language at all, and taking up minimal space; meanings can be fluid, so there is space to manipulate, adapt and change; signs can suggest several ideas at once, so they can be multi-purpose.

The ideas behind signs such as these – here, animals as having certain characteristics – are used frequently in literary texts as forms of symbolism: for example, a poem could use a bird image, described verbally, to call up ideas about personal freedom.

How does the poem 'Easter Wings', by the seventeenth-century religious poet, George Herbert, make use of the symbol of the bird?

Text: 'Easter Wings'

Lord, who createdst man in wealth and store,
Though foolishly he lost the same,
Decaying more and more,
Till he became
Most poore:
With thee
O let me rise
As larks, harmoniously,
And sing this day thy victories:
Then shall the fall further the flight in me.
My tender age in sorrow did beginne:
And still with sickness and shame
Thou didst so punish sinne,
That I became
Most thinne.
With thee
Let me combine,
And feel this day thy victorie:
For, if I imp my wing on thine,
Affliction shall advance the flight in me.

Commentary

The symbol of the bird is at the centre of this poem (even to the extent of the title and the physical shape of the text) in that the idea of Christ's Resurrection is likened to the flight of a bird – the lark. This flight – the Redemption – is seen as all the more powerful as a result of humanity having fallen so low. The idea of falling and rising is mirrored, not just in the look of the lines, but in their meanings, too: at the smallest point are the words 'poore' and 'thinne', before the lines 'take off' again to celebrate Christ's, and therefore humanity's, ultimate victory.

AS SIMPLE AS ABC

In looking at logos, it's clear that, even if readers are not consciously analysing and interpreting them, logos bring to mind a range of associations.

Just as logos are signs, so too are our common alphabetic letters and punctuation marks. But we don't go through the same process with them – or do we?

Activity

Look at the signs in Text: Signs and logos, which are all based on the English alphabet and punctuation system. Apart from the triangular road sign, these are all company logos.

Which alphabetic letters are being featured, and what do you think each of the signs is trying to suggest?

Text: Signs and logos

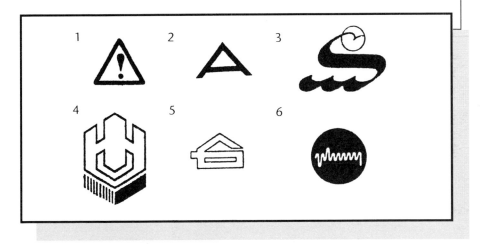

Then try to decide what possible meanings might be carried by the invented road signs below:

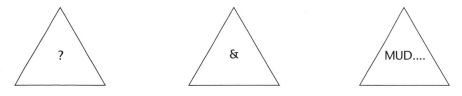

Commentary

1 The exclamation mark suggests emotive expression – presumably as a result of the shock or surprise that the driver may experience if s/he encounters the impending road feature unprepared. Notice how quickly we process the meaning of this sign, and how complex the meaning actually is. We know not to take this sign iconically – we do not expect to be showered by exclamation marks! This sign is therefore doubly symbolic – as a road sign, and as a punctuation mark.

2 This is a roofing company, using the letter 'A' to represent a traditional roof shape.

3 This is a South African cruise-line company. The letter 'S' is deployed very cleverly: to represent a ship and the sea in its shape, and to suggest **sound symbolism** (linking sounds with certain ideas) by calling up the 's' sound as well, to remind us of the sea. (See later in this unit for more exploration of sound symbolism.) In addition, the top of the 'S' becomes a seagull flying across the sun. Perhaps this company is capitalising on the fact that this has become a well-known symbol as a result of the success of another company – Thomson's – but hopes that we will associate the symbol with holidays in general rather than just the Thomson name.

4 and 5. These are both building-society logos, using an H and a G respectively. The associations we have may be for different types of building, the three-dimensional 'H' resembling a castle structure (an 'Englishman's home') while the 'G' appears as a more modest residence, such as a bungalow.

6 This is Plessey Radar. The writing looks like the company name, with the added suggestion of the kind of electrical impulse produced by a sophisticated piece of equipment – a radar screen, perhaps in a military installation. On the other hand, the machine could be registering a human pulse in a hospital context: a company with a scientific profile would benefit from being seen as humane and concerned with saving life.

The invented road signs could be as follows (note that there are no right and wrong answers for these): the question mark could suggest that there may be some impending danger, but that the author of the sign can't be quite sure; the ampersand, meaning 'addition', could suggest a traffic jam; 'mud . . .' could be hinting that mud is coming up, but something else might also occur after that.

Collect some company/institutional logos and categorise them according to headings which you yourself devise: for example, below is the official logo from Nottingham University, and there are two more of these from different universities in Unit 4 of this book. One heading, therefore, could be 'university logos' and your analysis would explore what the various establishments were trying to suggest about themselves by their logos.

English alphabetic letters are not symbols in the way the earliest forms of our writing were, where written symbols pictured what they represented: such symbols, called 'pictograms' or 'pictographs', have been discovered in many parts of the world — for example, Egypt (dated around 3000 BC) and China (1500 BC). The pictogram would be similar to one of the letters A, G or H in the previous activity standing for the whole concept of 'house' in all contexts and occurrences. In contrast to this, the English writing system is quite closely related to sound: there is a basic correspondence between written symbols (**graphemes**) and sounds (**phonemes**), although there are many exceptions (see later in this unit). Because of this relationship, knowing about speech in early childhood is a good basis for the acquisition of written language, the learning of which is a long, slow process.

FROM SPEECH TO WRITING

By the time we have reached adulthood, most of us have forgotten what it felt like to move from spoken to written language, and to encounter, not just a whole new set of conventions in terms of the features of writing, but a new set of rules about functions as well: just what are the purposes of written language? Why bother to have it at all? Why pay so much attention to it?

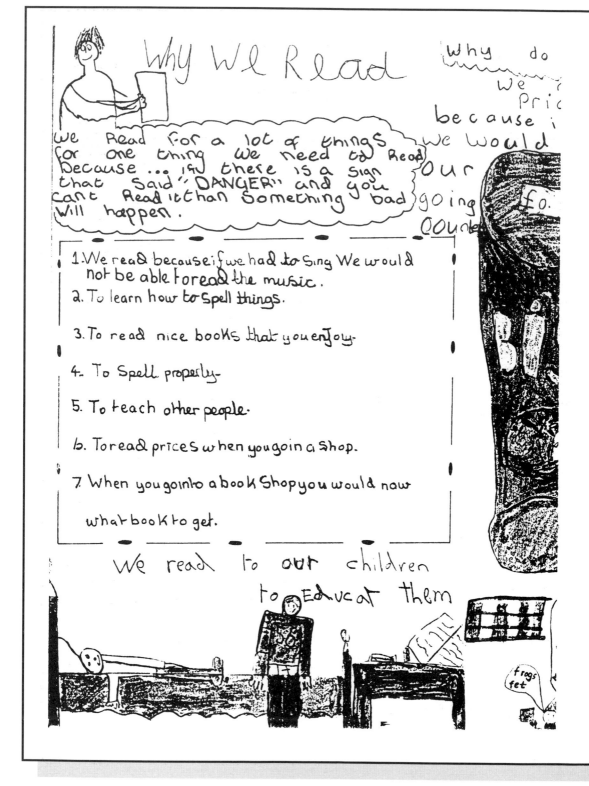

Why We Read

Why do We Pri because we would Our going f0. Counter

We Read for a lot of things for one thing We need to Read because ... if there is a sign that said "DANGER" and you cant Read it than Something bad will happen.

1. We read because if we had to Sing We would not be able to read the music.

2. To learn how to Spell things.

3. To read nice books that you enjoy.

4. To Spell properly.

5. To teach other people.

6. To read prices when you go in a Shop.

7. When you go into a book Shop you would now what book to get.

We read to our children to Educat them

frogs fet

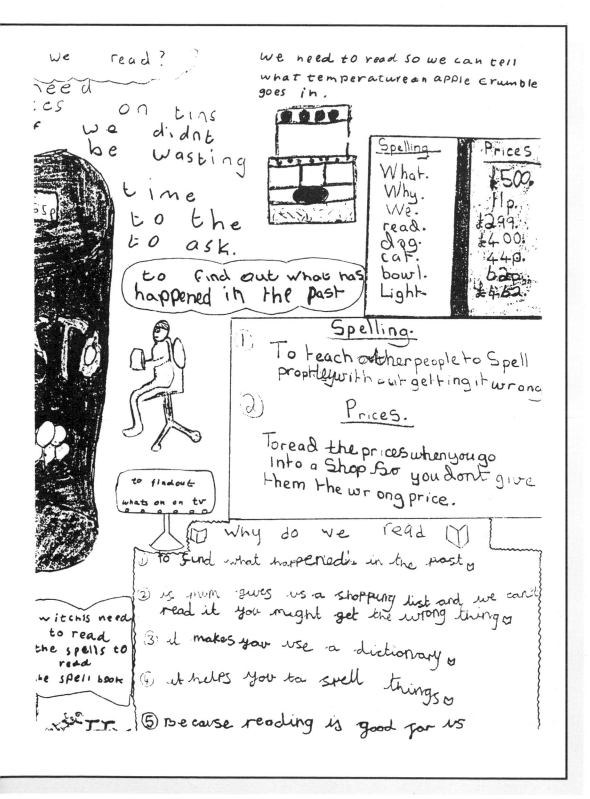

we read?

need
:es on tins
f we didnt
be wasting
time
to the
to ask.

to find out whats has happened in the past

We need to read so we can tell what temperature an apple crumble goes in.

to find out whats on on tv

Spelling	Prices
What.	£500.
Why.	11p.
We.	£299.
read.	£400.
dog.	44p.
cat.	62p.
bowl.	£4.62
Light.	

Spelling.

1. To teach other people to Spell properly without getting it wrong

2. ### Prices.

To read the prices when you go Into a Shop so you dont give them the wrong price.

witchis need
to read
the spells to
read
he spell book

Why do we read

1. To find what happened's in the past

2. if mum gives us a shopping list and we can't read it you might get the wrong thing

3. it makes you use a dictionary

4. it helps you ta spell things

5. Because reading is good for us

Text: Why do we/adults write?

in cause of checks and writing letters cards and to tell things to people they dont see.

They write to get atention and to cheques and lots of other things like that. Oh and Bills.

My mum writes crosswords.
my Dad writes cheques.
my Grandma writes bets for the horses.
So does my Grandad

My mother writes letters to her friends

Grown ups write crosswords and shopping lists.

They write cheques Letters Bank and holliday Letters.

They write to relitaves to tell them what happend.

Grown-ups write to the milk man

because they need to.

I dobt no

My mum and dad use a computer to write essays and important things for work.

Why do grown-ups write ?

Why do we write?

14

We write because in the future we will beadul to spell.

To become clever and Work.

you write to become clever and get a job

I write mostly for pleasure and because I want to. I write for school and to keep up ideas for my best stories.

Sometimes you write to communicate with people or to remember something.

for fun. and edjercashon. and writeing boobes

so People can read it instead of hearing it

Because it gives my hand excercise

I write to communicate

Sometimes I have to.

I write because it is relaxing and you sometimes learn from it

I write because its nice to know that you can and it gives my mind a rest.

because it is a way to explan.

Because I am told

We write so we can learn and if you cant write you cant read and then you can't learn.

I write because I enjoy writing sometimes.

I write because the teacher makes us.

15

Read through the comments in Text: Why we read, and Text: Why do we/ adults write? They are from classes of 7–8 year olds, asked about the purposes of writing and reading. What ideas come through here, and how do their ideas compare with your own – what do *you* see as the functions of written language?

Commentary

Some of the ideas that are expressed by the children could be grouped as follows:

1   The importance of literacy in terms of day-to-day functioning: reading recipes, seeing signs for danger, not being cheated in shops, finding out what's on TV, leaving notes for the milkman, writing shopping lists and cheques, and putting bets on. These are all ways of controlling and negotiating our world, and illustrate the importance of reading and writing as forms of instrumental, everyday communication.

2   Written language is seen as the repository of knowledge and therefore a means of educating ourselves. Writing produces tangible permanent artifacts – books – and as such is the archive of a culture's ideas and attitudes. To gain access to this store, we need to be able to read.

3   Written language is associated with being 'clever' and getting a job. In contemporary society, we take for granted the idea that literacy should be a universal entitlement. But compulsory schooling only started in 1870; traditionally, while spoken language was universal, writing was a very particular skill, learned only by those who were formally educated. In medieval times, writing was a professional skill – 'scribing' – for which money would be charged.

Even though we now view literacy as a basic skill for everyone, we still have a legacy which connects literacy with power in all sorts of ways, from the most obvious – the importance we give to written exams and application forms, the way we pay large sums of money to lawyers to write our legal documents and 'translate' them for us – to the slightly more subtle – the importance of signing your name (as opposed to giving a verbal agreement), the way libel is seen as a valid legal concept, while slander is not taken as seriously.

4   Both the pleasure and the labour of using literacy skills come across

here. Unlike speech, which is spontaneous and feels relatively effort-less, both writing and reading are skills which require concentration and subtle co-ordination of hand and eye movements, aside from all the different types of linguistic processing that they entail.

Observing children's transition from spoken to written language can give us many insights into how written texts work for us as adults.

Activity

Text: Jonathon is a piece of writing by Jonathon, age 4, reporting on his day out to Blackpool. In it, the writer uses initial letters to stand for whole words; the child's teacher wrote the full lines of text, after Jonathon read his writing back to her.

Using initial letters to stand for whole words is a common stage for early writers: it signals that a crucial connection has been made between speech and writing, but that not enough of each whole word can be mapped out in order to represent it graphically. Initial letters can be a useful aide-mémoire, to recall the whole word if necessary at some later stage (as here – it was two days later that Jonathon read his text back to the teacher); in learning the manual skill of writing, the hand quickly tires. This method is therefore a good way of writing a long text – something any teacher in the vicinity would be encouraging. Note also the impor-tance of drawing in early texts such as these, where pictures are often an integral part of the writing. It is only the adult world that puts strong boundaries around these two types of activity, putting them into the separate categories of 'art' and 'writing'; for children who have yet to learn about the way adults divide up the world of representation, one type of symbolic mark must be much like another. It is well known that early drawing (what adults sometimes disparagingly call 'scribbling') is good preparation for the very fine movements needed to produce alphabetic letters.

Text: Jonathon

Where, in adult texts, do we use single letters or abbreviated forms of words on a regular basis? How do such alterations work? Are our reasons for doing this the same as Jonathon's? To get you started, read through Text: Estate agent's advert, then abbreviate the words as far as you can without removing the ability of the reader to reconstitute them:

Text: Estate agent's advert

Beautifully restored nineteenth-century farmhouse with two reception rooms, a large kitchen, three bedrooms, a bathroom and separate toilet. There is gas central heating throughout the house. Outside the property, there is a substantial double garage, and extensive gardens and outhouses. All the carpets and curtains are included in the selling price, which is £85,000 or nearest offer.

Commentary

In abbreviating the description of the house, you will have omitted many of the vowels (except where a vowel starts a word) but retained many of the consonants. This approach is at the basis of other examples of abbreviation, such as in 'T-line' shorthand. However, some words have such a distinctive profile, or are used so often in abbreviated form, that we come to understand them even when given only the first part of the word, especially when we see them used in a particular context – for example, the estate agent's material could have had 'beaut', '19thC', 'rec', 'sep', 'ext' and 'incl'. Some phrases are often abbreviated to initial letters (called **initialisms**) where this occurs on a regular basis: for example, GCH regularly means 'gas central heating', and ONO 'or nearest offer'. The latter examples are not very different from the child's strategy of initial-letter use; this same technique is also used regularly in personal ads (where GSOH in lonely hearts' columns means 'good sense of humour' and WLTM means 'would like to meet'), and in road signs – such as P for 'Parking' and H for 'hospital'. **Acronyms** also feature single letters, but they are then pronounced as whole words, whether recognised as a collection of letters (as in NATO) or not (as in laser – 'light amplification by the stimulated emission of radiation').

The reasons for our uses of initialisms and abbreviations in adult texts could be determined by any one or several of the following factors: financial cost of advertising space (e.g. estate agents, personal ads); demands on the memory made by having to remember the whole word or series of words (e.g. acronyms); the need for speed in writing (e.g. shorthand), reading (e.g. roadsigns) or speaking (e.g. initialisms which enable us to refer quickly to institutions or artifacts – BBC, TV, CD-ROM, PC).

19

Extension

Collect as many examples as you can find of texts that use abbreviations, initialisms and acronyms. When you have collected your material, sort your examples into groups according to the techniques they use. Try to draw some conclusions about the reasons for the usages you have collected. If you are unsure about the comprehensibility of some of your examples, test them out on some informants of your own.

One area that hasn't been covered, but which you could explore in your data collection, is that of jokes, puzzles and riddles which involve playing around with written symbols. For example, some use single letters (but not necessarily initial letters) to stand for whole words, as in the following hoarding outside a church:

WHAT'S MISSING FROM THIS CH--CH?

You might find some more examples like this in children's comics and magazines, or in some types of English school textbook.

Activity

Another area where children can teach us a lot about the resources of written texts is that of sound effects. The writing system has a range of ways to call up some of the aspects of sound that we learn to pay attention to as part of the meaning of spoken language.

Read through the two children's stories in Text: Omar, and Text: Lauren.

How are these children using aspects of written language to try to suggest sound?

Text: Omar

Ones a ponc Tieem Therer
wes a hntb hous no one
went to the casel Be coos The
Spereit The Spereit
meycs pecPeL Then into
goost

Omar.s

21

~~The~~ ~~I~~ my brithday

When it was my brithday I went to
a island for a picnic.. I take
Simone and megan. We went in a boat
Ween we got there we played for
a bitr then we had. The picnic.
~~then~~ we came to going home the
boat had gone I Started to
cry. I whant to go home
Simone had a ~~they~~ I decu We can
make a ward out of pebbles.
What is the ward going to
Say ~~hdpt~~ help??? yes Side
megan. lasts get going I ho
I ho its of to work We
go There ~~we have~~ ~~work~~
Wave finish. At home mum
and dad had Send a
Sertch party. At the island
the were sitting woting.
A helicopter they Saw the
Words h.e.l.p then we all
Side hepp. the helicopter
came with laders we ~~clamd~~
Clamnd up.

Lauren.

Omar (age 5) enhances his story with a picture where a ghostly figure makes 'ooooo' sounds, in an attempt to provide something of an atmospheric soundtrack. This also occurs within the text itself: the reader knows that the words 'The Spirit, The Spirit' need to be pronounced in a 'spooky' way, as a result of their having wobbly lines round them. It's difficult to say exactly where this convention is from, but likely contenders could be comics and those science-fiction films where the screen 'dissolves' as the narrator goes back in time to remember 'when it all began'. (Note the very logical sound-based spelling, 'ones a pone tieem' for 'once upon a time'.)

Lauren (age 7) uses a range of devices to suggest features of spoken language: the enlargement of letters and the darker print in the words 'gone' and 'help?' suggest increased volume – in the first word, as a result of shock, and in the second, to signal a voice calling out. The question mark on 'help' indicates a speaker's raised voice when asking another character whether that is the right word to use. While the characters work to build their word out of pebbles, there is a soundtrack: 'Hi ho, hi ho, it's off to work we go'. This is particularly appropriate, as in *Snow White and the Seven Dwarfs*, from which the soundtrack comes, the dwarfs sing this as they go off stone-breaking in the mines. The sense of time passing, as the characters go through a laborious routine of repetitive work, is therefore achieved.

Towards the end, there is a clever use of full-stops to indicate that the letters in the word 'h.e.l.p.' are written (in pebbles, of course) rather than spoken.

Activity

If writers can use aspects of writing to suggest sound, this is unlikely to remain unnoticed by the advertisers of hi-fi equipment.

Text: Metz & Rahmen is an advert for personal stereos.

Identify the written language devices being used by the advertisers to refer to or represent aspects of sound. (Note: there is no commentary on this activity.)

Text: Metz & Rahmen

Lots of people settle for any old personal stereo —they jusst put up with the hissSing and accept that sometimes only one earpiece works at a time. They TURN UP THE VOLUME until the sound is so distorted that its just a NIGHTMARE Then, just when they're listening to their favourite music, their batteries *conk out on them*..... or their headphones drop to bits in their lap. Not with Metz & Rahmen.
EEZZZy listening that's a dream .

(((M&R)))

Activity

Writers of fiction often try to give the reader a sense of spoken language, in a variety of ways: they may want to construct a 'voice' for the narrator, so that the reader can distinguish this address from the language used by the characters; there are the various voices of the characters themselves when they are talking to each other; and there are 'inner voices' in the form of the thoughts of the characters, relayed to readers by the narrator.

Below is an extract from *Ladder of Years*, by Anne Tyler, published in 1996. It is the opening of the novel.

◎ How does the writer use graphological features – in particular, punctuation and variations in typeface – to suggest aspects of spoken discourse?

◎ How much cannot be conveyed by such features, but has to be explained by the narrator directly, in the form of description?

Text: *Ladder of Years*

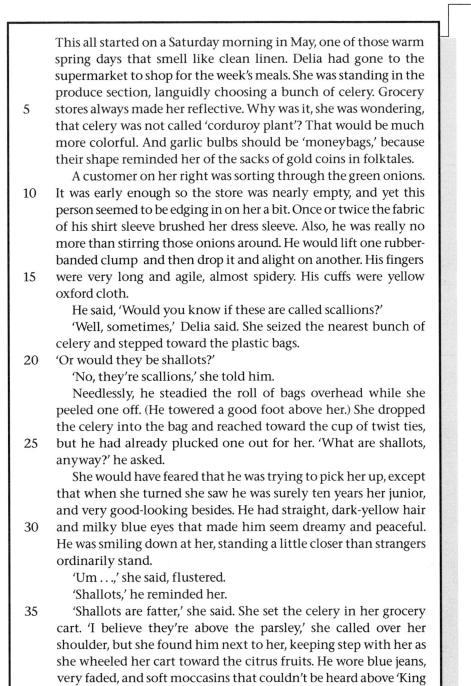

5

10

15

20

25

30

35

This all started on a Saturday morning in May, one of those warm spring days that smell like clean linen. Delia had gone to the supermarket to shop for the week's meals. She was standing in the produce section, languidly choosing a bunch of celery. Grocery stores always made her reflective. Why was it, she was wondering, that celery was not called 'corduroy plant'? That would be much more colorful. And garlic bulbs should be 'moneybags,' because their shape reminded her of the sacks of gold coins in folktales.

A customer on her right was sorting through the green onions. It was early enough so the store was nearly empty, and yet this person seemed to be edging in on her a bit. Once or twice the fabric of his shirt sleeve brushed her dress sleeve. Also, he was really no more than stirring those onions around. He would lift one rubber-banded clump and then drop it and alight on another. His fingers were very long and agile, almost spidery. His cuffs were yellow oxford cloth.

He said, 'Would you know if these are called scallions?'

'Well, sometimes,' Delia said. She seized the nearest bunch of celery and stepped toward the plastic bags.

'Or would they be shallots?'

'No, they're scallions,' she told him.

Needlessly, he steadied the roll of bags overhead while she peeled one off. (He towered a good foot above her.) She dropped the celery into the bag and reached toward the cup of twist ties, but he had already plucked one out for her. 'What are shallots, anyway?' he asked.

She would have feared that he was trying to pick her up, except that when she turned she saw he was surely ten years her junior, and very good-looking besides. He had straight, dark-yellow hair and milky blue eyes that made him seem dreamy and peaceful. He was smiling down at her, standing a little closer than strangers ordinarily stand.

'Um . . .,' she said, flustered.

'Shallots,' he reminded her.

'Shallots are fatter,' she said. She set the celery in her grocery cart. 'I believe they're above the parsley,' she called over her shoulder, but she found him next to her, keeping step with her as she wheeled her cart toward the citrus fruits. He wore blue jeans, very faded, and soft moccasins that couldn't be heard above 'King

25

40 of the Road' on the public sound system.

'I also need lemons,' he told her.

She slid anoher glance at him.

'Look,' he said suddenly. He lowered his voice. 'Could I ask you a big favor?'

45 'Um ...'

'My ex-wife is up ahead in potatoes. Or not ex I guess but ... estranged, let's say, and she's got her boyfriend with her. Could you just pretend we're together? Just till I can duck out of here?'

'Well, of course,' Delia said.

50 And without even taking a deep breath first, she plunged happily back into the old high-school atmosphere of romantic intrigue and deception. She narrowed her eyes and lifted her chin and said, 'We'll *show* her!' and sailed past the fruits and made a U-turn into root vegetables. 'Which one is she?' she murmured

55 through ventriloquist lips.

'Tan shirt,' he whispered. Then he startled her with a sudden burst of laughter. 'Ha, ha!' he told her too loudly. 'Aren't you clever to say so!'

But 'tan shirt' was nowhere near an adequate description. The

60 woman who turned at the sound of his voice wore an ecru raw-silk tunic over black silk trousers as slim as two pencils. Her hair was absolutely black, cut shorter on one side, and her face was a perfect oval. 'Why, Adrian,' she said. Whoever was with her – some man or other – turned too, still gripping a potato. A dark, thick

65 man with rough skin like stucco and eyebrows that met in the middle. Not up to the woman's standard at all; but how many people were?

Delia's companion said, 'Rosemary. I didn't see you. So don't forget,' he told Delia, not breaking his stride. He set a hand on her cart to steer it into aisle 3. 'You promised me you'd make your

70 marvelous blancmange tonight.'

'Oh, yes, my ... blancmange,' Delia echoed faintly. Whatever blancmange might be, it sounded the way she felt just then: pale and plain-faced and skinny, with her freckles and her frizzy brown curls and her ruffled pink round-collared dress.

75 They had bypassed the dairy case and the juice aisle, where Delia had planned to pick up several items, but she didn't point that out because this Adrian person was still talking. 'Your blancmange and then your, uh, what, your meat and vegetables and da-da-da ...'

> 80 The way he let his voice die reminded her of those popular songs that end with the singers just absentmindedly drifting away from the microphone. 'Is she looking at us?' he whispered. 'Check it out. Don't make it obvious.'
>
> Delia glanced over, pretending to be struck by a display of converted rice. Both the wife and the boyfriend had their backs to her, but there was something artificial in their posture. No one
> 85 could find russet potatoes so mesmerizing. 'Well, she's mentally looking,' Delia murmured. She turned to see her grocery cart rapidly filling with pasta. Egg noodles, rotini, linguine - Adrian flung in boxes at random. 'Excuse me . . .,' she said.

Commentary

David Crystal's *The Cambridge Encyclopedia of the English Language* (1995) lists four main functions for punctuation: grammar, where features such as full stops and commas mark out grammatical units; prosody, where such symbols as speech marks, question marks and exclamation marks indicate that someone is speaking, and that their voice is behaving in certain ways; rhetoric, where some forms of punctuation – most notably, colons – and semi-colons, map out aspects of argument or explanation (as in this paragraph); and semantic nuance, where features of emphasis such as quotation marks suggest a particular attitude to a word or phrase being 'marked out'.

Anne Tyler uses punctuation to mark out grammatical units in the same way as writers of many other types of text. There are two examples of the rhetorical function listed above: these are a colon in line 72, which points forward to the explanation that follows it, and the semi-colon in line 66 which balances the sentences either side of the punctuation mark, bringing them into more dramatic parallel than a comma would do, and leading up to a rhetorical question (a question posed for effect, rather than one requiring a real answer).

What is noticeable, however, is Tyler's extensive use of the prosodic and the semantic nuance functions. This is hardly suprising, given that these are concerned with constructing a sense of voice, and with establishing attitudes.

Examples of the prosodic function: within the language of the characters themselves – speech marks, lines of dots suggesting a voice trailing off, question marks, exclamation marks, italics to suggest emphasis; within the language used by the narrator, brackets and dashes in lines 23, 63 and 64, 88 and 89 to suggest a change in pace as a result of adding extra information.

Examples of the semantic nuance function: quotation marks in the narrator's report of Delia's thoughts in lines 6 and 7; the same in the narrator's commentary in lines 39 and 59.

Despite these extensive markers, there is still much about the way the characters speak that has to be described by the narrator. Here are some examples: 'she called over her shoulder'; 'he lowered his voice'; 'she murmured through ventriloquist lips'; 'he whispered'; 'he startled her with a sudden burst of laughter'; 'he told her too loudly'; 'Delia echoed faintly'; 'the way he let his voice die reminded her . . .'.

These examples illustrate that, in the end, written language cannot do justice to the subtleties of speech. All it can do is to give us some signposts as readers, via devices such as punctuation marks, to help us create the idea of speech in our heads.

Extension

Collect some texts that are using features of written language in order to suggest aspects of speech. You could focus on a particular area: for example, children's early writing; advertising; literature.

SPACE-SHIFTING

In computer language, space is treated as if it were a mark on the page; it therefore has the same status as a punctuation mark or a letter. The fact that this seems like an odd notion is evidence of how much we take space in written texts for granted, both in its existence and where it should occur: in English, words have gaps between them, lines of writing are separated by space, pages have no-go areas called 'margins', application forms announce sternly 'do not write below this line'. Rules about space are part of the way we formulate rules about textual shape.

Space is actually meaningful in a variety of ways. To begin with, different languages have very different rules about orientation - Arabic reads from right to left, Chinese from top to bottom - therefore ideas about where spaces should occur will be different, leading to different written patterns.

28

It's also clear that we have notions, as readers, of an appropriate amount of space in and around texts: for example, we talk about some forms of writing being off-putting because they look too densely packed, or some texts looking rather hectic and 'busy', perhaps because the writing in them is set at odd angles on the page or contains overlaps; we might also say that writing looks rather 'lost' on a page because it doesn't fill the space adequately. Such ideas about crowds and loneliness appear to vary according to a number of factors associated with the reader – age being one significant dimension: the size of print, the amount of space left on the page, and the ratio of verbal language to pictures will be very different in a children's reader compared with a book such as this one.

Activity

Space, defining the shape of a text, is also one powerful way of recognising different types of writing (also called **genres**). This activity will test out how far it is possible to identify different written genres without being able to read any of the actual words the texts contain. First, brainstorm as many distinctively different types of writing as you can think of. Here are some examples, to start you off:

◎ shopping list
◎ menu
◎ recipe
◎ letter
◎ poem
◎ newspaper article.

When you have exhausted your list, without writing any words, draw the shape of each of your texts by using lines to represent the shape of the writing, and boxes to show artwork such as photographs. You can use any number of different lines, plus asterisks, bullet points, arrows, or any ornamental features you want to include. Here is an example of a shopping list:

_____

_____

_____

_____

_____

_____

_____

When you have finished drawing your texts, swop them with those from other students in your group, without saying what the texts are: see how many can be guessed accurately. There may well be more than one possible outcome for a particular shape: where this happens, try to see what the various 'guesses' have in common in terms of their nature and purpose.

Activity

Because particular written genres are associated with certain shapes, the idea of textual shape can be used by one text to suggest another.

Look at Text: Tampax, which appeared in a magazine aimed at teen-age girls.

◎   How does this advert use aspects of shape and design to convey its message?

◎   What other texts might the advert be imitating?

Commentary

At first glance, this advert could be mistaken for a problem page.

It is well known that problem pages excite interest from magazine readers, so for an advert to imitate this feature is a good way to attract attention. (Where one text refers to or bases itself on another text this is called 'intertextuality'.) It does this very cleverly, by the use of variations in the boldness of type and by choosing a column format. Even when the reader realises that the text is not a problem page, the fact that menstrual issues often feature as 'problematic' means that the reader might still see a link between the advert and an 'agony aunt' feature. A problem–solution format is a very common approach in advertising texts in general. Here, menstruation is the 'problem'; the product is the reader's ally in helping her fight back with 'attitude'. In reinforcing the advert's assertive message, the cartoon figure and the figure's personal voice suggest a useful ambiguity: the girl is confident psychologically, in terms of her own allure, and physically, in her ability to protect herself in a fight.

Other texts which may be called up include news reports (for information value) and news articles setting out an individual's personal argument or opinion (for the idea of personal endorsement).

Beyond individual genres, the whole layout of this advert suggests assertiveness in going against established conventions: the image is on the right rather than the left; the 'hook' line is at the bottom rather than the top; the coupon starts, rather than finishes, the text. By these means, the advert's whole layout expresses 'attitude', fighting back against the traditions of its own genre in the same way as the girl is exhorted to fight back against traditional notions of menstruation.

Activity

As well as different written genres having particular shapes, certain genres of writing can exploit the nature of text shape as a form of art, iconic (representational) or otherwise. One example of this is concrete poetry, where the shape of the text draws a picture of the thing or idea being described: George Herbert's 'Easter Wings' (p. 8) used this strategy. A slightly more oblique approach is illustrated by Text: Road signs (2) (from the same Highway Code as the signs on p. 4), where the idea of a human form is suggested by the shape. Although this is not a direct picture of the idea 'halt', it was perhaps intended to soften the command element of the sign by giving it a human face, or to call up the idea of a policeman directing traffic.

Of course you have loads of things in your life other than boys, like er,......... well OK, like clothes for instance.

And isn't it nice just occasionally to wear that dress that isn't just drop-dead gorgeous but more drop-dead-roll-over-bite-the-furniture-and-drool-like-a-pathetic-dog gorgeous?

Let's be clear what we're talking about here.

It's the kind of dress you need attitude to wear.

It's the kind of dress you may even need a padded bra to wear.

And it's the kind of dress that you definitely do not need a towel to wear.

The trouble is, that party that HE is definitely going to be at and where HE will be knocked out by the sheer power of your sex appeal and HE will finally become putty in your hands, is on the same day that IT arrives.

Your period. With its impeccable sense of timing.

Tampax tampons are made for this kind of thing. Because you don't have to feel one jot less confident when you have your period than when you don't.

And no matter how short your skirt or how tight your PVC, no one will have a clue that it's anything other than a normal day of the month.

Tampax tampons thoughtfully come in four absorbencies to suit the various different stages of your period.

There are higher absorbencies for your heavier days, and mini ones for those lighter days.

So you can feel perfectly confident there's no danger of leaking.

And don't worry about inserting it correctly. The applicator always places the tampon in exactly the right place inside you. So you won't be able to feel or see a thing.

Although there's nothing more natural than your period, there are times when there is nothing more uncomfortable.

Tampons aren't about making your period disappear; they just stop it dictating what you have to wear and when you have to wear it.

After all, who says that just because you are having your period, you stop being

attractive to boys? Certainly not boys.

But you don't have to just take our word for it.

If you fill out the coupon at the top of the page and send it to us, we'll send you some free samples. In plenty of time for your next party.

Then you can get on with what you do best.

Inflicting some really serious damage on those floorboards.

just because i'm having my period, it doesn't stop me enjoying the sound of a chin hitting the floor.

Text: Road signs (2)

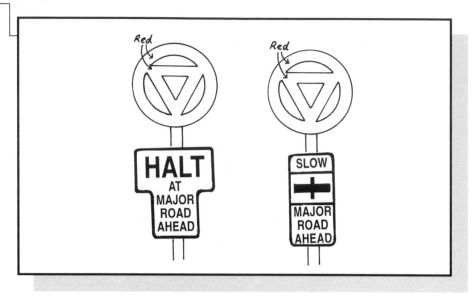

Read Text: Hine, which uses an eye-catching shape as part of its presentation.

What is the shape trying to suggest, and how does it work alongside the other aspects of the text?

Les Secrets Précieux de

HINE

LE CERF

The stag has always occupied a prime position among the symbols deployed by thirsty mankind. Its antlers graced the ale-halls of the Vikings, Gauls & Saxons. So when, 125 years ago the (originally English) Hine family were looking for an emblem for the century-old cognac house, there wasn't a single objection when some wag suggested a play on the family name. It couches on the label to this very day, reminding you to ask for Hine as in 'hind' & not, as some try to frenchify it, 'Een' when ordering this graceful & majestic of spirits.

COGNAC IS OUR HERITAGE.

Commentary

The shape could represent either the idea of 'spirit' (the heady perfume of the cognac being released; the 'genie' from the bottle) or the idea of filtration, depending on whether you read the text as emerging from the bottle or being poured down into it through a filter funnel. In either case, the symbol of the stag sits at the top as somehow connoting the quintessential qualities of the cognac, suggesting supremacy and majesty, appearing twice: once in the style of a classic painting or woodcut, and again as if part of an aristocratic coat of arms – the kind of stone carving that decorates the entrance to a stately home. The ideas of family and heritage are picked up in the verbal text in the references to the family name and in how to pronounce it.

The text expresses satisfaction in revealing that the name was originally English, thus overturning our association of all things French with 'the finer things in life'; and implying the cutting down to size of those English speakers who think themselves superior because they know that certain words are of French derivation, and insist on pronouncing them accordingly. The text therefore claims aristocratic heritage for its product, but is also appearing to champion the cause of the common man – found in the Viking and Anglo-Saxon drinking halls, fighting but certainly not 'Frenchifying'. The Hine family were ordinary folk, not averse to a waggish joke. The phrase 'common man' has been used advisedly in this commentary, for although the name is pronounced like 'hind' (female red deer), the product is being associated with male lineage, stag nights rather than hen parties.

At the bottom of the text is the slogan 'Cognac is our heritage'. It is interesting to consider whose heritage is being referred to.

Extension

Collect as many pieces of writing as you can find that use textual shape as part of their message. Draw your own conclusions about how the texts work, then test out your impressions on other people, by asking them to read the texts and comment on them.

WHO'S IN THE PICTURE?

So far, the focus has been on signs and symbols involving non-human images. But pictures can also feature people and, as with all the signs that have been studied so far in this unit, there is no such thing as any simple neutrality: the way people are represented can call up powerful connotations that work alongside the verbal language in a text. Analysing images in the form of photographs, paintings and drawings is clearly a large area in its own right. To do justice to this, a range of academic areas would need to be addressed – including art, media studies, cultural studies and anthropology. But the fact that analysing images may open up several more academic areas doesn't mean that language analysts can simply ignore visual aspects, since images form an important part of the way we 'read' the world. What is offered here, then, is a set of headings and questions as a starting point: if you want to explore this area further now, look through this book, fix on some of the texts that use images as part of their message, and apply the ideas below to them. On the other hand, you may decide to come back to these questions later, as you deal with the texts that form part of each unit.

Content: what is the content of the picture?

- ◎   What artifacts are in the picture?
- ◎   Are there any non-human beings in the picture?
- ◎   What people are included?: consider gender, age, ethnicity, occupation, social class, region, sexuality.
- ◎   What is the setting?

Genre: how is the content being presented?

- ◎   What is being suggested by the content and how it is set up? For example, does it involve a story of some kind, where certain types of people might own the artifacts in the picture, or where some action has occurred before the image was 'captured'?
- ◎   How does the reader use his/her cultural knowledge to make sense of the picture and the way the items relate to each other within it?

Techniques: what are some of the mechanisms and effects?

- ◎   What method of representation has been chosen, and why (for example, photograph, line drawing, painting, computer-generated image)?
- ◎   How is the viewer's position established by the techniques used (for example, camera angle, perspective, body language and eye

contact of the 'actors')? Is the viewer in a more or less powerful position than the people or things in the picture?

◎ Does the picture presume that the viewer is interacting with it in some way?

◎ What colours and dress codes are present? What technical treatments have been used (for example, glossy surfaces, sepia tints, soft focus photography)?

Inter-relationships

How do features of the image relate to the verbal aspects of the text? Does the whole text refer to or base itself on another text and, if so, why? If so, what part does the picture play in this?

Agencies and audiences

On the evidence of the answers to the previous questions, what cultural attitudes and values are being presented by the producers? What assumptions are made about the audience's views, interests and composition?

Sounds

Just as signs connote ideas for language users, so do sounds.

Sound as a system is primary: it is the first code learnt by individuals in their lives; it also came before writing historically as a system of communication for humans in general. However, the fact that speech is primary does not mean that our responses to sound are simple and straightforward. The way we talk about sound, for example, is often metaphorical, where we describe sounds not in terms of our hearing, but in terms of our other senses: we say some sounds are 'big', 'small' or 'rounded' (sight); some are 'piercing', 'hard', 'soft' or 'abrasive' (touch); others are 'sweet' (taste). We have developed systems for the interpretation of sounds that may or may not have a base in physical reality; in the end, whether our attitudes to sound are physically based or culturally constructed, the result is the same - sounds still have an *effect* on us. The aim of this unit is to familiarise you with the physical nature of sounds, so that you are more accurately able to assess the way we interpret them, both in speech and in written texts.

A SOUND ALPHABET

The Roman alphabet, which is what you are reading now, cannot represent the sounds of spoken English with total accuracy and uniformity. It has been estimated that there is only about a 40 per cent correspondence between the sounds and written symbols of English. For example, one spelling can have many different pronunciations (consider how 'ough' is pronounced in 'through', 'cough', 'dough', 'thorough' and 'ought'); one sound can be represented by different written symbols ('meat', 'meet' and 'metre' all contain the same vowel sound, but this sound is spelt in different ways).

Because of the problems outlined above, linguists use a set of symbols called the International Phonetic Alphabet, or IPA, to represent sounds. Even if you have never heard its official name, you will have come across the IPA in dictionaries, where the pronunciation of a word is often given in brackets, before the definition. The IPA covers the sounds of all the world's known languages. This book will only be using that part of it that describes the sounds of the English language. Some of the symbols will already be familiar to you because they exist in the Roman alphabet; others won't be, but they will be explained later. When you work with the symbols that follow, remember that the underlined part of the word given as an example of each sound refers to how that sound would be produced by someone with a Received Pronunciation (RP) accent. This is the accent you would be likely to hear when listening to a national TV news broadcaster. It is an accent which does not mark the speaker as coming from a particular region (but does give messages about the user's social-class membership). If you speak with a regional accent, you may find some differences between the chart and the sounds you would make in pronouncing certain words.

Text: IPA symbols

IPA symbols for English sounds

Consonants		Short vowels	
p	- pip	ɪ	pit
b	- bib	ɛ	pet
t	- ten	æ	pat
d	- den	ɒ	pot
k	- cat	ʌ	putt
g	- get	ʊ	put
f	- fish	ə	patter
v	- van		
θ	- thigh	**Long vowels**	
ð	- thy		
s	- set	iː	bean
z	- zen	ɜː	burn
ʃ	- ship	ɑː	barn
ʒ	- leisure	ɔː	born
h	- hen	uː	boon
tʃ	- church		
dʒ	- judge	**Diphthongs**	
m	- man		
n	- man	aɪ	bite
ŋ	- sing	ɛɪ	bait
l	- let	ɔɪ	boy
r	- ride	əʊ	roe
w	- wet	aʊ	house
j	- yet	ʊə	poor
		ɪə	ear
		ɛə	air

(Note: the headings under which vowels are grouped will be explained later)

In order to become familiar with the alphabet, write your name using the appropriate symbols. Forget the spelling of your name, and concentrate on the sounds that are produced when you say it aloud. Exchange your writing with someone else, and get them to read back what you have written.

Then have a go at transcribing the sentence below, assuming that the speaker had an RP accent. In some cases, the sounds in a word will be influenced by the words either side of it, so take notice of how the sounds blend together as the sentence as a whole is said, rather than taking each word strictly in isolation. This instruction itself says a lot about the difference between speech and writing: we don't necessarily speak in 'words' with pauses around them – the very concept of a word is an idea derived from writing.

> Would you please queue at the end of the corridor?
> (Answer and commentary on p. 66)

SPEECH PRODUCTION AND DESCRIPTION: CONSONANTS

Sounds in English are produced as a result of air from the lungs coming up through the vocal cords and being manipulated in various ways. We describe consonants by answering three questions about how they are produced physically:

1 How is the airstream manipulated? *Manner of articulation*
2 Where does this happen? *Place of articulation*
3 Are the vocal cords vibrating or not? *Voiced or voiceless sound*

Plosives: p b t d k g

These sounds (or 'phonemes') are all explosions: they are created by obstructing the flow of air by bringing parts of the mouth together, then letting go suddenly. To explore this, place the palm of your hand in front of your mouth and, one by one, make each of these sounds in an exaggerated way. You should be able to feel the air from your mouth hitting your palm. English plosives (also called 'stops') are differentiated from each other in two ways: they are made in different places in the mouth (place of articulation, above), and they use different amounts of voice (as 3, above). While /p/ and /b/ are produced using the two lips (bilabial), /t/ and /d/ involve contact between the tongue and the teeth ridge (alveolar); /k/ and /g/ are made by closing off air at the back of the mouth (velar). See the diagram below.

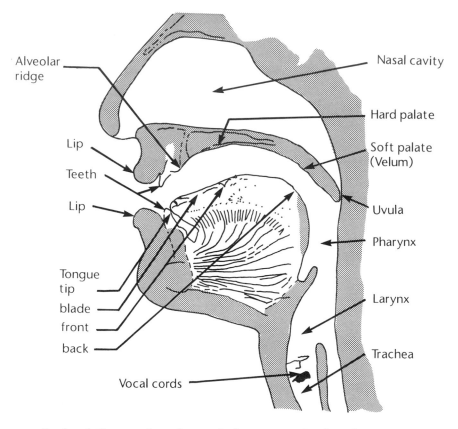

Each of these pairs of sounds has one voiced and one voiceless phoneme, as follows:

Voiceless	Voiced
p	b
t	d
k	g

To understand the idea of voice, put your fingers on your 'Adam's Apple' and alternate between the voiceless and voiced phonemes several times: you should be aware that your vocal cords are vibrating when you say the voiced sounds. If all the plosives sound voiced to you, this will be because you are adding a vowel (which are all voiced) and your voiceless plosives are picking up some of the vowel's voiced quality. For example, you might be adding the vowel /ə/. If you are doing this, make the voiceless sounds as if you were whispering them.

Fricatives: f v θ ð s z ʃ ʒ h

While plosives are produced by completely obstructing the airflow, fricatives involve a lesser obstruction where air is forced through in a steady stream, resulting in friction rather than explosion. Plosives cannot be kept going in the way fricatives can: to illustrate this idea, say an /s/ until you run out of breath; now try to keep a /p/ sound going. You will find that all you can do for the latter is to produce a number of separate /p/ sounds, one after the other.

Fricatives, like plosives, are distinguished from each other by their place of articulation, and by voice, each pair below being made up of a voiceless and voiced phoneme – apart from 'h', which is voiceless but has no voiced partner:

Voiceless	Voiced
f	v
θ (as in 'thigh')	ð (as in 'thy')
s	z
ʃ (as in 'ship')	ʒ (as in 'leisure')
h	

As with plosives, go through these phonemes, exploring where they are made in the mouth and sounding out their differences in terms of voice. (If your version of 'h' sounds voiced, this is because you are adding a vowel again, and saying something like 'huh'. The 'h' sound above is the sound that you would make if you were whispering.)

Some linguists regard /h/ as a weak and vulnerable fricative because of its isolation, and point to its absence from many regional accents to support the view that it may eventually drop out of the English language altogether.

Affricates: tʃ (as in 'church') dʒ (as in 'judge')

There are only two of these consonant sounds in English. They have double symbols to represent the fact that each one is a plosive followed by a fricative. If you make these sounds in very slow motion you may be able to hear this sequence. /tʃ/ is voiceless and /dʒ/ is its voiced partner.

Nasals: m n ŋ (as in 'singing')

The distinctive feature of these sounds is that they are produced in a particular manner: the airstream comes out through the nose rather than the mouth. They differ from each other in being made in different places: /m/ is bilabial, /n/ is alveolar, and /ŋ/ is velar. When you have a cold and air cannot escape from the nose, nasals become plosives, as in the second version of 'good morning' below:

gʊd mɔːnɪŋ
gʊd bɔːdɪg

Laterals: l

This sound is sometimes referred to as a 'liquid' sound, and is made by placing the tip of the tongue on the teeth ridge and sending air down the sides of the mouth. The easiest way to experience this airflow is to put the tongue in the right position to say an /l/, then breathe in instead of out: you should be able to feel the air flowing along the sides of your tongue. This is the reverse of what happens when you say an /l/ normally.

Approximants: r w j

The final three consonants are usually grouped together because they share the property of being mid-way between consonants and vowels; in some linguistic descriptions you will see them called 'semi-vowels'. They all involve less contact between the organs of speech than many of the other consonants: compare /r/ with /p/, for example. While /r/ and /j/ are produced in the palatal area (roof of the mouth), /w/ is a bilabial.

Glottal: ʔ

This does not appear on the list of symbols because it doesn't represent a sound as such. It is a closure of the vocal cords, resulting in shutting off the airstream, and it is sometimes produced as an alternative to certain plosive sounds. To explore this, say the words 'butter' and 'water', but 'swallow' the /t/ in the middle of each word. The glottal stop is a strong feature of some regional accents, and written texts often represent it by an apostrophe: for example, 'I've go' a lo' of li'le bo'les'.

Below is a summary of the consonant system in English. The chart shows place and manner of articulation; a colon marks voice, where there is a pair of sounds contrasted by this feature, voiceless sounds being to the left and voiced to the right. /r/ and /j/ are together because they are both palatal sounds, but they are not separated by a colon because they are not a voiceless/voiced pair.

| Manner of articulation | *Place of articulation* | | | | | | |
	Bilabial	Labio-dental	Dental	Alveolar	Palatal	Velar	Glottal
Plosive	p : b			t : d		k : g	p
Affricate					tʃ : dʒ		
Fricative		f : v	θ : ð	s : z	ʃ : ʒ		h
Nasal	m			n		ŋ	
Lateral				l			
Approximant	w				r : j		

IT'S NOT WHAT YOU SAY, IT'S THE WAY THAT YOU SAY IT

Some of the sounds you have been studying vary considerably on a regional and ethnic basis: for example, Cockney and Afro-Caribbean Patwa speakers have no /h/ phoneme; /ŋ/ is regularly replaced by /n/ in the West Country, and by /ŋg/ in some northern accents; glottal stops are a common feature in many regional accents, including Geordie. Such regional variations are often stigmatised, being regarded as 'bad', 'sloppy' or 'lazy' speech in some quarters. It's important to realise that these judgements are social, rather than linguistic: they are examples of how language can be used as a shibboleth – a way of more powerful groups marking out their own forms of language as prestigious and 'correct' and that of others as inadequate in order to forestall social movement and prevent others' access to power.

Being able to describe these aspects of language phonetically can help you to understand and explain the differences between linguistic facts and social attitudes. One aspect that should be apparent, if you work further on accent variation using the IPA, is that quite extensive and complex sets of attitudes are based on rather small features of language: for example, that a speaker has specific character traits, a certain degree of social status, or a particular level of intelligence as a result of whether s/he uses one phoneme or another.

Activity

In Text: Mother of the Nation, and Text: Leader's speech, both cartoons by Steve Bell, a certain type of accent is suggested by altering the spelling of words (known as 'eye-dialect'); this accent is then linked with particular attitudes and values as expressed by the speakers.

Discuss the stereotypes that are often associated with this type of accent. Compare the stereotypes you have identified with those often associated with regionally accented speakers.

Text: Mother of the Nation

Text: Leader's speech

Extension

1   Collect some written material where the writers have tried to represent accent on the page, and analyse their approaches: for example, have they altered the spellings of words, or used apostrophes to show glottal stops? How do their strategies compare with the real phonetic features of that accent? (If you can't spend time doing some phonetic analysis yourself, you can find information on accent variations in linguistic textbooks.) You will find further work on the representation of speech in Unit 5.

2   Record some TV adverts, and analyse how differently-accented speakers are used. For example, which products are sold by the use of regionally accented voiceovers or actors, and which by RP-accented voices? What qualities are associated with particular accents? Are male and female regional and RP speakers used in the same ways? What accents are given to non-white speakers of English in adverts? How are foreign-accented speakers used?

SOUND SYMBOLISM

Another important use of the IPA is to help us understand any possible basis for sound symbolism. This is the process by which we use the different sounds produced by our speech organs to stand for some of the sounds around us in our environment. When we form these sounds into whole words that themselves stand for noises, like 'bang', 'crash', and 'thud', this is called **onomatopoeia**. This area is by no means clear cut, however. Take, for example, the sound effects often seen in comics, as in Text: Comic 'noises'. Are these really an accurate description of noises, or do we just interpret them as such because we are used to the convention of the words meaning specific things? Are they understandable outside the context of the page where they occurred, without all the picture and story cues to support comprehension? Would someone who had never read a comic understand them? And are they language-specific: would someone who isn't an English speaker interpret them the same way, even though that person's organs of speech produce all the same sounds as ours? (You might be interested to know that German cockerels go 'kikeriki', while the French for a dog's 'woof-woof' is 'oua-oua'; and that the Spanish for 'bang' or 'crack' is 'pum' or 'paf'.)

48

Text: Comic 'noises'

Activity

The aim of this activity is to look carefully at the relationship between the sounds we produce and the sound effects we try to achieve in texts.

Read the poetry extracts in Text: Sound effects.

In each case, the language is highlighting certain types of sound, which have been underlined. Look back at the phonetic information given earlier, think about the way the sounds are produced physically and decide why the writers might have used them:

49

Text: Sound effects

1   From a poem by Wilfred Owen describing a battle in progress:

>   Only the stuttering rifles rapid rattle

2   From a poem by Geoffrey Hill about the Crucifixion:

>   While the dulled wood
>   Spat on the stones each drop
>   Of deliberate blood

3   From a poem by Peter Redgrove describing wind around a house:

>   Limped up the stairs and puffed on the landings
>   Snuffled through floorboards from the foundations

4   From a poem by Sylvia Plath addressing a sleeping baby:

>   All night your moth breath
>   Flickers among the flat pink roses

5   From a poem by Tennyson describing the sounds of doves and bees:

>   The moan of doves in immemorial elms
>   And murmuring of innumerable bees

6   From another poem by Wilfred Owen describing the sounds of a summer's day:

>   By the may breeze murmurous with wasp and midge

Commentary

Examples 1 and 2 are plosives, 2 using more voiced sounds. Example 1 suggests the explosive force of bullets (compare this with the sounds in 'rat-a-tat'); 2 tries to evoke the duller thud of drops on a hard surface.

Examples 3 and 4 use voiceless fricatives, suggesting the light friction of wind and breath.

Examples 5 and 6 use nasals, 5 suggesting the repeated and over-lapping calls of doves and continuous hum of bees; 6 uses nasals in combination with fricatives and an affricate. The humming of wasps is combined with the lighter hissing noises of smaller insects.

Summary of broad categorisations

◎ Voiced/voiceless: louder, heavier, a fuller sound/softer, lighter, a thinner sound
◎ Plosives: percussive sounds – banging, striking, tapping
◎ Fricatives and affricates: friction – hissing, scratching
◎ Nasals and approximants: continuous sound or motion – flowing, rippling, humming

Activity

Some of the effects in Text: Sound effects are cumulative: particular sounds are repeated within a short space (termed 'alliteration' when the sounds are at the beginnings of words). Individual words occurring on their own may or may not have in-built sound effects: for example, while 'murmur' may suggest the hum of mumbled talk – as 'mumble' itself may – the word 'immemorial' has no particular sound profile.

But it appears that some groups of words have acquired an 'aura' of meaning, as a result of an accumulation of another kind: that of simple force of numbers in the lexicon. These are much harder to explain. To explore this, brainstorm as many words as you can that belong to the following sets, then try to draw some conclusions about the operation of certain sounds. (Note: there is no commentary on this activity.)

slip, slide . . .
glitter, glow . . .
flip, flutter . . .
twist, twiddle . . .
bump, lump . . .
smash, crash . . .
puff, bluff . . .

Activity

'Meeting at Night' (1845) is a poem by Robert Browning.

How does Browning use sound – particularly consonants – to reinforce the action that takes place in the poem and the emotions that are involved?

Text: 'Meeting at Night'

The grey sea and long black land;
And the yellow half-moon large and low;
And the startled little waves that leap
In fiery ringlets from their sleep,
As I gain the cove with pushing prow,
And quench its speed I' the slushy sand.

Then a mile of warm sea-scented beach;
Three fields to cross till a farm appears;
A tap at the pane, the quick sharp scratch
And blue spurt of a lighted match,
And a voice less loud, through its joys and fears,
Than the two hearts beating each to each!

Commentary

The poem is organised into two 6-line rhyming stanzas. In stanza 1 the narrator is rowing his boat at night across the sea towards land. Stanza 2 describes his journey across land and culminates in the lovers' meeting of the title.

The dominant consonant sounds in the first stanza are:

- ◎ the voiced lateral /l/, sometimes referred to as a 'liquid' and associated with the flowing, rippling qualities of water
- ◎ the voiceless plosives /k/ and /p/ – soft percussive sounds
- ◎ the voiceless fricatives /ʃ/ and /s/ – soft hissing sounds
- ◎ the voiceless affricate /tʃ/ – soft percussive, immediately followed by soft hissing.

The way that these sounds are distributed across the lines of the stanza helps to suggest the action and sound of the oars. The plosives enact the vigorous movement of the oars entering and pulling through the water and the fricatives are suggestive of the sound made by the disturbed water after the oars are taken up ready for the next stroke. The 'soft' voiceless quality of most of the sounds contributes to the emotional atmosphere of the poem – the action takes place at night imparting an air of secrecy to the proceedings and the oarsman is perhaps driven by a sense of quiet determination. In line 5 the poet describes the boat coming to a halt as it drives into the sand of the beach. Here he introduces the voiced plosive /g/ in the word 'gain' – a loud percussive sound – and follows this with a concentration of voiceless plosives (/p/), fricatives (/ʃ/ and /s/) and the affricate (/tʃ/) – sounds that suggest the sudden stopping of the boat, the disturbance this creates in the water (the affricate /tʃ/ which involves both a plosive and fricative sound) and the gradual restoration of the sound and motion of waves lapping gently onto the beach and around the finally stilled boat.

In the second stanza the narrator crosses the beach and fields to arrive at the farm. 'A tap at the pane' echoes the rhythm of his action and the voiceless plosives /t/ and /p/ suggest that his tapping is cautious and muted. He doesn't want to alarm the occupant. The following line and a half use another series of voiceless sounds to describe a match being struck inside the house in response to his tapping. Think about striking a match. It involves friction (scratching sounds) and combustion (percussive sounds). The fricatives and affricates reinforce the sound of a match being rubbed against sandpaper and the plosives contribute to the image of the match bursting into flame. All these sounds are voiceless until the point where the match takes light. We could perhaps interpret this as the moment when the lovers recognise each other, the tension that has built up in the poem is released, the door is opened and the 'two hearts' are united in the final two lines.

Extension

Explore the use of sound symbolism based on consonants by collecting a range of data. Here are some areas to consider:

1   Plosives are often used in newspaper headlines to give a sense of energy and drama: for example, in words like 'probe', 'cut', 'hit', 'snap', 'quit', 'scoop' and 'block'. (These words are also monosyllabic, giving them extra force.) Collect some headlines and

investigate the types of words used in them.

2   Product brand names are carefully chosen by manufacturers to have a certain 'ring'. Choose some different products and list their brand names and slogans. Do certain sounds recur, or are certain sounds associated with particular types of product? For example, the names 'Twix', 'Crunchie', 'Snickers', 'Kit Kat' and 'Picnic' all contain plosives, perhaps because the manufacturers want to suggest a crisp, cracking noise. Are fricatives used for scouring creams and liquids, or air fresheners?

Slogans can often use alliteration, for example:

Best Buy Bold (washing powder)
P-P-Pick up a Penguin (chocolate bar)
The Power to Hit Pain Precisely (analgesic)

3   Some newspapers also use phoneme substitution as a regular technique in their headlines. Rather than exploiting sound symbolism, this process is one of rule-breaking: the reader expects one sound and gets another which creates a new and relevant word or phrase – sometimes with deliberately comic effect. You can see this process in certain kinds of 'corny' joke:

Q: What did the duck say as it flew upside down?
A: I'm quacking up.
Q: What do sea monsters live on?
A: Fish and ships.
Q: What do cats read?
A: The Mews of the World.

But the same technique can be used for serious purposes too. Adverts can exploit the way phoneme substitution can call up two phrases at once, as in using 'Limited Emission' to describe a car with a catalytic converter (and calling up the sophistication and exclusiveness of 'Limited Edition' at the same time).

See if you can find some examples of sound substitution from newspaper headlines, advertising copy and jokes.

4   The jokes above are one example of how much we like to play with sound. Collect some further examples of sound play, in the form of tongue twisters and popular sayings.

SPEECH PRODUCTION AND DESCRIPTION: VOWELS

Vowels also play their part in our interpretation of language.

Vowels are always voiced. Unlike consonants, they do not involve any obstruction of the airway; vowel sounds are more to do with the shape and position of the tongue, and whether the lips are spread or rounded.

English vowel sounds are grouped into two categories: 'pure' vowels and 'diphthongs'. While the former are single sounds, diphthongs are a combination of two sounds where the speaker starts with one sound and glides towards the other. Here are the relevant symbols:

Short vowels		Long vowels		Diphthongs	
ɪ	pit	i:	bean	aɪ	bite
ɛ	pet	ɜ:	burn	ɛɪ	bait
æ	pat	ɑ:	barn	ɔɪ	boy
ɒ	pot	ɔ:	born	əʊ	roe
ʌ	putt	u:	boon	aʊ	house
ʊ	put			ʊə	cruel
ə	patter			ɪə	ear
				ɛə	air

(Note: the phonetic system in this book marks long vowels with a colon (:). You may encounter descriptions in other textbooks where this mark is not used, but you will still be able to understand the sounds because the symbols themselves do not differ.)

In order to get a sense of these sounds, go through them, first alternating between short and long vowels and trying to feel the difference between them – for example, contrasting the vowel sound in 'pit' with that in 'bean'; then sound out some diphthongs, trying to feel the way these sounds are sequences of vowels.

The diagrams below show where English vowel sounds are made in the mouth. The shape of the diagram (called a 'vowel trapezium') is an abstract version of the space inside the mouth: 'high', 'mid' and 'low' refer to how near the tongue is to the roof of the mouth or bottom of the jaw; 'front', 'central' and 'back' refer to how far forward or retracted the body of the tongue is; the shapes drawn around the sounds themselves are explained below.

○ = made with rounded lips

☐ = made with spread lips

◖ = starting with rounded lips and ending with spread lips

◗ = starting with spread lips and ending with rounded lips

'Pure' vowels

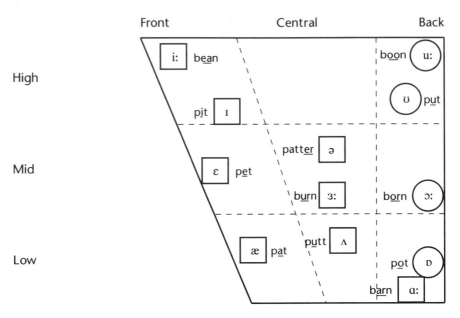

Diphthongs

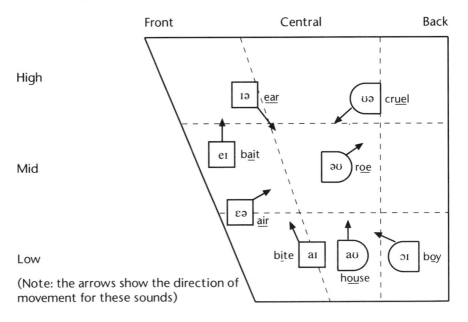

(Note: the arrows show the direction of movement for these sounds)

How now brown cow

As with consonants, vowels can mark out the region of origin, ethnicity or social class of a speaker: for example, Northern speakers have no /ʌ/, so will pronounce 'put' and 'putt' in the same way; speakers of Afro-Caribbean Patwa will use /aː/ instead of /ɒ/; an older form of RP, characteristic of the language of the royal family and upper-class speakers from years ago, is sometimes called 'marked RP'. In this accent, speakers would use /ɔ/ instead of /ɒ/.

Activity

Now that you have looked at vowels, read through the Steve Bell cartoons again (on pp. 46–47). Previously, you discussed the stereotypes that are associated with this 'marked RP' accent (there is a reference to this accent as an older form, often heard on early radio and TV broadcasts, in the first cartoon strip).

Now map out the way Steve Bell has altered the vowel sounds in order to construct the idea of this accent for the reader. List the words whose spelling has been altered, then compare this pronunciation with the regular RP version. An example has been done below, to start you off:

Word	Marked RP	RP	Word

Word	Marked RP	RP	Word
hellay			hello
ailed			old
gaying	eɪ	əʊ	going
thrait			throat
lair			lower

(Answers on p. 67)

Extension

Choose an accent that you know well, and write some 'eye dialect' yourself, where you try to simulate the accent by altering the spelling. Think about vowel sounds as well as consonants.

In a previous activity, you collected some texts in order to examine

57

how accent is represented on the page. How far did you find alterations in spelling to suggest vowel sounds? Are vowel alterations in 'eye dialect' more likely to be done in humorous texts than in those for serious purposes? What strategies are used in dialect poetry?

A bit of a teeny weeny ding-dong

As with consonants, vowels are used to suggest certain ideas: for example, /i:/ is often associated with diminutive size, as in the words 'teeny', 'weeny', 'wee'. We often put /i:/ on the ends of words in 'baby talk', using 'cardies' for 'cardigan', 'jarmies' for 'pyjamas', 'drinky' for 'drink', 'walkies' for 'walk', and so on.

As well as individual sounds appearing to have symbolic value, vowels also have cumulative force, either in repetition or in contrast: for example, 'teeny weeny' as a phrase is more effective for the repetitions in it; 'ding dong' draws attention to itself partly through the contrast of the high front /i:/ with the low back /I/. (Note the effect of the consonants here, too: the striking note of the voiced plosive, followed by the drawn out resonance of the nasal.)

Activity

We have many expressions that exploit vowel sounds by using either repetition or contrast. Below is a list of some of them. Sort them out by referring back to the vowel trapezium and symbols you studied earlier: which of these use repetition, and which use contrast? Group them into categories, identifying which vowels are being used. When you have finished, think about the nature of these terms: what type of language do they represent? Where would they be used – by whom, and in which contexts?:

---

helter skelter   flip flop   topsy turvey   wishy washy   fat cat
hoity toity   lovey dovey   hip hop   see saw   mishmash
spick and span   big wig   knick knack   harum scarum   tick tock
tit for tat   jet set   eebie jeebies   hanky panky   sing song
willy nilly   shilly shally   nitty gritty   ping pong   hotch potch
pitter patter   namby pamby   hugger mugger   collywobbles
hoi polloi   jim jams (for pyjamas)   airy fairy   arty farty   roly poly

(Answers on p. 68)

Rhyme, pararhyme, assonance and reverse rhyme

Some of the expressions above use rhyme as part of their effect: for example, willy nilly, nitty gritty. This aspect of patterning is learnt early as part of our childhood experience of language, via songs, nursery rhymes and the chants that accompany play. As well as full rhyme, though, there are other types of near-rhyme that set up relationships between sounds, and these can be used where full rhyme may seem too neat and tidy or childlike (although sometimes full rhyme can be very effective in serious texts, as a deliberate device).

First, it's important to realise that rhyme of all kinds is based on the sounds of words rather than the spelling. Here, the operation of **homophones** (words that are spelt differently but have the same sound) can have an important role.

Activity

The following are homophones in RP. How many different words can be represented by these sounds?

```
 1   ni: dz
 2   a: mz
 3   bru: z
 4   kɔ: s
 5   səʊl
 6   kɔ: t
 7   lɛsən
 8   kwɔ: ts
 9   kɔ: z
10   rəʊz
11   sɛnt

(Answers on p. 68)
```

The following words are homophones for some regional speakers, who would pronounce both words in each case as the first example. Can you identify where the speakers would be from? A random list of possibilities is given after the wordlist:

59

1   ant   aunt
2   stir   stair
3   moo   mew
4   caught   cot
5   tree   three

Liverpool; Afro-Caribbean Patwa; Northern England; Norfolk; Scotland.

(Answers on p. 69)

The homophonic principle can work across word boundaries as well as within them. For example:

Q: Where did Humpty Dumpty leave his hat?
A: Humpty dumped 'is 'at on the wall.
Q: Where do all policemen live?
A: Lettsby Avenue.
Q: What did Neptune say when the sea dried up?
A: I haven't a notion.

and the book title *Dangerous Cliffs,* by Eileen Dover.
Supply your own answer to this question:

Q: If frozen water is iced water, what's frozen ink?

(Answer on p. 69)

Supply the answers to the following jokes, and identify the homophones involved:

> *Q:* What trees come in twos?
> *Q:* What fly has laryngitis?
>
> (Answers on p. 69)

Some of the expressions you sorted earlier use contrasting vowels within the framework of the same consonants: for example, 'sing song', 'shilly shally'.

This is known as **pararhyme**, and can be found in many different types of text as a shaping strategy. For example, it is used in the poem 'Strange Meeting' (1918) by Wilfred Owen in order to set up echoes between words, without providing the sense of completeness that would come with full rhyme. The narrator describes an imaginary journey down into hollow spaces in the earth where he encounters a dead enemy soldier who was one of his victims during the battle.

Identify some examples of pararhyme in these initial lines of the poem, and try to describe the effects produced.

Text: 'Strange Meeting'

> It seemed that out of battle I escaped
> Down some profound dull tunnel, long since scooped
> Through granites which titanic wars had groined.
> Yet also there encumbered sleepers groaned,
> Too fast in thought or death to be bestirred.
> Then, as I probed them, one sprang up, and stared
> With piteous recognition in fixed eyes,
> Lifting distressful hands as if to bless.

These lines also use a form of sound patterning called **assonance** – the repetition of vowels, without the other components that entail full rhyme: for example, the vowel sounds in 'down' and 'profound'; or in 'dull tunnel'. This pattern is seen in the expression 'collywobbles', from the earlier list.

A final aspect of patterning that can be useful to focus on when explaining sound effects in language is **reverse rhyme**. This is the repetition of an initial syllable rather than the final one which is necessary to full rhyme: for example, <u>star</u> and <u>star</u>ling, or <u>grey</u> and <u>gra</u>iny.

Activity

The two texts for this activity – the poems 'Kubla Khan' (1816), by Samuel Taylor Coleridge (the first thirty lines have been printed here), and 'Ballade Made in the Hot Weather', by the late nineteenth-century poet W.E. Henley – both use sound as a strong element in their construction of sensation.

Explore how sound contributes to the overall meaning of the poem in each case. (Note: there is no commentary for this activity.)

Text: 'Kubla Khan'

Kubla Khan or, A Vision in a Dream, A Fragment

In Xanadu did Kubla Khan
A stately pleasure-dome decree:
Where Alph, the sacred river, ran
Through caverns measureless to man
   Down to a sunless sea.
So twice five miles of fertile ground
With walls and towers were girdled round:
And here were gardens bright with sinuous rills,
Where blossomed many an incense-bearing tree;
And here were forests ancient as the hills,
Enfolding sunny spots of greenery.

But oh! that deep romantic chasm which slanted
Down the green hill athwart a cedarn cover!
A savage place! as holy and enchanted
As e'er beneath a waning moon was haunted
By woman wailing for her demon-lover!
And from this chasm, with ceaseless turmoil seething,
As if this earth in fast thick pants were breathing,
A mighty fountain momently was forced:
Amid whose swift half-intermitted burst
Huge fragments vaulted like rebounding hail,
Or chaffy grain beneath the thresher's flail:
And 'mid these dancing rocks at once and ever
It flung up momently the sacred river.
Five miles meandering with a mazy motion
Through wood and dale the sacred river ran,
Then reached the caverns measureless to man,
And sank in tumult to a lifeless ocean:
And 'mid this tumult Kubla heard from far
Ancestral voices prophesying war!

Text: 'Ballade Made in the Hot Weather'

Ballade Made in the Hot Weather

To C.M.

Fountains that frisk and sprinkle
The moss they overspill;
Pools that the breezes crinkle;
The wheel beside the mill,
With its wet, weedy frill;
Wind-shadows in the wheat;
A water-cart in the street;
The fringe of foam that girds
An islet's ferneries;
A green sky's minor thirds –
To live, I think of these!

Of ice and glass the tinkle,
Pellucid, silver-shrill;
Peaches without a wrinkle;
Cherries and snow at will,
For china bowls that fill
The senses with a sweet
Incuriousness of heat;
A melon's dripping sherds;
Cream-clotted strawberries;
Dusk dairies set with curds –
To live, I think of these!

Vale-lily and periwinkle;
Wet stone-crop on the sill;
The look of leaves a-twinkle
With windlets clear and still;
The feel of a forest rill
That wimples fresh and fleet
About one's naked feet;
The muzzles of drinking herds;
Lush flags and bulrushes;
The chirp of rain-bound birds –
To live, I think of these!

*Envoy**

Dark aisles, new packs of cards,
Mermaidens' tails, cool swards,
Dawn dews and starlit seas,
White marbles, whiter words –
To live, I think of these!

*An envoy is the summarising final stanza of a poem.

Glossary

mill	a water mill (a construction involving water falling onto a large wheel causing it to revolve. The wheel itself was attached to machinery which was set in motion as it turned.)
water-cart	at the time the poem was written, the village pump would have been the main source of water. In a hot summer the pump might run dry and water would have to be brought in by cart from elsewhere.
girds	surrounds or 'girdles'
ferneries	damp places containing ferns
minor thirds	a combination of musical notes producing a melancholic sound
pellucid	transparent or translucent
incuriousness	a word of the poet's own making suggesting a lack of curiosity or active interest
sherds	same as 'shard', a broken piece or fragment
vale-lily, periwinkle, stone-crop	native English plants
rill	a brook or stream
wimples	ripples
fleet	fast
flags	traditional name for native English iris, a plant that grows in shallow water
swards	areas of mown grass

Extension

Collect some non-literary texts that use sound patterning involving vowels: for example, advertising slogans that use rhyme or pararhyme. You may also find that you see new aspects of sound patterning in the texts that you collected earlier in order to explore consonants.

This unit has not had the space to explore the effects of stress and rhythm in language, but these are often important ingredients in how sound patterns work. When you are collecting and analysing material, give some thought to the way these larger patterns contribute to the overall effects.

Answers to activities

Sentence for transcription (p. 41)

wʊdʒuː pliːz kjuː (w) ət ðiː (j) ɛnd əv ðə kɒrɪdɔː

According to how exactly this utterance was said (particularly, how strongly some of the vowel sounds were stressed), there could be some alternatives: for example, the vowel in the word 'you' could be /ə/; the vowels in 'at' and 'of' could be /æ/ and /ɒ/ respectively.

The symbols in brackets are linking sounds, enabling smooth transitions between words.

Steve Bell cartoons (p. 57)

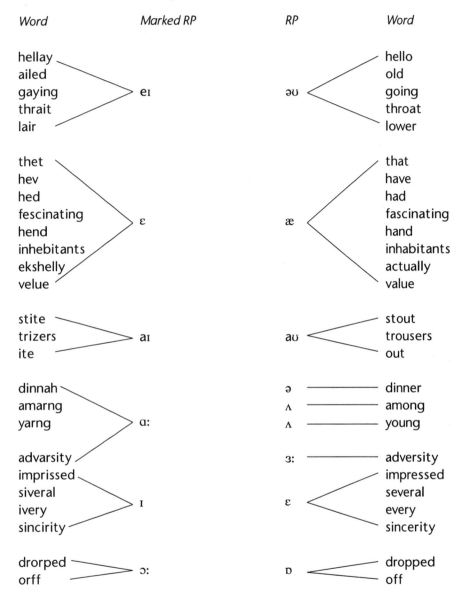

Word	Marked RP		RP	Word
hellay ailed gaying thrait lair	eɪ		əʊ	hello old going throat lower
thet hev hed fescinating hend inhebitants ekshelly velue	ɛ		æ	that have had fascinating hand inhabitants actually value
stite trizers ite	aɪ		aʊ	stout trousers out
dinnah amarng yarng	ɑː		ə ʌ ʌ	dinner among young
advarsity imprissed siveral ivery sincirity	ɪ		ɜː ɛ	adversity impressed several every sincerity
drorped orff	ɔː		ɒ	dropped off

Sorting vowel sounds (p. 58)

Repetitions

/ɛ/ helter skelter   jet set   harum scarum   airy fairy
/ɪ/ willy nilly   big wig   nitty gritty
/æ/ hanky panky   fat cat   namby pamby
/ɑ:/ arty farty
/ɒ/ hotch potch   collywobbles
/ʌ/ lovey dovey   hugger mugger
/i:/ eebie jeebies
/ɔɪ/ hoity toity   hoi polloi
/əʊ/ roly poly

Contrasts

/ɪ/ → /ɒ/ flip flop   hip hop   sing song   ping pong   tick tock   wishy washy
/ɪ/ → /æ/ shilly shally   pitter patter   mishmash   spick and span   knick knack   jim jams   tit for tat
/i/ → /ɔ:/ see saw
/ɒ/ → /ɜ:/ topsy turvey

These terms belong to the informal, spoken area of language. Some are so unfamiliar on the page that their spelling is uncertain: for example, is it 'colliewobbles' or 'collywobbles'? 'hoy polloy' or 'hoi polloi'? This is the language of personal anecdote rather than public lecture, although many a public lecture would benefit from the liveliness and energy contributed by these vigorous little items. Many express motion, emotion, muddle and incoherence − 'helter skelter', 'eebie jeebies', 'mishmash', 'hotch potch'; others strike arch attitudes about certain types of people − 'fat cat', 'hoi polloi'; some are straightforwardly onomatopoeic − 'tick tock'. They are all cheeky.

Homophones (p. 59)

1   kneads, needs
2   arms, alms
3   bruise, brews
4   course, coarse
5   sole, soul
6   caught, court

7   lesson, lessen
8   quarts, quartz
9   cause, cores, caws
10 rose, rows, roes
11 sent, scent, sent.

1   Northern England /ænt/
2   Liverpool /stɜː/
3   Norfolk /muː/
4   Scotland /kɔːt/
5   Afro-Caribbean Patwa /triː/

Iced ink / I stink
Pear / pair
Horse / hoarse

Words and things

Aim of this unit

The aim of this unit is to provide a brief overview of the complex area of the English vocabulary. Analysis of text often starts at the level of the word. Words are clearly visible units in written text, and distinguishable units in spoken text. However, the task is not always that simple. What is a word? Are simple definitions such as 'the smallest meaningful unit of language' helpful or even accurate? Is there a straightforward one-to-one relationship between word and meaning? Where does the vocabulary of English come from in the first place? This unit attempts to address some of these issues, and to look more closely at the way words work within texts.

71

Contents

Historical dimensions

This section looks at the origins of the English word stock.

1 *Got any spare words?*
   This explores the way English has borrowed words from other languages, and looks at these words in a range of texts.
2 *Words mean what I want them to mean*
   Here, the way that words change their meaning over time is explored.
3 *Get your new words here!*
   This explores the different ways in which new words can be created.

Texts used

◎ Shop and business names
◎ Articles and headlines
◎ Extracts from novels including graphic novels
◎ Students' writing
◎ Advertisements
◎ Notices, letters, menus, etc.
◎ Old English text
◎ Extracts from speeches

What are words made of?

Some questions about words, like 'What is a word?' might be answered by looking at ways in which words in the English language are structured. The study of the structure of words is called **morphology**.

Most users of English would assume that words are the smallest units of language to carry meaning. This, however, is not necessarily the case, which makes questions such as 'What is a word?' even more difficult to answer.

Activity

Look at the following sentence:

> The plogs glorped bliply.

What do the words in this sentence mean?

Commentary

Apart from the first word, apparently nothing. They are units of text that currently have no meaning attached to them, unlike units such as 'dog', 'deckchair' or 'grip'.

Now look at the text again, and answer the following questions:

1   How many plogs were there? One or more than one?
2   What were they doing?
3   Were they doing it now or in the past?
4   How, or in what way, were they doing it?

Most speakers of English will have very little trouble answering these questions. There was more than one plog, because this word carries the plural marker 's'. 'Glorped' is marked as a verb by the use of the past tense marker 'ed', so the reader knows what the plogs were doing, and the fact that they were doing it in the past. Finally, the reader can tell how or in what manner the plogs were glorping – bliply – because the word carries the adverb marker 'ly'.

Just a brief look at text can establish that units smaller than words are carrying meaning. These units are **morphemes**.

Words may be made up of one or more morphemes:

One morpheme	dog, elephant, establish, child
Two morphemes	dog s, elephant ine, establish ment, child ish
Three morphemes	dis establish ment, child ish ness.

In theory, there is no limit to the number of morphemes a word can have, but logic and comprehensibility mean that there tends to be an upper limit, and six morphemes is about it for English:

anti dis establish ment arian ism

There are exceptions found in highly specialised areas of language, for example, terms used in organic chemistry.

Activity

Identify the individual morphemes in the following word list.

pigs, barked, unlikely, motherhood, salty, cherry, taller, hammer, displease, hardship, superheroes, player

Commentary

pig s, bark ed, un like ly, mother hood, salt y, cherry, tall er, hammer, dis please, hard ship, super hero es, play er.

Activity

Now classify the morphemes into the following groups:

1   Independent or free. These morphemes can stand on their own.
2   Dependent or bound. These morphemes must be attached to another morpheme.
3   Grammatical. These give grammatical information and mark the role of the word in the sentence.
4   Creative or derivational. These form new words.

Commentary

Many morphemes can constitute words by themselves: pig, bark, like, mother, salt, cherry, tall, please, hard, super, hero, play. These are usually referred to as **free morphemes**.

Others are only ever used as parts of words: s, ed, un, ly, hood, y, er, dis, ship, es, er. These are usually referred to as **bound morphemes**.

It is easy to confuse some bound morphemes with free morphemes that have an identical sound and structure. For example, English has free morphemes 'hood' (a head covering) and 'ship' (a sea going vessel). It also has the bound morphemes '-ship' and '-hood', that are both used to form nouns. 'Hardship' means a state of deprivation or difficulty, 'hard ship' means something different, a vessel that is difficult to sail, perhaps. 'Motherhood' means the state of being a mother, not the head covering that a mother might wear.

It is also easy to confuse part of a word that is a single morpheme, like 'hammer', with a bound morpheme, in this case '-er', that is used to create nouns of agency (as in 'play', 'player') or adjectives of comparison or degree ('tall', 'taller').

Bound morphemes have two functions. One is to act as a grammatical marker, giving information about number, verb tense, aspect and other grammatical functions. These are **inflectional morphemes**. Examples in the data are -s, -ed, -er (comparative), -es. The second is to form new words. These are called **derivational morphemes**. Examples in the data are un-, -ly, -hood, -y, dis-, -ship, -er (to create a noun of agency).

Summary

Meaning therefore exists in units of language smaller than the word, in morphemes. Users of English frequently use the term 'word' when, strictly speaking, they are referring to morphemes. If someone looks a word up in the dictionary, for example 'dogs', they don't look up the plural form, they look up the base morpheme 'dog'. For this reason, and for reasons looked at later in this unit, many linguists prefer the term 'lexeme' to the term 'word'. **Lexeme** refers to a unit of meaning that may be smaller or larger than the traditional term 'word' implies. This unit (i.e. Unit 2) could, therefore, be more accurately called 'Lexemes', but 'Word' is used as being more familiar.

Word and meaning

The previous section looked at meaning in units smaller than the word. This section looks at the relationship between word and meaning, and the way meaning operates in units that are larger than the traditional definition of 'word' allows.

LEXICAL AMBIGUITY: SAY WHAT YOU MEAN, OR MEAN WHAT YOU SAY?

In *Alice through the Looking Glass*, Humpty Dumpty says:

> 'When I use a word, it means just what I choose it to mean - neither more nor less.'

At first, Humpty Dumpty's point seems ridiculous. Common sense tells that each word in the English language has a meaning, and that meaning is well established. Look in any dictionary. Why is it, then, that even the most skilled and experienced users of language can get into trouble, by meaning one thing and saying another. What did Margaret Thatcher really mean when she said that every Prime Minister needed a Willie? (William Whitelaw, usually known as Willie Whitelaw, was a trusted senior member of Thatcher's government at this time.)

Activity

The examples of text below all apparently intend one meaning, but give another. Try to identify the word(s) that have caused the difficulty, and say why this has happened.

These examples are all from letters sent to housing departments.

> I request permission to remove my drawers in the kitchen.
>
> Will you please send a man to look at my water. It is a very funny colour and not fit to drink.
>
> The person next door has a large erection in his back garden which is unsightly and dangerous.

Commentary

If two words in English have the same meaning, this is known as **synonymy**, and the words are called **synonyms**. Examples of synonyms are skin/hide, purchase/buy, obstinate/stubborn. A problem can arise when a word has more than one synonym. 'Hide' means the same as (i.e. is synonymous with) (1) conceal, (2) skin, (3) place for watching wildlife. If these synonyms aren't closely related in meaning, then the result can be **ambiguity**.

Synonyms

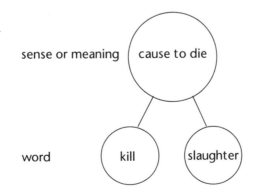

If a word has more than one meaning, this is known as **polysemy**, and the word is called a **polyseme**. An example of a polyseme is pupil (part of the eye, school child).

Polysemy

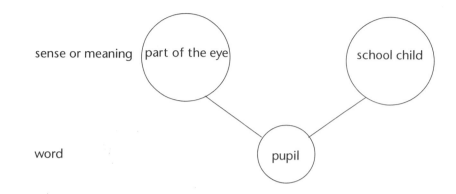

sense or meaning (part of the eye)   school child

word   pupil

If the synonyms aren't closely related in meaning, or if the intended meaning of the polyseme isn't clear, then the reader or listener may not be able to identify which meaning is intended. There are many kinds of ambiguity, but this section is concerned with **lexical ambiguity**, that occurs when it is not possible to decide on the intended meaning of a word.

In the activity above, some of the words used in these letters have synonyms, or are polysemes. 'Drawers' is synonymous with 'part of an item of furniture' but is also synonymous with 'item of women's underwear'. 'Water' can mean any amount of water from the flow from a tap to the ocean; but also by association 'urine'. 'Erection' can mean 'building' or 'sexual arousal'. If the producer of a text intends one meaning, but the context in which a word is used implies another, the result is confusion, because the text becomes ambiguous.

The examples above are presumably unintentional, but what about examples produced by people whose profession is language? Anyone can make a mistake if they are talking spontaneously, as the following examples show:

GLR reporter	What should you do if your children want to talk about solvent abuse?
Brian Mawhinney	Take a deep breath ...
George Bush	I'm for a stronger death penalty
Jason Donovan	The lights went up and there I was standing flat on my face.
Brian Gould	We're not the sort of party that does deals behind smoke-filled doors.

But written text is more considered, usually proof read, and it is unlikely that double meanings pass unnoticed. Were the following headlines intentional or not?

Activity

Look at the following newspaper headlines. They are all ambiguous in that there are at least two potential meanings for each one. Try to identify the word(s) that have caused the problem, and say why the problem has arisen.

THREE BATTERED IN FISH SHOP

EIGHTH ARMY PUSH BOTTLES UP GERMANS

MOUNTING PROBLEMS FOR YOUNG COUPLES

FIELD MARSHALL FLIES BACK TO FRONT

The English language, then, has a broader capacity for meaning than a simple one-to-one word and meaning relationship. Producers of text are aware of this capacity and make use of it.

Activity

Text: Shop names is a list of names of various shops, businesses and services. Discuss the ways in which words and meanings are used here. Are all these examples synonyms or polysemes, or can you find other ways of using the relationship between word and meaning? What effects are created by using language in this way?

Text: Shop names

Hairdressers
Curl up and dye, Fresh hair, Look ahead, Kuttin' kru,
Headlines, Making waves, Highlights

Bed salesrooms
Bedside manor, Bedlam

Heating
Gas flair, Power dressing

Fur shop
Hide and sheep

Services
Nappy cleaning service: Wee care
Chimney sweep: Clean sweep
Drain clearing: Watershed, Blockbusters
HGV driving instructors: Road train
Dry cleaners: Suits me
Plumbers: Plumbing your way

Commentary

All of these names are playing games with the language, and exploiting
its capacity to produce ambiguous meanings, in many cases by using the
capacity of the language to develop synonyms and polysemes.

Another cause of ambiguity arises in the use of words that are
spelled differently, have different meanings, but have the same pronunciation. These words are homophones. Some examples in the data are dye,
die; wee, we; manor, manner.

The creators of these names are playing on our ability as users of
language to create a meaning link where, strictly speaking, none should
exist. The effect of this is to entertain the recipient, and to make the
names memorable, whilst using words that give a positive view of the
product or service on offer.

Homophones

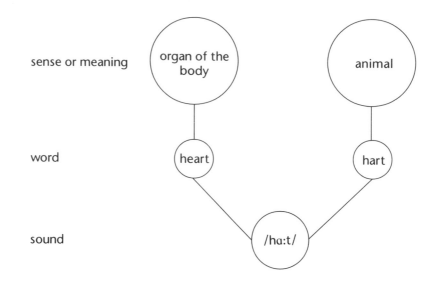

There are some words that are close to homophones placed in a context where the reader or hearer would expect another word. For example, plumbing rhymes with coming. Placed in the phrase 'Plumbing your way', the language draws on both meanings, giving the effect of an identified service that is close at hand.

Activity

Collect examples of names of shops and services that exploit the capacity of words to create ambiguous meanings.

Invent names for the following:

> an undertaker, a baker, a fruit shop, a pest controller, a fish and chip shop, a solicitor.

Check in a local *Yellow Pages* directory. What names do these shops and services use? Which ones do, and which ones don't, play meaning games with language?

These are some examples of names that students invented in response to this activity:

Solicitors	Doowie, Cheetham and Howe. Silk 'n' Briefs
Undertakers	U. Killham and I. Berryem. Croakers. The body shop. Graves 'R' us. Coffin up
Fruit shop	Going bananas
Pest controller	Make mice day

The use of this kind of word play is often humorous, almost always light-hearted. Certain trades and professions must give the clearest indications that they take their work seriously. It is, therefore, extremely unlikely that firms such as undertakers or solicitors would play games with language.

Summary

Humpty Dumpty may not be right, but the study of words in use demonstrates quickly that the relationship between word and meaning is more complex than it seems at first. This section looked at the ambiguity that can be created (accidentally or deliberately) by the existence of synonyms and homophones. The situation is even more complex than this, as the next section will discuss.

METAPHOR: LIFE'S A BEACH, AND THEN YOU FRY

This section looks at the way words can be used to create connections between areas of meaning that may have no direct link, but offer a useful comparison or connection that helps to enhance, clarify, make more vivid or even reinforce existing ideas and concepts.

The existence of metaphor allows for a further expansion of meaning. By linking words or concepts that don't generally have a semantic link, a new meaning can be expressed. Metaphor allows producers of text to make connections in a few words, that would take lines of writing, or long stretches of speech, to make in a more literal way. The literal translation of a metaphor rarely produces the same effect as the metaphor. Metaphor can be used to make comments on aspects of human behaviour or society without the writer having to spell out

83

literally the point he/she is trying to make.

Metaphor is often seen as something that is more likely to exist in the domain of literature, and not as something that has a lot to do with everyday life. It isn't unusual for people to associate metaphor with written language, and particularly with written language that is literary or has literary associations. Advertising, for example, is often very creative; tabloid newspapers are known for their inventive ways of using the phonological and lexical levels of language. However, metaphor is much more a part of day-to-day uses of language.

Activity

Look at the example of dialogue in Text: Graphic novel (from *The Sandman – The Doll's House* by Neil Gaiman, Mike Dringenberg and Malcolm Jones III). A group of violent criminals are meeting for a convention. They are casually chatting to each other before proceedings begin.

Identify any standard phrases or sayings you recognise. (The first two have been underlined.) What is the literal meaning of these?

Why has the writer used these particular phrases in this context?

Commentary

A lot of language that is used regularly is metaphor. It isn't unusual for somebody describing a situation that has embarrassed them to say, 'I could have died,' or to hear someone say, 'It nearly killed me,' when talking about some major effort. This is not meant literally, but gives a clear expression to the strong feelings aroused by, for example, social embarrassment.

This writer has chosen everyday uses of metaphor that relate to death and violence. The examples used are deliberately commonplace – as readers we probably wouldn't notice them except that so many are used. The effect is interesting. It enhances the role of the participants in the narrative. These are people for whom violence is a way of life, but by drawing attention to the sheer 'everydayness' of such language, the writer is enforcing a point he makes further on in the narrative: violence is so much a part of our lives that we almost fail to notice it.

86

Activity

The examples of language in Text: Metaphors are all ready-made phrases that are a familiar part of the day-to-day experience of language. They have been classified according to topic. What metaphors are used here? What connections are made to enhance meaning? How does the metaphoric use of language here reflect our cultural attitudes?

Text: Metaphors

Women
Mutton dressed as lamb
She's a bitch.
She's a cow.
She's a slag.

Countries and places
America is our ally.
The rape of Sarajevo
Cuba is the victim of the American blockade.
The evil empire

War
Surgical strike (attack)
Ethnic cleansing
Friendly fire (killed by your own side)

Government and politics
The economy is ailing.
The trade figures are healthy this month.
The Government does not realise how much is at stake.

Commentary

There is clear metaphoric use of language in these examples. Countries and places are treated as people (ally), they suffer as people (rape, victim).

What is more revealing, though, is the connections that are made through these metaphoric uses. Women are associated with animals (cow, bitch), meat (mutton, lamb), or with rubbish discarded after the valuable content has been extracted (slag).

War becomes a medical or beneficial act (surgical, cleansing). Something that kills you becomes benign (friendly). Countries and places become friends or enemies (ally, evil).

Government and politics is described in terms of gambling (at stake), or in terms of health and disease (healthy, ailing).

Cultural attitudes to particular areas of human activity can often be seen in the choices of metaphor used when that activity is discussed. A useful linguistic concept to be aware of here is that of **semantic field**, sometimes called just field, or field of meaning. Particular topics, trades, concepts are associated in the mind of the user of language with particular groups of words. Texts that belong to a particular area of meaning draw from a range of words that relate specifically to that area of meaning. For example, a text that used the words chop, fry, stir, simmer, season, taste, would almost certainly belong to the semantic field of cooking. However, writers can also draw on semantic fields to create metaphorical effects and associations that can enhance the meaning of the text.

Activity

Look at the following word list. All these words were taken from the same text. What topic does this text address?

> attrition, sudden death, barbed-wire entanglements, defence, threat

Most people assume that these words are from a text about war, possibly the 1914–18 war.

The complete text is given in Text: Newspaper report.

Text: Newspaper report

ENGLAND v SPAIN

An early goal will open up any game but the longer this Wembley quarter-final today remains scoreless, the more it will become a contest of attrition, with the winners likely to be decided by sudden-death overtime or a penalty shoot-out. England are better equipped for an exchange of goals, with Shearer at last producing his prolific league form at international level. Spain have yet to find a consistent striker but the depth of their strength is formidable. They will hope to draw England on to the barbed-wire entanglements of their defence and then use Sergi to catch the opposition on the break. Hierro, Amor and Caminero will pose a threat to Adams coming from the deep. Terry Venables could have done with Ince against Nadal.

Forecast: England 2, Spain 0.

Comment on the use of metaphor in Text: Newspaper report, and the way in which the writer has drawn upon the semantic field of war to create these metaphors.

Commentary

The semantic field of war and battle is one that sports writers often draw on. Sport, particularly football, in our culture is also associated with conflict and violence. Football teams, for example, have close regional connections (Sheffield Wednesday, Wolverhampton Wanderers), their fans link their support of the team with their regional affiliation, the pseudo-battle of the game is frequently mirrored by the real battle of the supporters before and after the game. People are hurt, and sometimes die. Even when the injury and death occur for reasons that are not to do with football violence (as when the organisation and policing of the crowd led to fatal overcrowding at Hillsborough), the injured and dead are identified by their team affiliation (the Liverpool supporters . . .).

In other words, it isn't just the writer using a device of language, metaphor, to bring a description to life; the writer is coding in language the role that football plays in our society today. Does this work in other fields and areas?

Activity

Text: Wine, and Text: Grunge, are from a Sunday colour supplement and a music magazine respectively. The first text is part of an article about wine, the second is a review of Nirvana, a grunge group. Which text uses the most metaphor? What aspects of wine and music attract the highest use of metaphor? What associations are the writers making with the metaphors they select?

WINE BY PAUL LEVY

KEEP IT SWEET

We had all these in our tropical fruit salad. The brief to our wine merchants was to complement their exotic, musky perfumes and flavours. It wasn't easy. One imaginative firm sent a smart Australian chardonnay. Its own oaky, tropical fruit flavour ought to have married beautifully. It didn't, though, for the same reason that the clever choice of a dry red Lambrusco di Sorbara failed: sweetness in the wine is essential. This is one case when contrasting dry with sweet just doesn't work.

Those who add alcohol in the form of eau de vie to fruit salad are on to something. We found that 'rich, full, high alcohol wines and fortified wines are the most successful'. I think this probably has something to do with the warmth of the alcohol matching the sultriness of tropical fruit.

We all agreed that the best match was with the 20-year-old Moscatel de Setubal of Jose Maria da Fonseca (H. Allen Smith, £11.95), a fortified (18 per cent alcohol by volume) wine variously described by authoritative writers as 'raisiny-nutty-apricoty' and 'rich and unctuous with the flavour of caramelised oranges'.

This was the last wine of 12 in our blind tasting, and we were particularly impressed by its amber-pink colour, which held out the (subsequently delivered) promise of caramel. The bouquet is 'huge, aggressive and spirity'. In the mouth, 'though old and weighty, it is fresh and attractive; it's a bit like eating toffee with the fruit, and adds another dimension to the fruit flavours.'

Text: Grunge

Once there was The Grunge. It was massive and messy and emanated like a rumbling from your nightmare. An aural chaos spewed forth from a bucketful of hopes and realisations. Prepared with a handful of loud guitars, propelled through a clutch of prehistoric amps and speakers, and penetrated into a desperate core of rattling hearts, The Grunge spoke authentically to the longhaired kids of America. And I don't mean the ones who wore hairspray. The Grunge meant bloody business.

Nowadays you don't hear so much about The Grunge. Fever broke and melted, like it always does, bands rose and fell, like they always do. The Sub-Pop romance turned sour for some (although Mudhoney still stay true) and the geographical phenomena was put to bed. But a brave A & R man at MCA/Geffen remembered something. How he was struck by Nirvana! How he wanted to sign them up, tune them in and turn them over into stardom! And so he did. Nirvana - welcome to the big, bad, boy with guitar eating world of major label record business!

Commentary

The metaphor in the wine article focuses very much on the senses, obviously on taste and smell, but also on touch. This occurs to a greater extent in the adjectival description, with words such as exotic, musky, oaky, unctuous. The tastes of the wine are evoked by the use of words like toffee and caramelised, suggesting foods that are pleasant, but frivolous and unhealthy. The wines are also personified, as they 'hold out' and 'deliver' a promise. The descriptions imply sensual pleasure, over-indulgence, possibly with sexual overtones (musky, married, sultry).

The metaphor in the music article is much more pervasive. There are associations of disease and decay, the breakdown of order, noise and violence, but many of the metaphors draw on several images at once: 'spewed forth from a bucketful of hopes and realisations'; 'prepared with a handful of loud guitars, propelled through a clutch of prehistoric amps and speakers, and penetrated into a desperate core of rattling hearts'.

Wine, therefore, attracts metaphor that carries implications of pleasure and guilt, rather in the way of the 'naughty but nice' campaign that was used to sell cream cakes. Grunge music, like many developments in modern music, operates against the rules — rules of order, structure, acceptability. Does the chaotic use of metaphor in the review reflect this both in the images chosen, and in the apparent disregard for order and clarity in the images themselves?

Encoding views and opinions about the world, aspects of society, in metaphor, gives the producer of text scope to make opinions and ideas implicit, and often to express complex ideas in an economical and accessible way.

Activity

Write a short description of a city scene. It can be any time of day, it can be busy or deserted; you can focus on small detail or give a more general description.

Use metaphor to 'code' into your description some comment on modern urban society. It can be an optimistic comment about progress and development, it can be a pessimistic comment about the decay of such a society, or any other kind of comment you feel you would like to make. The important thing is to use metaphor to describe the scene in a way that carries the message you are trying to get across to your reader.

When you have written the text, read it to the rest of the group. Do they pick up the message you have tried to put into your description?

Here are some examples of text produced by a group of students who carried out this activity.

> I was surrounded by tower blocks that punched the sky and loomed over me, threatening and dark. Cars snarled at each other and tussled for space on the roadways, veering round each other, hooting and shouting. The stink of their battle filled the air.

> The market square bloomed in green. The voices of the traders mixed with the busy chatter of the birds, swooping and diving over the city centre. The sun shone on the clean buildings, the bright colours, and the people, who carried the joy of this city on their backs, their faces turned up to the life-giving wash of the light.

Metaphor, then, is very much a part of the day-to-day language, so much so that its presence is often not even noticed by users of language.

93

It serves to encode and possibly reinforce our attitudes to many aspects of life. Given this, metaphor has the capacity to be a very powerful tool of language.

Metaphor to persuade

The previous section looked at the way in which metaphor encodes our attitudes to aspects of our society, and the way in which language can be manipulated to reflect attitudes or influence the opinion of readers or listeners. This section will look more closely at the way metaphor can be used to manipulate or influence, and particularly to persuade.

Activity

One of the most effective ways of persuading people is to present them with an image of themselves that they find desirable, or that they aspire to (flattery); or to present them with a self-image they want to change.

How does Text: Hewlett Packard use metaphor to present the reader with a self-image? How does this make the text more persuasive?

Commentary

This text uses metaphor to present the reader with an image of him/ herself. With the help of the graphology, it allows the reader to see his or her business as a lion, a strong, carnivorous animal, the 'king of the jungle'. Thus the world of business is presented as a harsh, natural environment, where only the strong or the fit will survive.

The company that wants a Hewlett Packard printer is 'hungry', it has 'new bite', it will 'bite deep'. All of these concepts fit in with the image desired by businesses in the 1990s – hard-hitting, strong and successful. By suggesting that the reader runs such a company (or that such companies will want this machine), the advertisement is creating a desirable self-image for the reader. The catch is that the possession of the printer is essential to the image.

Summary

When metaphor is brought into the picture, the complexity that exists in the relationship between word and meaning becomes apparent. It is not surprising that a computer program that can respond to human language is proving so elusive. How does a computer respond to metaphor? What does the metaphor 'Time flies like an arrow' mean? A computer program found five potential meanings for this.

◎ Time proceeds as quickly as an arrow proceeds. (The meaning most competent users of English would find with no difficulty.)
◎ Measure the speed of flies the same way you measure the speed of an arrow.
◎ Measure the speed of flies the same way an arrow measures the speed of flies.
◎ Measure the speed of flies that resemble an arrow.
◎ A particular species of fly, time flies, are fond of an arrow.

People are adept at making decisions about language meaning, so that despite the complexity of potential meanings for a particular word, most of us can decide which meaning is intended, and make the links that metaphorical uses ask of us without too much confusion.

IDIOMATIC LANGUAGE: FLOGGING DEAD CROCODILES AND KEEPING YOUR FEET UNDER WATER

The section on metaphor above looked briefly at the daily use of metaphor that is so commonplace that it goes almost unnoticed. A lot of these structures have a fixed and expected form. Some are so fixed that it is not possible to change a word or the structure without losing, or irretrievably changing, the meaning. Such structures are called **idioms.**

Idioms are units of language with a fixed grammatical and lexical content. Their meaning cannot be worked out from a study of the individual words contained in the idiom, and they frequently operate on a metaphorical level.

Idioms therefore function more like individual words than like phrases or sentences, and can be considered as lexemes according to the discussion at the beginning of this unit.

Activity

Complete the idioms in the list below by providing the missing words. Translate the idioms into clear, non-idiomatic English. Is a dictionary helpful here?

1	It's raining _____ and _____.
2	Don't feel sorry for him. Those are only _____ tears.
3	You should always call a _____ a _____.
4	Do it now before you get cold _____.
5	Since I gave up smoking, I feel as fit as a _____.

Commentary

Idioms present problems of direct translation. It is unusual to be able to substitute one word for another and provide a translation into non-idiomatic English. Frequently, a whole phrase has to be rewritten. Possible translations for the above examples are:

1   very heavily
2   insincere, hypocritical

97

3   speak plainly
4   get frightened
5   really well

What problems do idioms present to learners of a language?

Very real ones! First, it is not always possible for listeners or readers to recognise that an idiom exists, and they may assume the literal meaning. Second, without access to a good dictionary that gives examples of idiomatic uses, an idiom is untranslatable.

Activity

The examples in Text: Translations are all from translations into English by people for whom English is not a first language.

Text: Translations

> 1   On the menu of a Swiss restaurant: Our wines leave you nothing to hope for.
> 2   On the menu of a Polish hotel: Roasted duck let loose; beef rashers beaten up in the country people's fashion.
> 3   On the door of a Moscow hotel room: If this is your first visit to the USSR, you are welcome to it.
> 4   In an Acapulco hotel: The manager has personally passed all the water served here.

In some cases, these texts have gone wrong because the translator was unaware that he/she was dealing with idiom. In other cases, the translator has unwittingly produced an idiom that has a different meaning from the one that the combination of words would logically suggest.

Try to rewrite these texts into clear English. Identify the idiom that has caused the translation to go wrong.

Commentary

1   'Hope' is synonymous with 'desire'. Unfortunately, 'leaves nothing to be desired' means the opposite of 'nothing to hope for'. A translator who was not fluent in English, and who was working with a thesaurus, could easily fall into this trap.

2   'Free-range' is an expression of very fixed meaning. It may appear to mean the same as 'let loose', but it doesn't.

    The second mistranslation in this example is not a matter of idiom, but is a problem of lexical ambiguity (see p. 77 above). 'Battered' is synonymous with 'covered in batter' and with 'beaten up'.

3   'You are welcome' and 'you are welcome to it' have more or less opposite meanings. An inexperienced user of the language would have no way of knowing this.

4   The word 'pass' has the meaning 'to adjudicate or make judgement'. However, the phrase 'pass water' has a very specific meaning that presents a trap to both the fluent and the inexperienced user of the language.

Idioms are useful devices. They provide users of language with ready-made phrases that communicate a clear, agreed meaning. They add colour and variety to the language. Because of the fixed structure and lexis of most idioms, they function more like words than phrases, and in any discussion or analysis of word and meaning, it is useful to treat idioms as words.

DENOTATION AND CONNOTATION: WHAT ARE WORDS WORTH?

This section looks at the way words can carry value judgements with them. Each word will have its straightforward dictionary definition, but a large number of words will also carry extra associations, often personal or emotional, that the use of the word brings to mind. The dictionary definition of a word is its **denotation**. The denotation of the word 'dog' (noun) is 'carnivorous quadruped of the genus canis'. The personal or emotional meaning that a word may carry is its **connotation**. The connotations of the word 'dog' will vary from individual to individual. To one person, 'dog' may connote loyalty, bravery, faithfulness, love; to another person, it may connote noise, nuisance, filth, danger.

Some words carry strong connotations, and those connotations are generally agreed on by users of the language. Such words are often described as 'loaded'. Loaded words have strong negative or positive connotations, and can have a powerful emotional impact.

Activity

Look at the following words. Decide whether they have (a) no particular connotations, (b) strong negative connotations, (c) strong positive connotations.

> vehicle, slavery, democracy, was, photosynthesis, torture, the, brat, morphophonemics, Rolls Royce, fascism, building, freedom, hovel, a

Compare your analysis of the list with someone else's. Do you agree on which words are loaded, and whether they are positive or negative in their connotations?

Commentary

As discussed above, connotation depends to a certain extent on individual response. However, certain words do tend to evoke similar responses from individuals. Here is an analysis of the list produced by a group of students who did the activity collectively:

No connotations	vehicle, was, the, morphophonemics, building, a, photosynthesis
Negative	slavery, torture, brat, fascism, hovel
Positive	democracy, Rolls Royce, freedom

There was some disagreement about Rolls Royce, fascism and democracy. The group felt that Rolls Royce had connotations of wealth and luxury that could be used in either a negative or a positive way. They agreed in their response to fascism and democracy, but decided that people with different political beliefs might think differently.

What characterises the words that are not loaded? Grammatical words such as articles and auxiliary verbs are less likely to carry connotations, as their meaning is grammatical rather than lexical. Therefore 'was', 'a', 'the' carry no connotations.

Words that are highly specialised and are restricted to a particular area of meaning are less likely to be loaded. 'Morphophonemics' and 'photosynthesis' are probably too restricted and specialised in their use to carry any emotional loading. The majority of English speakers will not have 'morphophonemics' in their vocabulary, and though 'photosynthesis' is more widely known, it still has a restricted range.

Words that are highly general are also less likely to be loaded. There are a lot of words that have a classification function, in that they are general terms that encompass more specific terms.

'Vehicle' is a general term that encompasses car, bus, bicycle, lorry, truck, van, etc. 'Car' encompasses sports car, saloon, hatchback, and a whole range of specific names such as BMW, Rolls Royce, Lamborghini, that have a wide range of cultural connotations.

Words that have this classification function are called **hypernyms**. Examples of hypernyms are:

fruit, animal, bird, flower

The words with a more specific meaning that can be classified by the hypernyms are called **hyponyms**. Examples of hyponyms are:

apple, orange, banana
dog, cat, buffalo, warthog
robin, vulture, eagle

Hyponyms are more likely to carry strong connotations than hypernyms, though this is not an invariable rule. The word 'animal' can carry negative connotations in metaphors such as 'He behaved like an animal.' However, more specific connotations can be carried by the use of more specific words. 'He ate like a pig.' 'You rat!' 'She's a bitch.'

The section on synonyms above looked at the way the English language often has a range of words that focus around the same area of meaning. There are historical reasons for this that the next section will discuss, but often this wealth of synonyms allows speakers or writers to express an opinion by choosing a synonym that is loaded in a negative or positive way.

Look at Text: Amnesty. Identify words used for feelings and emotions, words used to name individuals, and words used to name groups of people. How does the word choice work to make the text effective?

Rewrite the text, substituting proper names for the nouns relating to groups of people (e.g. for 'soldiers' substitute a person's name). Has this changed the impact of the text? How?

What is the effect of the use of personal pronouns 'we' and 'you'?

Text: Amnesty

The reason you join Amnesty is not words, but pain.

It's the pain of children like 16 year old Sevki Akinci, literally barbecued alive by Turkish soldiers who came to his village looking for guns which they didn't find.

It's the tears of 17 year old Ravi Sundaralingam, tortured by Indian troops in Sri Lanka – tied upside down with a fire lit beneath his head and electrodes sparking at his genitals.

It's the anguish of Angelica Mandoza de Ascarza, whose teenaged son was taken from home by the security forces in Peru, never to be heard from again. He joined the hundreds who have simply 'disappeared.'

It's the terror of a 23 year old Tibetan nun, raped by Chinese soldiers with an electric cattle prod.

It's the agony of children like Walter Villatoro and Salvadore Sandoval, street children in Guatemala City, whose eyes were burned out by police cigars, their tongues ripped from their heads with pliers.

Maybe you simply don't realise that such vile things go on.

But for two years now, we have been running appeals in this newspaper. With one exception, all of these cases were mentioned in previous appeals.

Amnesty International

Commentary

Most of the words used for feelings and emotions are abstract nouns with connotations of great suffering. The suffering is closely linked to the people whose proper names are given. The text does not, therefore, talk about pain and agony in an abstract way, but about the pain and agony of named individuals. The perpetrators, however, are anonymous groups: soldiers, troops and police.

These are comments made by students who carried out this task:

The anonymous groups are more sinister, more frightening.

The groups make it sound official, as though the people in charge wanted it to happen. Names could just be criminal killers, and that's different.

The groups are all employed by governments. They are supposed to protect people, not torture them. That makes it worse.

The use of 'we' and 'you' helps to establish a sense of exclusion in the reader. The function of the text is to persuade people to join Amnesty International, and the initial exclusion, in this context, makes the reader feel guilty and in some way responsible. If you, as a reader, feel this, then it is likely that you will want to become included, one of the 'we' not one of the 'you'.

Activity

Look at the Amnesty text again, and the word 'barbecued' in line 3. Make a list of the connotations of this word (as it stands alone, not as it is used in the text).

Commentary

'Barbecue' has connotations of pleasure. Barbecues usually take place in good weather, often occur in party or celebratory situations, and are good fun. The object of the action is an item of food, often meat, and the effect of barbecuing is to brown and sear.

To talk about a person being barbecued gives them the status of a

103

piece of meat. This emphasises the contempt the perpetrators have for their victim. It is only too easy to visualise the effects implied by the use of this verb. The celebratory context that we associate with barbecues emphasises the shock the word creates, and also further dehumanises the perpetrators who could perform such an act.

The meaning of a text can, therefore, be strongly influenced by the connotations of the words that the producer of the text has chosen to use.

LINGUISTIC DETERMINISM: WORDS AND VIEWPOINTS

A very important aspect of the relationship between word and meaning is the cultural context in which the word occurs. It has been suggested that the language we speak may influence or determine the way we perceive the world. In other words, we are trapped in the maze of our own language because speakers of different languages code the world in different ways.

This concept is often exemplified by the idea that 'Eskimos have fifty words for snow'. The implication of this is that the perception of snow for this group is different from, say, a native English speaker who has only one word for snow. The problem with this example is that it is just not true. It is a bit of linguistic folklore. The Inuit language has about the same number of words for snow as English.

In fact the theory of linguistic determinism as it is often expressed is just not supported by the evidence. What does happen, though, is that we encode our prejudices and beliefs in language (see Metaphor, p. 83 above) in a way that may foster and reinforce such beliefs.

An example of this is the way gender is expressed in the English language. Many collective nouns for people are masculine (e.g. man, mankind). English no longer has a suitable ungendered third person pronoun in the singular, only 'he' and 'she'. Forms such as 'man' and 'mankind' are often called generic, that is, they are general terms that apply to both sexes. Feminists have argued that this can exclude women from the discussion, where such terms are used.

Activity

Look at the following short texts. Which ones are you happy with as constructions in English, and which ones do you feel are incorrect?

> This study looks at the development of the uterus in pigs, sheep and man.
>
> Any delegate may bring his husband or wife with him.
>
> The chairman must wear a dinner jacket or evening gown.

Commentary

Most people who do this activity find these texts problematic. Where a specifically female role is identified, the so-called generic form does not seem to work. This suggests that it is not truly generic and helps to foster the view that there are areas of human activity from which women are excluded, or to which they are peripheral.

Groups that have a lower status in society are frequently subjected to derogatory or demeaning terms. Words relating to women often undergo a process by which the original meaning is lost, and a new, derogatory meaning is acquired, or the original meaning is retained, but the new meaning becomes the more central one. This process is known as **pejoration**. Words relating to men, on the other hand, frequently retain their original meaning, or even undergo a process whereby the original meaning acquires extra status. This process is known as **amelioration** (see p. 118 below).

Activity

The following pairs of words are all originally equivalent in meaning, except that the first list refers to women, and the second to men. What range of meanings do these words currently have?

mistress	master
hostess	host
governess	governor
spinster	bachelor
lady	lord

Commentary

The words 'master', 'governor' and 'lord' have all retained their meaning of power and prestige. The female terms, 'mistress', 'governess' and 'lady' have acquired primary meanings that are non-prestigious. 'Mistress' has acquired connotations of illicit sexual relationships; 'lady' has become a more general term, occasionally derogatory. The word is frequently used in relation to employment in a way 'lord' is not, for example cleaning lady, dinner lady, lollipop lady; but not cleaning lord, dinner lord or lollipop lord.

'Hostess' has retained its original meaning, but has also acquired a meaning that has connotations of prostitution.

'Spinster' is a mildly derogatory term and is not used with any frequency, unlike 'bachelor' that has (or had until recently) positive connotations.

Language applied to ethnic minorities also has this quality, as the racist attitudes within a group are encoded in the language used.

Activity

In Text: Attitudes, the narrator, a woman, is in a Manhattan bar with two detectives, Malloy and Rodriguez. How does the word choice reflect the attitudes to race and gender that the writer is trying to depict?

Text: Attitudes

Malloy smiled. 'She's a good kid. She writes out my messages three times.'

...[Rodriguez]...looked around the room again, and he, too, saw the black girl. He smiled at her. Malloy caught me watching Rodriguez and winked at me.

'I thought you only liked dark meat on Thanksgiving,' Malloy said to him. He ordered another round. 'We know each other twenty years,' Malloy said to me.

'Longer,' said Rodriguez, not taking his eyes from the girl.

'Where's Marty?' Malloy asked him.

'He called in for a Twenty-eight. Said his mother was sick.'

'There was a homicide in the Three-Four,' Malloy said. 'A ground ball. Some spic did his wife. The captain went up.'

Rodriguez nodded. 'She must not of known when to shut up.'

I wondered if Rodriguez throught of himself as a spic.

Rodriguez looked away from the girl and said, 'You know, all you really need is two tits, a hole and a heartbeat.'

Malloy said mildly, 'You don't really need the tits.'

Rodriguez said, 'You don't even need the heartbeat.'

I reminded myself that Pauline says they have to despise us in order to come near us, in order to overcome their terrible fear of us. She has some very romantic ideas. I tried hard, but there must have been something a little pinched in my face, a momentary faltering, because Rodriguez said to me, 'You're one of those broads, right? You know, man, one of those feminist broads.' Working a lot of gender into one sentence.

Susannah Moore, *In the Cut*

Commentary

Moore depicts here a culture in which both racism and sexism are endemic. The words used by the men to name women either diminish (kid), demean (meat, broad), or identify by family role (wife, mother).

Women are also depersonalised into body parts, mainly sexual. The choice of the word 'hole' is interesting here. A hole is a nothingness. It is something that is defined by an absence. There are several possible terms the men could have used for female genitalia. The one chosen is not obscene or taboo, although the connotations are disturbing. The other parts of the woman are dismissed as unessential, most tellingly her heart-beat. We are left with an image of nothing – hole.

The language used in relation to race is also disturbing. It is demeaning both to women and to race, and is racist.

Some of this depiction is metaphoric (see p. 83 above). As discussed earlier, metaphoric description often encodes social and cultural attitudes and prejudices.

The selection of these words gives the passage the connotations that Moore is after, of a violent, misogynist, racist society. The words relating to these attitudes are put into the mouths of the people whose role it is to protect the social order – the police.

Summary: words and meanings

The term 'word' is, therefore, not as easy to define as it first seems. Any analysis of text that is looking at word level needs to be done with an awareness of the complicated relationship that exists between word and meaning, the ways in which this relationship can be used, and the existence of smaller units and larger structures that need to be considered in relation to the word.

Historical dimensions

This section looks at the origins of the English word stock, and the ways in which the language gains new words through the processes of borrowing, changing the use of existing words and creating new words.

GOT ANY SPARE WORDS?

English has often been described as having a very rich and extensive word stock. For political and historical reasons, it has borrowed from other languages all over the world, and still does. For example, Chinese food became popular in this country towards the middle of this century. This brought a whole range of new words into the language, many of them borrowed directly from one of the many dialects of Chinese. The word for the deep round-based pan used for stir frying, 'wok', is one of these.

For this activity, you will need an up-to-date dictionary that gives etymological information (information about the origins of a word).

Using a dictionary

1   2   3   4   5
CAMEL (kæməl). [Late Old English, adapted from Latin camelus adoption of

       6
Greek adopted from Semitic]

The section of a dictionary entry in square brackets gives information about the origin of a word. In the example above, 1 is the word itself, 2 is the phonological representation, 3 is the period it first arrived in English, 4, 5 and 6 show the route this word followed to arrive in the English language.

A full etymological dictionary, such as the *Oxford English Dictionary,* will give all the meanings a particular word has had since it came into English.

Look up the words in the following lists, and locate them on a world map according to their country and language of origin. Some words may not be located in a specific country, but a more general area such as North America, e.g. Wampum, N. American, from Algonquin, wampumpeag.

List 1 contains words that are comparatively recent additions to the language. You may not be able to find them if your dictionary is not a very recent one, but you should be able to identify the place of origin.

List 1

balti, barbie (barbecue), couch potato, fatwah, glasnost, internet, intifada, karaoke, macho, tandoori, tuckus

---

List 2 contains words that have been in the language for a relatively long time, and therefore should be in any comprehensive dictionary.

List 2

attorney, banjo, barbecue, brogue, budgerigar, bungalow, butter, cartoon, coleslaw, concerto, dilemma, dirge, dragon, geisha, gorilla, junta, kettle, kimono, knapsack, macaroni, mediator, moccasin, mosquito, paprika, pound, samovar, scot (as in scot-free), sinecure, scorch

---

A short dictionary investigation of this kind shows how widely the English language has borrowed from other languages. The borrowing is world-wide; in fact there are very few languages English has not borrowed from at one time or another. The reason for this lies in the history of both the language and the country. The earliest borrowed words, or **loan words**, are from Latin, with a very small number from the original Celtic languages of Britain.

The Viking invasion introduced Scandinavian words. The Norman conquest introduced a massive number of French loan words. Later contact with other European languages through cultural exchange, trade, political contacts and exploration gave the language Portuguese, Dutch, Spanish and Italian loan words. Languages from the Near East – Arabic, Turkish, Persian, Hindustani, Indic, Tamil – came via trade, exploration, colonisation and, sadly, the slave trade.

How long has this pick 'n' mix approach to our lexicon existed? The English language has always borrowed from other languages, so are there any words that are 'truly' English?

This concept, 'truly English', is a difficult one to define. The earliest language spoken in Britain was the ancestor of modern Welsh. The earliest words that are identifiably English come from the Germanic languages from which English developed. It is probably reasonable to say that these earliest words from the Old English period are 'truly English'.

Read Text: *Beowulf*; an extract from the Old English poem *Beowulf*, in which the monster, Grendel, comes to the King's hall in darkness and kills one of the warriors.

Text: *Beowulf*

> 710 Ðā cōm of mōre under misthleoþum
>   Grendel gongan, Godes yrre bær; . . .
>   . . . Nē þæt se āglæca yldan þōhte,
> 740 ac hē gefēng hraðe forman sīðe
>   slǣpendne rinc, slāt unwearnum,
>   bāt bānlocan, blōd ēdrum dranc,
>   synsnǣdum swealh; sōna hæfde
>   unlyfigendes eal gefeormod,
> 745 fēt ond folma.

Obviously, to the modern reader this looks like, and in many ways is, a foreign language. It is made more complicated by the fact that some of the letters have changed, the spellings are very different and the grammar of Old English required a lot of word endings (and some beginnings) that we no longer use. Can you identify any of the words? Try modernising the spelling and the word structure. Remove -e, -es, -a, -an, -um. Break the words into syllables to see if you can recognise parts of a word. Change the letters <Ð> ,<ð>, <þ>, to <th>, and <æ> to <a>. Do any words now look familiar, even if you can't give them a precise meaning? Do any look completely strange?

   Text: Translation (1) is a translation that is, as far as possible, word for word. How many words from the Old English text are still in use today?

Text: Translation (1)

> Then came over the moor under the mist bank
> Grendel going God's ire bore; ...
> ... Not that the fiend of delay thought
> but he seized quickly at the first opportunity
> the sleeping man slit greedily
> bit the bone-lock blood from the veins drank
> huge pieces swallowed soon had
> the unliving eaten completely
> feet and hands.

Text: Translation (2) is a translation into good modern English.

Text: Translation (2)

> The Grendel came across the moors under the cover of darkness. The anger of God was upon him. ... He didn't hesitate, but at the first chance, grabbed the sleeping man and greedily tore him apart, biting into the muscles, swallowing huge pieces and drinking the blood from the veins. Almost at once he had devoured the dead man completely, feet and hands.

Commentary

English has clearly lost a lot of words since the Old English period, but a large number have come down to the present day, particularly grammatical words such as articles and prepositions. There are also lexical words from this period in Modern English; commonly used verbs: come, go, think, drink, swallow, sleep; nouns to do with the body, weather and landscape, emotion and religion.

It is interesting to find so many in a passage that certainly doesn't relate to everyday experience. Modern English contains a lot of words from the Old English period, and interestingly the hundred most frequently used words are almost all Old English.

Even in this early period, English was borrowing from Latin and Greek, and this process continues to the present day. For historical reasons, Latin has been associated with learning and **formality**; words of Latin and Greek origin have become associated with a formal register. Look at the activity relating to levels of formality in Unit 4 (p. 179 ff.), and look up the origins of the words used in the texts. How many of them are of Latin or Greek origin?

Activity

The two extracts in Text: Speeches are taken from speeches made by Ronald Reagan (text 1) and Martin Luther King (text 2). Look up the origins of the underlined words. Which speech uses more Latin or Greek loan words? What is the overall effect? Which, in your view, is the most effective text?

Text: Speeches

Text 1

We're <u>approaching</u> the end of a <u>bloody century</u>, <u>plagued</u> by a <u>terrible invention</u> - <u>totalitarianism</u>. <u>Optimism</u> comes less easily today, not because <u>democracy</u> is less <u>vigorous</u>, but because democracy's <u>enemies</u> have <u>refined</u> their <u>instruments</u> of <u>repression</u>. Yet optimism is in order because day by day, democracy is proving itself to be not at all a <u>fragile flower</u>.

Text 2

I have a <u>dream</u> that one <u>day</u> on the <u>red hills</u> of Georgia the <u>sons</u> of <u>former slaves</u> and the sons of former slave owners will be able to <u>sit</u> down <u>together</u> at the <u>table</u> of <u>brotherhood</u>. . . . I have a dream that my four <u>little children</u> will one day live in a <u>nation</u> where they will not be <u>judged</u> by the <u>colour</u> of their <u>skin</u> . . .

Commentary

There is a very clear difference between the two texts. Reagan's speech has a high proportion of Latin or Greek loan words, or words that came into English from Latin via French.

King's speech, on the other hand, though it does contain some Latinate words, draws very much on the older forms that come from Old English or Old Norse.

Reagan's speech seems in some way more elaborate, perhaps more difficult to follow than King's speech, which draws on the language of everyday usage.

This does not mean that King's speech is more simple or less complex. It has a complex pattern of metaphor and of rhetorical devices that help to give it its impact. King, however, choosing to select words from the day-to-day vocabulary of his audience, has produced one of the most famous and memorable speeches of the twentieth century.

Activity

Using a thesaurus and a dictionary, replace the Old English and Old Norse words in King's speech with Latinate ones (e.g. I have a fantasy . . .). How has the impact of the text changed? Is it more or less effective in your view?

The origins of a word can often, therefore, be reflected in its use. It is not just a matter of formality. After the Norman conquest in 1066, the French language became associated with the court, the aristocracy, the wealthy and sophisticated. Our later contacts with and perceptions of French culture mean that English has often acquired words from the French language that relate to concepts of fashion, wealth and sophistication.

Activity

Text: Chanel is from the fashion pages of the *Observer*. Identify the origins of the underlined words. How do the origins of the words reflect the topic and the function of the text?

Coco Chanel first introduced the <u>androgynous</u> look to <u>womenswear</u> back in 1930s Paris; her pioneering appropriation of <u>masculine tailoring</u> for <u>female attire</u> has since become a staple of the working <u>woman's wardrobe</u>. This summer, city-boy <u>chic</u> looks good in or out of the office, with <u>briefcase</u> or <u>mobile</u> phone as optional <u>accessories</u>

Commentary

Many of the underlined words, words relating to the specialism of fashion, are loan words from French. Most of these are very much part of the day-to-day vocabulary. 'Fashion', 'attire', 'tailoring' may all be from a specialist field, but cause no problems to the reader.

As noted above, as early as the eleventh century, French words became associated with sophistication and fashion, and it is interesting that new words for artifacts that are not immediately associated with fashion but have clear connotations of 'style' to the modern reader have been taken from French. For example, why 'mobile' (French) phone, rather than 'portable' (Latin) phone?

Continued borrowing from French means that we tend to go to the French language when a word for a fashion concept is needed. 'Chic', for example, has its first recorded usage in 1856. Its status as a more recent arrival can be identified by its pronunciation, which has not become anglicised: /ʃik/ rather than /tʃɪk/.

French loan words came into English in great numbers as the language of a successful invader, and are well assimilated into the language. Loan words from other languages can often reflect the cultural contact that resulted in the borrowing. Thus, for example, words to do with music, particularly classical music, are often Italian in origin – aria, concerto, duet, opera, piano, violin – reflecting the interest that English culture had in Italian music.

Later borrowings from Italian reflect a recent interest in Italian cuisine ('cuisine' is a French loan word): lasagna, pizza, scampi are all recent arrivals, though spaghetti and gorgonzola have been in the language since the nineteenth century.

Dutch loan words have given English nautical terms and words to do with cloth (buoy, cruise, skipper; cambric, duffel).

Loan words from Eastern languages relate to science or trading goods (particularly fruits and spices): algebra, almanac, amber, camphor, orange, saffron, syrup.

English is often described as a language that has a very rich and versatile vocabulary. One of the reasons for this is the extent of the borrowing from other languages. English has probably more loan words in its word stock than any other language, and this gives the language a lot of scope for subtle shades of formality, tone and meaning.

WORDS MEAN WHAT I WANT THEM TO MEAN

The English language doesn't only acquire words by borrowing from other languages, though as the previous section demonstrates, many new words came into the language via that route. Another route is that of **semantic change**, or a change in the meaning of a word over time. A fairly recent example is the word 'gay', which used to have the primary meaning of happy or carefree, but now has the primary meaning of homosexual.

Activity

The following text appears to be nonsense. This is because the underlined words have been used with their original or earlier meaning. Look up the original meanings of the words, and rewrite the text into modern English.

> The <u>girl</u> wore his best <u>frock</u> to the dinner-party. He was a healthy young man with a healthy appetite, and he was in danger of eating so much he would <u>starve</u>. There was plenty of <u>meat</u> to suit his vegetarian tastes. After the meal, his <u>disease</u> was so bad he had to go and lie down.

Commentary

This text demonstrates the extent to which the meaning of a word can change. The problem faced by language purists who object to change of this kind is that many of the words that are commonly used have undergone the process they are objecting to, and unless they demand that the language should be subjected to some kind of 'purification' process in which all words were restored to their original meanings, the purists' position is a bit illogical.

There are patterned and recognised ways in which the meanings of words can change.

Generalisation and specialisation

A very common way for semantic change to occur is where a word either expands its meaning to include a wider range (generalisation) or narrows

117

its meaning to become more specific (specialisation). Examples of this include 'wife', a word that used to mean woman in the general sense. The word gradually specialised to mean 'a woman of humble rank or low employment', giving the language constructions such as ale-wife or fish-wife. The word now means married woman. The word 'tail', on the other hand, has generalised in meaning. It used to mean a hairy tail, as that of a horse or a fox. It has come to mean any tail.

Activity

Look at the text from the last activity again. Say whether the underlined words have generalised or specialised in meaning.

Beware of the word! Taboo and euphemism

An important influence in the semantic change of words is the change of meaning brought about by the associations a word may have. There are certain concepts a culture may be uneasy about, and words associated with these concepts may attract censure. When this happens, such words can develop negative connotations. They may then be replaced by other words that are seen as a better or 'nicer' way of expressing the concept. Unfortunately, once the new word becomes associated with the concept, it too begins to attract negative connotations and needs to be replaced in turn. This process is known as **pejoration**. The reverse process, whereby a word acquires a 'better' meaning, is known as **amelioration**. (See p. 105 above.)

Activity

The following words refer to the act of human excretion, and the place where this should take place. Classify the words into groups under the following headings: casual/slang, technical/medical, formal/polite.

pee, piss, urine, shit, crap, faeces, wee, pass water, urinate, defecate, go to the toilet/lavatory/bathroom, powder my nose, rest room, comfort station, w.c., ladies, gents, loo, lavatory, bog.

Which words or phrases would be acceptable in a fairly formal situation?

Commentary

A quick analysis of this word list suggests that excretion is a social mine-field in the English-speaking world (or parts of it). A group of students doing this activity decided that in informal, peer-group situations, English is well equipped with words (though there are many groups who would not find these terms acceptable, even in very informal situations). Most of the informal terms are slang, except for 'crap', 'shit' and 'piss'.

Interestingly, 'crap', a word that is mildly taboo, is probably a euphemism in origin. Its original meanings were husk, weeds and residue. 'Shit' has not changed its meaning over time, but is described in the *Oxford English Dictionary* as 'not in decent use'. 'Piss' is also an old form that has become mildly taboo.

Therefore, one word associated with a socially difficult concept began as a euphemism and has become taboo, while words that carry the original meaning have been considered taboo for some time. Presumably, newer euphemisms will also become taboo in turn.

'Piss' and 'shit' also seem to be acquiring new, non-taboo meanings. 'Pissed' is a well-known English slang term for drunkenness, and more recently American English has developed the meaning belongings, detritus, the rest, etc., for 'shit', as in the following examples:

'Bring all your shit with you.'
(part of an invitation from a New Yorker)

Cornelius looked at me. 'That means I'm getting an A. Now that I know the difference between ain't and aren't and shit.'
(Susannah Moore, *In the Cut*)

Technical and medical terms, urinate and defecate, would appear to be clear and direct in meaning. Urinate has just the meaning to pass urine, but defecate has the original meaning of to purify.

119

The formal terms are all euphemistic. The group noted that there is no polite way to say what you are going to do. In this context, the use of a technical term will not help. 'I am going to urinate' would not be seen as socially acceptable. There are only polite ways of saying where you are going or asking directions. Even the most apparently direct words for the place are euphemisms.

'Toilet' originally meant a piece of cloth in which clothes were wrapped, then a cloth cover for a dressing table, then the dressing table itself. Its current meaning is fairly recent and is American in origin.

'Lavatory' used to mean a place to wash yourself (compare with current use of bathroom). Both 'toilet' and 'lavatory' have become socially a bit difficult, and the language has acquired a newer range of euphemisms: ladies, gents, powder room, bathroom, rest room, etc.

Semantic change, as with borrowing, is a continuous process, and far more complex than the brief outline above suggests. An awareness of the capacity of words to shift and change their meaning helps the receiver of text to be aware of change as it has occurred, or as it is occurring.

GET YOUR NEW WORDS HERE! CREATING NEW WORDS

A third way in which English acquires new words is by word creation, either through invention following existing word patterns, or through the direct creation of new words. As with semantic change, this is a massive area, and this section will only address aspects of it.

Activity

Text: Invented words lists words that don't actually exist in the English language, but could do according to existing routes for word creation. Discuss the ways in which these words may have developed. Can you identify any words that do exist in the language that may have arrived via similar routes?

Text: Invented words

Word	Definition
Spide (verb)	To move like a spider
Bookaholic (noun)	Someone who is addicted to reading
Pimad (noun)	A personally identified multiple aerial device
Buscar (noun)	A car that is used as part of a car pool
Busc (verb)	To drive a buscar
Gummer (noun)	Someone who makes children eat food they don't want (reference to the then Minister of Agriculture, John Gummer, who fed his daughter a burger on TV in an attempt to allay fears about BSE)

Commentary

Spide

Words follow patterns (see section on morphemes p. 74 above). Many words in English follow the pattern verb, verb + -er (noun of agency). For example, there are pairs like dance (verb) and dancer (noun), play and player, sing and singer. Some nouns have the -er agency ending but have no corresponding verb. Hammer is a good example. It is conceivable, then, that such words might at some time generate their own verb. So 'spider' might generate 'spide', or 'hammer' might generate 'ham'.

Bookaholic

A common way in which new words are created is by adding affixes (prefixes or suffixes) to existing words. Prefixes such as after-, be-, un-, under-; suffixes such as -er, -like, -hood, -ing, are just a few of the possibilities. All of these affixes go back to the earliest days of the language. However, the language is developing new affixes. The suffix -aholic/ -oholic is an interesting one. The original source of this is the word alcoholic, from alcohol, the Latin adaptation of an Arabic word for a powder used to stain the eyes, from which we also get kohl, and -ic, a suffix used usually for forming adjectives, as in artistic, neurotic. However, for some reason modern users of English have seen the word structure as alc-oholic, and created a new suffix meaning 'addicted to'. A similar process has occurred with 'marathon', a word of Greek origin that

121

came into the language as a single morpheme (see p. 74 above), but has given English the new suffix -thon, thus telethon, congathon, etc.

Pimad

Another fairly recent way of forming new words is via initials. Words created this way are called acronyms. Examples are scuba (self-contained underwater breathing apparatus), AWOL (absent without leave). A very recent example is twoc, to take a car, usually for joy-riding. This word comes from the charge, taken without owner's consent.

Buscar

Existing words are often combined to create new words. This can be done as with the example above, by combining whole words (though bus is an example of another method of word formation, shortening; the original word was omnibus). Examples in the language are doorman, greenhouse. Joy-riding (see above) is another example, its recent status marked by the use of a hyphen. It can also be done by combining parts of existing words. 'Daisy' is a combination of 'day's' and 'eye', the day's eye.

Busc

This kind of formation, back formation, is similar to the way spide might be formed. The word 'buscar' sounds as though it is a noun of agency, and should have a verb: busc. In fact, this would be to mistake the origin and structure of the word. This doesn't prevent such a process from happening. 'Burgle' is a back formation from burglar, for example.

Gummer

New words are often formed from a proper noun, the name of the inventor or of a person particularly associated with a concept or idea. The word hoover, for example, was originally a brand name for a particular make of vacuum cleaner. It has become an alternative term for vacuum cleaner, and has also become a verb (interestingly, despite the patterns identified above for nouns of agency, we hoover the carpet, not hoove it). If the original vacuum cleaner had been invented by Mitsubishi or Hotpoint, would we hotpoint or mitsubishi the carpet?

Summary: historical dimensions

The English language is over a thousand years old. Its word stock is wide and varied, with immense capacity for expressing subtle shades and wide ranges of meaning. As a living language, English will continue to develop and expand its word stock in response to social change and development, technological change, changes in cultural and religious beliefs, and all those other factors that operate to make a language a tool that its users need.

Unit three

Sentences and structures

The main aim of this unit is to introduce you to some of the most significant patterns of English grammar. It is, of course, impossible to introduce all the patterns, but those selected here are generally likely to be significant in the organisation of texts. Knowing about these patterns and understanding how they function will help you to see how meanings are made in texts and can provide a basis for interpreting what the texts mean to you.

Grammar is only one level of linguistic analysis, and interpreting the use of grammar in the text is not the same as interpreting the text. To do this we need to consider other patterns of language too, such as vocabulary, phonology and discourse. But grammar is a central resouce for making and communicating meaning, and the more you understand how it works the more systematically you can work with texts that interest you.

Many students are frightened of grammar and of the terminology used to discuss it. Some consider that its study is no more than a mechanical exercise. The aim in this unit is to show how interesting and useful grammatical knowledge can be. The specific aim is to teach you some grammar by showing you how it works in different texts and contexts of use, not simply to name individual parts and forms out of context. To do this we need some language to talk about grammar, and part of that language will involve words and terms which are new and are explained in the 'Index of terms' at the end of the book. Most of these terms will be discussed and explained but some are emboldened. We aim to give you regular practice in using those terms so that you will feel comfortable and confident in talking and writing about grammar and working with grammar in texts.

Contents

In this unit you will learn about the following grammatical forms:

1   *Nouns and patterns*: nouns and noun phrases; modifiers; main verbs; tense; pronouns; simple and complex noun phrases
2   *Verbs and patterns*: tense; the verb 'to be'; modal verbs and modality
3   *Sentences and patterns*: sentence and clause structure; deictics
4   *Texts and patterns*: active and passive voice; transitivity; repetition

Texts used

◎   Poems, prose extracts
◎   Newspaper news reports
◎   A note from your milkman
◎   A charity appeal
◎   A campaign leaflet from an environmental organisation
◎   Advertisements
◎   An official notice

Activity

Grammar and patterns

The following sentence does not make sense. It is not grammatical. Put all the words in an order so that it does make sense overall. Then ask yourself how you did it.

weekend going am to I next disco the.

One way to do it is to look for groups of words which belong together in a pattern and then to put all the groups of words together. For example:

going am I   = I am going (or am I going?)
the to disco   = to the disco
weekend next   = next weekend

Sentences are made up of individual groups of words which form *patterns* with other groups of words. The patterns can be fixed; that is, they must follow a certain order. Or the patterns can follow different orders (though if they do, the meaning is normally changed).

For example, *to the disco* is a fixed pattern; but *I am going* can also be formed as *Am I going?* which turns a statement into a question. *I am going to the disco next weekend* can also be written as *Next weekend I am going to the disco,* which, by putting the reference to the time at the beginning, stresses *next weekend*.

Nouns and patterns

Activity

Write out a shopping list for shopping for your family at your local supermarket. List the ten items which you think your family would judge to be the most essential items. Look at the list you have produced and consider what the words have in common. The words will be mostly consumable or usable items but try to identify what they have in common as words. What does the list look like on the page?

127

Commentary

In this section we will examine **nouns** and patterns involving nouns. Nouns are one of the most prominent of forms in a language. In fact, quite a few texts can be made up just of nouns; for example, 'London' is a noun and can stand quite meaningfully on its own on a signpost, or in answer to a question or on a train or air ticket or as the title to a book. 'School' is a noun and can stand on its own on a road sign, for example. 'Apples' is a noun and can stand quite independently on a shop ticket or shop sign. Take any word from the first sentence in this paragraph and try to make a meaningful text. You will see that it is difficult to make a meaningful list with words like *we* or *this* or *in* or *involving* when they occur on their own.

The shopping list you wrote probably consisted of nouns such as

milk
bread
teabags
oven-ready chips.

As we have seen, nouns are not just single words; they form patterns with other words to form **noun phrases**. Again such phrases can stand on their own: for example, as titles to a book or story such as 'The Man with a Scar', or on a menu in a phrase such as 'Home-made celery soup', or on a shop front name such as 'The Body Shop' or 'The Vegetarian Restaurant'. Or on a shopping list such as 'oven-ready chips' or 'semi-skimmed milk'. Writers of all kinds of different texts regularly make creative and communicative use of nouns and noun patterns. A good example is the poem 'Off Course' (1966) by Edwin Morgan.

Text: 'Off Course'

```
          the golden flood      the weightless seat
          the cabin song      the pitch black
          the growing beard      the floating crumb
          the shining rendezvous      the orbit wisecrack
     5    the hot spacesuit      the smuggled mouth-organ
          the imaginary somersault      the visionary sunrise
          the turning continents      the space debris
          the golden lifeline      the space walk
          the crawling deltas      the camera moon
    10    the pitch velvet      the rough sleep
          the crackling headphone      the space silence
          the turning earth      the lifeline continents
          the cabin sunrise      the hot flood
          the shining spacesuit      the growing moon
    15       the crackling somersault      the smuggled orbit
             the rough moon      the visionary rendezvous
             the weightless headphone      the cabin debris
             the floating lifeline      the pitch sleep
             the crawling camera      the turning silence
    20       the space crumb      the crackling beard
             the orbit mouth-organ      the floating song
```

Edwin Morgan

The most striking feature of the poem is its layout. The arrangement of the words on the page, or what is termed the 'graphology' of the poem, is especially distinctive and leaves the reader a little uncertain as to how it is to be read. For example, you could read across the page, which is the more conventional 'direction'; but you could also read down the page, reading the two columns one after the other almost as if the words were part of some inventory or list, rather like the shopping list which you created above. The layout of the lines is unusual and disorientating. The second column does not have the clear order and pattern of the first column, and at line 15 it looks as if a new paragraph begins. The lines move in a different direction and, as in the title of the poem perhaps, appear to go 'off course'.

Extension

1 Why do you think the writer has laid out the text as described above?

2 Why are there no punctuation marks used in the poem?

Commentary

The new direction appears to be a disturbing one for there is no obvious structure or ending to it. The movement of the second column of words is even more markedly laid out to suggest disorder, and this suggestion is reinforced by the fact that the poem has no real *punctuation*. There are no commas or colons or semi-colons or capital letters anywhere in the text. And the absence of full stops, especially at line 21, suggests that there is no ending to the text; it remains free-floating, searching for a pattern rather then clearly following an already existing one.

Yet closer inspection of the poem reveals that there are patterns. There are patterns of grammar across the whole text which are remarkably consistent and unchanging. Most striking is the pattern of **noun phrases**. In each case the structure is that of *d m n*, where *d* = definite article, *m* = modifier and *n* = noun. In fact, this structure is repeated in every line in the poem.

The most basic examples of this *d m n* pattern are in lines such as the following:

the hot flood

where 'flood' is the noun (*n*), 'hot' the modifier (*m*) and 'the' the definite article (*d*). Or:

the weightless headphone

where 'headphone' is the noun, 'weightless' the modifier and 'the' the definite article.

One reason why the term 'modifier' is preferred here to the more usual term 'adjective' is that 'modifier' is more inclusive. For example, nouns can be modified by other nouns as in 'the space silence' and the 'orbit wisecrack', where 'space' and 'orbit', which are both nouns, fill in these noun phrases the position of modifier, defining more precisely the nouns to which they are attached.

Activity

As we have seen, this basic structural pattern pervades the whole poem, and repetition of this pattern is a key feature of the poem. But there are variations within the repeated patterns. Take a basic pattern such as

> the *pitch* black   (2)
> the *pitch* velvet   (10)
> the *pitch* sleep   (18)

and then find similar patterns in the poem in which a word is repeated with various partners. List as many of these patterns as you can. Why are there so many repetitions and what is suggested by the constant changes and variations?

Commentary

Here are some of the main patterns:

> the floating *crumb*   (3)
> the space *crumb*   (20)
> the space *debris*   (7)
> the cabin *debris*   (17)
>
> the *space* debris   (7)
> the *space* walk   (8)
> the hot *space* suit   (5)
> the *space* silence   (11)
> the *space* crumb   (20)

These are fairly straightforward repetitions, involving the same word classes in each case (for example *crumb* is a noun and is still a noun when it is repeated with a different partner word). But some of the words are in different patterns when they are repeated. For example:

> the *orbit* wisecrack   (4)
> the *smuggled* orbit   (15)

— where *orbit* is both a noun (15) and a modifier (4). But we can notice how the repetitions are in effect no simple repetitions. The repetition of words helps to tell a story. The *space debris* referred to in line 7 has

131

become the *cabin debris* in line 17. Bits and pieces floating in outer space are relatively normal but the presence of debris in a cabin works to suggest a kind of narrative in which events may have taken a turn for the worse.

In other words, the basic grammatical pattern provides a structural frame within and across which there are changing partnerships of words which in turn cumulatively create patterns of meaning. An increasingly prominent pattern is one in which there are suggestions of disaster or at least suggestions of things going seriously 'off course'. For example, headphones which crackle because of decreasing reception as the spacecraft moves further away from earth appear to become detached:

the *crackling* headphone   (11)
the *weightless* headphone   (17)

A *beard* which was *growing* normally (3) now collocates with *crackling* in an unusual and disturbing formation (20), possibly suggesting the movement of the hairs of a beard on the face of a dead body or on a body which has been subjected to electrical shocks or freezing air. The changing words within the same basic grammatical pattern enable the poet, Edwin Morgan, to embody changes to events and to perceptions of what is happening.

Activity

We should now consider other patterns which might go along with the noun phrases. For example, if we were to put the following nouns in a sentence, would you be able to make sense of the sentence?

> the tall man the black dog

What other words would you need to add to the sentence in order to make it make sense?

Take the verbs out of the following sentences. What are the results? Do the sentences make sense without the verbs?

> The girl kissed the boy.
> They lost the match 4-1.
> My friend's daughter has broken another vase.
> Paris is the capital of France.

Commentary

There are no main **verbs** in 'Off Course'. One effect of this omission of main verbs is that no clear relation seems to exist between the objects referred to in the noun phrases. Objects either seem not to act upon one another or have no particular 'action' of their own. Verbs create links. The links are usually between a grammatical 'subject' and a grammatical 'object'. In this example the subject 'man' is linked by a main verb 'walked' to the object 'dog':

> The man walked the dog

If the main verb is taken away, then the relationship between the noun 'man' and the noun 'dog' is no longer clear. Similarly, in the sentence

> My friend's daughter   has broken   another vase
>   (subject)   (verb)   (object)

if the verb phrase 'has broken' is removed, we are left with 'My friend's daughter another vase', where we cannot work out the precise relationship between 'My friend's daughter' and the 'vase'.

So it is with the noun phrases in 'Off Course'. Verbs generally work to connect things, and so in this case the main effect is that of normal relations being suspended and disconnected. The poet has suspended the normal rules of grammar to create a world in which everything is turned upside down and suspended. In one sense this is appropriate to the conditions of outer space in which there is no gravity, but it may also suggest a space journey in which actions and events have become disturbingly abnormal.

The absence of main verbs in a text also removes any sense of time. Verbs are normally marked when something is taking place or took place. Thus, 'walked' tells you that the action is completed and is in the past tense. If there are no verbs in a text then there is no **tense**, and if there is no tense it is difficult to work out within what timescale things are happening. The poem 'Off Course' has as a result a certain timeless quality, as if normal temporal relations are suspended too.

However, it is not true to say that there are no verbs in the poem. There *are* verbs in the poem. For example, there is another distinct pattern in the text formed from the following groups of words:

> the floating song
> the growing beard
> the shining rendezvous
> the turning continents
> the crackling headphone
> the crawling deltas

and so on. The words ending in -ing are all what are termed present participles. The differences between the two verbal items in the following sentences:

> the world turns
> the turning world

underline that present participles function to create a sense of continuing, if suspended, action. In the poem they convey a feeling of things continuing endlessly or, at least, without any clear end. It may not be inappropriate, therefore, that the final line of the poem contains the group of words:

> the floating song

which, with an absence of punctuation, possibly reinforces the idea of an endlessly drifting journey without a conclusion.

Notice, too, how many film titles contain present participles: for example, *Leaving Las Vegas*, *Boxing Helena*, *Being There*, *No Turning Back*. There are many more similar titles to check out in a local video shop, but consider why such forms are so common.

PRONOUNS AND PATTERNS

Although we interpreted the previous text 'Off Course' as being about a space journey which involved the lives of astronauts, there are, in fact, no actual references in the poem to people. The nouns refer to actions which we take to involve humans but the poem does *not* contain lines such as

> His rough sleep
> His growing beard
> Your hot spacesuit
> Her cabin song
> Our floating lifeline.

Words such as 'you', 'my', 'your', 'his', 'her' are **pronouns**. The main personal pronouns are: I, you, he, she, it, we, they. They are the main means of identifying speakers, addressees and others. The main possessive pronouns are: my, your, her, his, their, our. They indicate ownership. (Other types and functions of pronouns are explored in Unit 4 pp. 192 ff.) One possible effect of the absence of pronouns from 'Off Course' is to make the poem a little impersonal and cold, almost as if we are hearing a list of facts.

Activity

Text: Milk message also presents a number of facts but does it in a different way.

Find all the pronouns in this text and list them. Whom do they refer to? Why are so many pronouns used in the text?

135

Text: Milk message

Dear Valued Customer

A MESSAGE FROM YOUR CO-OP MILKMAN

You are probably aware of some of the major changes happening to the British Dairy Industry. I would like to take the opportunity to explain the action CWS Milk Group have taken to protect our service relationship with you, despite the increases in the cost of milk to us from the Milk Marketing Board (Milk Marque).

On the 1st July 1994 there was a rise in the price of milk charged to all dairies. Since this date we have held back on any increase to you, our valued doorstep customer.

Whilst we face still further increases in milk prices charged to us, *we are at present only increasing our price by 1p per pint. I hope that the action we have taken will give you confidence to continue to support us during these difficult times safeguarding our unique British service.*

The Co-op home delivery service performs a valuable social role within the community to all sectors, particularly to the aged, disabled and households with children. To all customers I offer on a daily basis a full range of milk types and a very competitively priced range of essential food items.

Please find enclosed coupons worth £2.00, as a special thank you for your continued support.

YOUR FRIENDLY CO-OP MILKMAN

Effective date Sunday 30th October 1994

Commentary

The strategy of the CWS Milk Group here is to address the customer directly and to show their sensitivity to their customers as individuals. In this message personal pronouns such as 'I', 'we' and, in particular, 'you' are extensively employed. A key sentence is:

> Since this date we have held back on any increase to you, our
> valued doorstep customer.

The message manages to describe the sale of milk to customers as if it were a collaborative venture. The use of the plural pronouns 'we', 'our', 'us' underlines the sense of the CWS group, the individual milkman and the customer as a 'team', and this is further emphasised by the description of the delivery of milk as an essential social and community service. At the same time the message is still a subtly individualised message. The 'letter' is written as if it is from each individual milkman who uses the singular personal pronoun 'I' (complete with personal photograph) to personalise the relationship with 'you', the customer. It is an effective piece of writing and it is all the more effective for personalising a message which informs us that the price of milk is to go up. The resigned expression on the face of the milkman tells us that there is little anyone can do about this state of affairs but we can continue to look positive and good-humoured. Holding his milk crate like a trophy also establishes a clear pride in his job and in his relationship with his customers.

One other very obvious grammatical difference between the 'Milk message' and the poem 'Off Course' is that the message is written in complete sentences and makes use of much more familiar and conventional patterns of paragraphing and punctuation. The use of upper-case (capital) letters at the beginning and end of the message also emphasises the personal and individual nature of the relationship between the milkman and the customer.

Activity

Now read the 'Milk message' and see how many noun phrases you can find which have the same *d m n* pattern as those in 'Off Course'. If they are the same, consider why they are the same and, if the patterns are different, consider how and why they are different. It may help to list all the nouns that you can find in the text and then all the modifiers which occur in front of these nouns. Here are two examples to start you off:

the CWS Milk Group
the Milk Marketing Board.

Here the nouns are *Group* and *Board*; the modifiers are *CWS Milk* and *Milk Marketing*.

Commentary

In 'Off Course' the noun phrases are written, as we have seen, in the same pattern of *d* (definite article), *m* (modifier) and *h* (headword); in the 'Milk message' text the pattern is more complex. Here are some examples:

> the CWS Milk Group
> the Milk Marketing Board
> our valued doorstep customer
> the Co-op home delivery service
> a valuable social role
> a very competitively priced range of essential food items
> households with children.

These examples illustrate the much wider range of noun phrases which are possible in English, and they also illustrate that modifiers can occur after the main noun as well as in front of the main noun. The modifiers which occur before a main noun are called **pre-modifiers** while the modifiers which occur after a main noun are called **post-modifiers**. In these examples 'with children' and 'of essential food items' are post-modifiers. On the surface they help to make the text a little more dense and complex to read than 'Off Course'.

Compared with 'Off Course' the 'Milk message' also employs more pre-modifiers in front of the main noun. This feature allows description to be a little more detailed and precise. Several of these pre-modifiers are also themselves nouns; and we should note that the pre-modifying nouns cluster in phrases which describe organisations or which provide a more technical definition of actions or entities (for example, the *Co-op home delivery* service). Normally, the more nouns which are used in a pre-modifying position the more technical or specialised the reference will be. You can often identify writing in science and engineering by the amount and density of this kind of pre-modification. For example, here are some terms from a car maintenance manual:

> metal hub-bearing outer race
> low-friction disc brakes
> aluminium precision dial gauge.

Although the letter to customers from their milkman is designed to be a personal letter, it nonetheless suggests that it is from a company which is in some way also specialised and efficient.

1   Text: Reebok trainers is an advertisement for training shoes. There are a number of interesting features of this text but your first task is to underline all the personal pronouns contained in it. How many pronouns are there? What kinds of pronouns are there? Are the pronouns singular or plural pronouns? What seems to be the purpose of the writer of the advertisement in using pronouns?

What is the shape of the advert? Why are capital letters in the centre and why does it seem as if the whole is like a wheel with spokes linking the centre and the perimeter? How many of the words at the centre are pronouns? Why?

2   Your second task is to underline the noun phrases in the text. When you have done this, write a short paragraph in which you say what you think the main effect is of noun phrases such as:

Hexalite lightweight cushioning
medially posted dual density midsole
Graphlite arch.

3   Your third task is to write a brief advertisement yourself. You may choose the product for which you wish to write the advertisement but your text should make particular use of personal pronouns and of pre-modified noun phrases. Your choices of language should be appropriate to the product you wish to advertise.

Text: Reebok trainers

AZTREK: Running is your life.

Here's your life support. The Reebok Aztrek.

A rugged running shoe with a medially posted dual density midsole

and Hexalite lightweight cushioning

Life is hard. So is asphalt.

One of them just got easier.

Maybe two.

You've got heart. You've got drive.

R E E B O K

BELIEVES
in the athlete
IN ALL OF US.

You've got desire. We've got shoes.

SATELLITE:

You play, you lift,

you train and you run.

And you wear

the Reebok Satellite,

a lightweight

cross training shoe

with a running profile and Hexalite

to cushion the heel,

because it's a truly

runnable cross trainer.

And you keep on running.

AEROSTEP PRO:

You never compromise.

You wear the Reebok Aerostep Pro.

With its Graphlite arch,

there's no compromising

weight for support.

So it's perfect for

Step Reebok™ class

or any aerobics class.

In fact, it might even

be the most versatile

shoe in its class.

TELOS:

What you've got in your head

is a whole planet full of mountains, trails; challenges.

So what you need on your feet

is a serious hiking shoe

made from a whole bunch of recycled and environmentally sensitive materials.

The Reebok Telos. How close to the earth do you want to get?

FOR MORE INFORMATION ABOUT REEBOK PRODUCTS FOR WOMEN, CALL 1-800-843-4444.

Reebok™

©Reebok International Ltd. All rights reserved. REEBOK, HEXALITE, and GRAPHLITE are registered trademarks and STEP REEBOK is a trademark and a servicemark of Reebok International.

Verbs and patterns

One of the most striking features of the poem 'Off Course' (see p. 129) is the absence of a main verb. In that poem one of the effects created by the omission of a main verb is a sense of suspension and disorientation as it becomes increasingly difficult to work out, grammatically, what are the objects and what are the subjects in the text (for discussion of 'subjects' and objects', see pp. 133). Readers find it difficult to know where they are.

Text: *Bleak House* (1852–3) is the opening four paragraphs from Charles Dickens's novel. Dickens is one of the major English nineteenth-century novelists who saw the legal system of the country as a source of corruption and as a major obstacle to progress. Here the 'Lord Chancellor' is the head of the legal system.

One of the most striking features of Dickens's use of the language is that the opening three paragraphs do not contain a single main verb. Is the effect which is created for the reader the same as that created in the poem 'Off Course'?

Text: *Bleak House*

London. Michaelmas Terms lately over, and the Lord Chancellor sitting in Lincoln's Inn Hall. Implacable November weather. As much mud in the streets, as if the waters had but newly retired from the face of the earth, and it would not be wonderful to meet a Megalosaurus, forty feet long or so, waddling like an elephantine lizard up Holborn Hill. Smoke lowering down from chimney-pots, making a soft black drizzle, with flakes of soot in it as big as full-grown snowflakes – gone into mourning, one might imagine, for the death of the sun. Dogs, undistinguishable in the mire. Horses, scarcely better; splashed to their very blinkers. Foot passengers, jostling one another's umbrellas, in a general infection of ill-temper, and losing their foot-hold at street-corners, where tens of thousands of other foot passengers have been slipping and sliding since the day broke (if this day ever broke), adding new deposits to the crust upon crust of mud, sticking at those points tenaciously to the pavement, and accumulating at compound interest.

Fog everywhere. Fog up the river, where it flows among green aits and meadows; fog down the river, where it rolls defiled among the tiers of shipping, and the waterside pollution of a great (and dirty) city. Fog on the Essex Marshes, fog on the Kentish heights. Fog creeping into the cabooses of collier-brigs; fog lying out on the yards, and hovering in the rigging of great ships; fog drooping on the gunwales of barges and small boats. Fog in the eyes and throats of ancient Greenwich pensioners, wheezing by the firesides of their wards; fog in the stem and bowl of the afternoon pipe of the wrathful skipper, down in his close cabin; fog cruelly pinching the toes and fingers of his shivering little 'prentice

141

boy on deck. Chance of people on the bridges peeping over the parapets into a nether sky of fog, with fog all round them, as if they were up in a balloon, and hanging in the misty clouds.

Gas looming through the fog in divers places in the street, much as the sun may, from the spongey fields, be soon to loom by husband-man and ploughboy. Most of the shops lighted two hours before their time – as the gas seems to know, for it has a haggard and unwilling look.

The raw afternoon is rawest, and the dense fog is densest, and the muddy streets are muddiest, near that leaden-headed old obstruction, appropriate ornament for the threshold of leaden-headed old corporation: Temple Bar. And hard by Temple Bar, in Lincoln's Inn Hall, at the very heart of the fog, sits the Lord High Chancellor in his High Court of Chancery.

Commentary

There are, of course, verbs in this opening to the novel. It is, in fact, difficult to construct a text without verbs and this passage is no exception. In the opening paragraph alone there are verbs such as 'retired', 'waddling', 'splashed', 'jostling', 'slipping', 'sliding', and so on. The verbs all serve to create an atmosphere of constant action and movement in the big city. Yet there are no **finite verbs** in main **clauses** in the text. There is thus a difference between the following two sentences, the first of which (1) contains a main finite verb, the second of which (2) does not:

(1)   Foot passengers jostled one another's umbrellas and lost their foothold at street corners.

(2)   Foot passengers jostling one another's umbrellas and losing their foothold at street corners.

Main finite verbs provide, as it were, a kind of anchor for the action. You know clearly when something took place and that the action was completed. In the second sentence above you are left suspended, knowing that the action is ongoing, but awaiting a main verb to give you your bearings. A sentence such as the following provides that kind of 'anchor' for the action in the verb *arrived*, which is the finite verb in the sentence:

Foot passengers jostling one another's umbrellas and losing their foothold at street corners *arrived* at the bank.

A finite verb is thus a verb which tells you when something happened (past or present), how many were/are involved (singular or plural) and who the participants are (you/we/I, etc.). By contrast, when a **non-finite** -ing form is used the verb can be referring to any number, or tense, or first, second or third person. For example:

She is singing.
They have been singing.
You might be singing.

In these examples, *singing*, *been* and *be* are the non-finite forms; *is*, *have* and *might* are the finite forms.

Sentence (2) above is a kind of model for many of the sentences in the first three paragraphs. Sentences such as the following therefore serve to create a sense of both disorientation and dislocation. We feel that all the activity of London is confused and directionless; and we do not know what timescale we are in. The present participles in particular convey a feeling of continuous action which could almost be timeless.

London.
Implacable November weather.
Smoke lowering down from chimney pots . . .
Dogs, undistinguishable in the mire.
Foot passengers, jostling one another's umbrellas
Fog in the eyes and throats of ancient Greenwich pensioners, wheezing by the firesides . . .
Gas looming through the fog in divers places . . .

Given the timeless character which is imparted to these descriptions it is perhaps not surprising that Dickens can suggest that London has an almost prehistoric feel to it — 'and it would not be wonderful to meet a Megalosaurus, forty feet long or so, waddling like an elephantine lizard up Holborn Hill'.

In the final paragraph of this opening to *Bleak House* main finite verbs are restored to the sentences of the text. In particular the main verb 'to be' is repeated: 'The raw afternoon is rawest, and the dense fog is densest, and the muddy streets are muddiest . . .'. The presence of a main verb is most noticeable in the final sentence:

143

And hard by Temple Bar, in Lincoln's Inn Hall, at the very heart of the fog, sits the Lord High Chancellor in his High Court of Chancery.

Here the main finite verb is *sits*. The action and location of the Lord High Chancellor is thus clearly situated. Indeed, the sentence is structured so that the location of the main subject of the sentence ('the Lord High Chancellor') comes first in the sentence. He sits:

hard by Temple Bar
in Lincoln's Inn Hall
at the very heart of the fog.

Structured differently, the sentence might have read:

The Lord High Chancellor sits hard by Temple Bar in Lincoln's Inn Hall at the very heart of the fog.

This structure would be more normal and would follow the conventional word order for sentences in English in which the subject ('The Lord High Chancellor') occurs first and is then followed by a main finite verb ('sits').

One of Dickens's purposes may be to delay the subject so that it has more impact as a result of its occurrence in an unusual position. It also has a very particular impact as a result of being in the simple present tense ('sits') when readers of a novel or of any kind of narrative might expect verbs to be in the simple past tense ('sat').

'Sits' suggests, however, that the Lord High Chancellor always sits there and is a permanent landmark in this landscape. The simple present tense in English carries this sense of a permanent, general, unchanging truth, as in scientific statements such as:

Oil floats on water.
Mice have long tails.
Two and two make four.

In this final paragraph one of the main effects which Dickens creates may be to imply that the legal system of the country is in a state of permanent confusion or creates states of confusion which cannot be changed. And both in these opening paragraphs and in the novel as a whole *fog* assumes symbolic importance, reinforcing a sense both of general confusion and of not being able to see clearly. The Lord High Chancellor is always 'at the very heart of the fog' and nothing will alter this position. For this reason perhaps choices of language and of the structure of the sentence position 'the Lord High Chancellor' and 'the heart of the fog' together.

Activity

Text: Oxfam an advertisement for a charitable organisation. Its main slogan is: This envelope changes lives. The main verb is in the simple present tense. The simple present tense is also used extensively throughout the advertisement (for example, 'buys', 'pays for', 'helps'). Why does the writer use the present tense?

Text: Oxfam

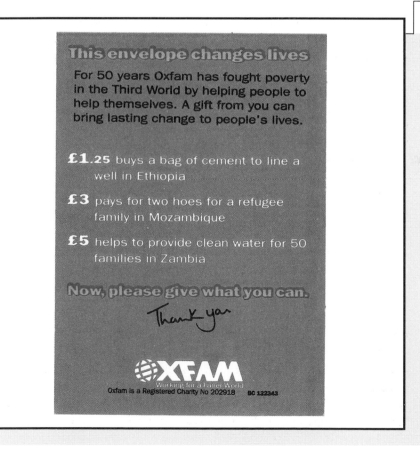

145

Commentary

The simple present tense is used to make action sound definite. In a world in which so many different charitable organisations are appealing to us for money and where donors may question the use to which their contributions are put, it is important that Oxfam conveys certainty and authority. '£1.25 buys a bag of cement . . .' is an unambiguous statement. Part of the effectiveness of the language on this appeal envelope derives from the way in which the simple present tense is used to inspire confidence in the donor that their money will make a difference.

MODALS AND MODALITY

Text: Severn Trent Water communicates information; in this case the information concerns an interruption to the water supply and is on behalf of a water company. Whenever instructions are given, a **modality** enters the relationship between the writer and reader of a text. Modality takes a number of different forms in English but the presence of **modal verbs** is particularly significant. Here are some of the main modal verbs in English:

can, could, will, would, must, should, shall, may

Activity

What is the function of modal verbs in Text: Severn Trent Water?

What other verb forms work, in particular to establish a relationship between the water company and the customers to whom it has distributed this notice?

146

Text: Severn Trent Water

Severn Trent Water

Notice of interruption to supply

We are sorry to inform you that necessary mains repairs in the area may cause an interruption to your water supply between the hours overleaf.

1. Every effort will be made to keep inconvenience and the duration of the shut-off to a minimum.

2. Do not draw more water than your minimum requirements.

3. If the water does go off, do not leave taps open or flooding may result when the supply is restored.

4. You may use water from the hot water system but it must be boiled before drinking.

5. Even if the domestic hot water supply runs dry there will be no risk of damage to the system, but as a precaution keep a low fire where a back boiler is installed and turn or switch off other sources of heating the water by gas, oil or electricity.

6. Central heating systems can continue to be used at moderate temperatures.

7. The main will be flushed before the supply is restored but discolouration and or chlorine may persist for a short time. Allow your cold tap to run for a few minutes to clear this water from your service pipe.

8. Do not use your washing machine or other appliances during the discolouration.

We apologise again for any inconvenience this may cause you and request your patience and co-operation. In case of any difficulty please contact the Nottingham District Office on the telephone number 608161, extension 4012.

Please remember neighbours who may be older or disabled - they may need your help.

ST,6253

Commentary

This text is in a curiously mixed mode. The water company has to inform its customers that repairs are unavoidable. It has to give its customers instructions which they need to follow both in their own interests and in the interests of other consumers. At the same time the company needs to reassure its customers that a more or less normal service is still available, that, in spite of the interruption to supply, the company still provides a good service and, above all, that there are no safety or health risks involved for its customers so long as they comply with the guidelines and instructions issued with the notice. It is important therefore that the company is clearly seen to be in control. This 'mixed mode' is inscribed in the different modal verbs in the texts along the following general lines:

◎ *Mode of reassurance/possibility*: *may* cause an interruption; *may* persist for a short time; they *may* need your help; every effort *will* be made; flooding *may* result; any inconvenience this *may* cause you.

◎ *Mode of control*: *must* be boiled before drinking; the main *will* be flushed; *can* continue to be used.

Notice that some modal verbs can signal possibility and control, depending on the other words which surround them as well as on the context in which they are used. For example, 'you may use water' (primarily control); 'they may need your help' (primarily possibility).

'Control' is also established through an extensive use of imperative forms of the verb which unambiguously inform us what to do and what not to do. For example:

Do not leave taps open
Allow your cold tap to run
Do not use your washing machine
Please remember neighbours.

Activity

Collect examples of further texts in which you would expect modal verbs to be used quite extensively. For example:

◎ horoscopes
◎ weather forecasts
◎ problem pages
◎ school notices
◎ recipes
◎ legal texts.

What other examples can you find? Why are modal verbs concentrated in some texts but not others?

Sentences and patterns

In this section we explore the role of grammatical patterns within larger patterns of language. We will consider the role of individual grammatical words and phrases but will focus on complete sentences.

Activity

Read Text: Christian Aid, an advertisement for making a will. Make a list of the main patterns you can find in the text. For example, the patterns can consist of repeated words and phrases, grammatical patterns (same type of pronoun or verb or noun phrase) as well as typographic and other patterns of layout. What do you think are the main effects produced on the reader by the patterns you have noticed?

Text: Christian Aid

Will your only legacy be upset, confusion and paperwork?

Without a Will, your wishes could count for nothing.

Without a Will, the State could take everything.

Without a Will, your family could lose out.

Without a Will, the taxman could easily benefit.

Without a Will, you can't remember your friends.

Without a Will, you can't remember Christian Aid.

Without a Will, life may be difficult for those closest to you.

Without a Will, life may be impossible for those far away.

- -

If you would like to find out how easy it is to make a Will, send for our free new booklet 'A Will to Care' to Christian Aid, Freepost, London SE1 7YY or phone Glenn McWatt 071-620 4444 ext 2226.

Name Mr./Mrs./Ms./Miss _____

Address _____

Postcode _____ **Christian Aid**

150

The poem 'This is a Photograph of Me' is by the Canadian writer Margaret Atwood. As you read the poem and start to work out what it means to you, you might think about the following questions:

1 Who is the 'me' in the poem? Who is being shown the photograph?
2 Can you take the words of the poem literally?
3 Why is the speaker only 'just under the surface', if she/he has drowned the day before? Why can we 'eventually' see the subject of the poem if we 'look long enough'?

Text: 'This is a Photograph of Me'

It was taken some time ago.
At first it seems to be
a smeared
print: blurred lines and grey flecks
blended with the paper;

then, as you scan
it, you see in the left-hand corner
a thing that is like a branch: part of a tree
(balsam or spruce) emerging
and, to the right, halfway up
what ought to be a gentle
slope, a small frame house.

In the background there is a lake,
And beyond that, some low hills.
(The photograph was taken
the day after I drowned.

I am in the lake, in the center
of the picture, just under the surface.

It is difficult to say where
precisely, or to say
how large or small I am:
the effect of water
on light is a distortion
but if you look long enough,
eventually
you will be able to see me.)

Commentary

The title to this poem is intriguing. You might consider that its meaning is quite straightforward. You might consider that the line is spoken by somebody who is showing somebody else a photograph. You might consider that the poem is the photograph. Answers to these questions seem to be basic to our understanding of the poem. But it is not impossible that all the references in the poem to things being vague '(balsam or spruce)', 'a thing that is like a branch', and to outlines and shapes being 'blurred' and 'smeared' and 'blended' are deliberate, that everything is not as it at first seems and that we should perhaps not always assume that everything we see is obvious.

And in this connection you might also think about the word *drown*. Has the speaker literally drowned or are we invited to think of other meanings for the word drown? For example, we can drown in a sea of paperwork or letters to be written or we can drown in unsolved problems. However we choose to interpret the poem we cannot ignore such words; and we are likely to remain intrigued, in particular, by a word like *this* which is ambiguous. 'This' is a **deictic**. Words like *this, that, those, here, there* are all deictics. Deictics are directing or pointing words in so far as they direct our attention to particular points of reference. In this poem 'this' points to something which is near to us, maybe even to what is in front of our eyes, but it is not clear exactly what it refers to.

Several grammatical choices made in the poem by the writer also underline a tone of uncertainty and lack of clarity. For example, the poem refers twice to when the photograph 'was taken'. The choice of voice is that of the passive voice; and the subject, that is, *who* took the photograph, is not declared. In English a passive sentence allows actions to be described without the main agent of those actions needing to be mentioned; and sometimes the omission of the agent can be deliberate because we may not know the agent or because we choose not to mention by whom or by what means something is done. The use of the passive voice here in the sentences

> It was taken some time ago

> The photograph was taken
> the day after I drowned.

adds to the apparent vagueness and indefiniteness of the experiences described.

References to time are also vague and not entirely logical and consistent. The tense of the poem, although mostly in the present, alternates between past and present. For example, 'the day after I drowned' contrasts with 'I am in the lake'. The reader is consequently not sure of the temporal order or dimension in which they are placed by the poem.

This commentary continues after the next activity.

Activity

We have observed above that there are several means open to us in language to register certainty and uncertainty, definiteness and indefiniteness. Before looking at the extract below from a conversation between university students, look back to the activity on p. 146 and to the commentary on pp. 147 and 148 where there is discussion of different degrees of certainty in language use. Now read the extract below and underline all those words and phrases which allow the speakers to sound deliberately vague, tentative and 'politely' indefinite (students are discussing how they've changed since coming to university).

153

> *A:* But you don't notice so much in yourself, do you? I don't think so, on the whole.
>
> *B:* I don't know, I definitely feel different from the first year. I don't think I look any different or anything.
>
> *A:* You're bound to keep changing, really, all your whole life hopefully.
>
> *B:* I don't know, I think it's probably a change coming away, I suppose ...

Commentary

Likewise, what is certain and what is less certain is written into contrasts in modality in the poem. Modality in language underlines our subjective assessments of things; for example, adverbs like *probably, perhaps, generally, apparently, definitely* and phrases like *it is certain, I am sure* or *I don't know*, verbs such as *it seems* or *it appears* or the use of the present tense (e.g. Oil *floats* on water) encode different degrees of subjective response in the viewpoint of a speaker or writer. More specifically too there are modal verbs such as *must, will, can, ought to, should, bound to*. In 'This is a photograph of me' there are contrasts between a viewpoint in which everything is definite ('... you *will* be able to see me'; '... there *is* a lake') and a way of seeing where there is greater vagueness and unclarity ('... it seems to be'; 'It is difficult to say where precisely'). The speaker in the poem knows what 'ought to be' but things do not seem straightforward.

A note of strangeness and uncertainty is also created by the poet by putting the conclusion to the poem in brackets. And after the definiteness and confidence of the short penultimate sentence:

> I am in the lake, in the center
> of the picture, just under the surface.

the final sentence is in distinct contrast. It is longer, more complex in structure and mixes subordinate and main clauses (the 'if' conditional clause is a subordinate clause), so that the grammar meanders as if 'it is difficult to say' where things are going and what they might mean.

We perhaps need to ask why the poet is making so much of uncertainty of viewpoint and the difficulty and unreliability of seeing clearly. (Notice by the way the number of times that there are references to 'seeing' ('see', 'scan', 'look').) We also perhaps need to ask who the speaker is and who is being spoken to. And in so doing we need to accept the seemingly improbable situation of someone who has already drowned showing us a picture of him/herself.

A basic interpretation of this poem might begin by saying that the 'I' in the poem is appealing for help and, in particular, for another person who will take the trouble to look closely at her situation. To do this requires another person prepared to see beneath the material surface of things and to adopt a more spiritual perspective. Only then might the identity and problems of the 'I' emerge more clearly.

The above analysis should not suggest, of course, that there are no other significant patterns or that they do not have a part to play. What is, however, evident is that a skilful and careful use of grammatical patterns is a key starting point for recognising significant meanings in the poem and that such analysis can provide a basis for further exploration and interpretation.

Activity

1   Write a couple of paragraphs about Text: Friends of the Earth, a campaign leaflet inviting people to join this environmental group. In your paragraphs say what effect the leaflet has on you. Pay partic-ular attention to the choices of language. (For example, you may like to comment on some or all of these features: present tense; noun phrases; present participles; modal verbs; pronouns.)
2   Write three or four paragraphs which form the introduction to a *Rough Guide to A-Levels and How to Survive Them* or write a one-paragraph horoscope under two or three different star signs. Think carefully about *how* you make language choices and *which* language choices you make in order to capture your reader's interest and attention.

Text: Friends of the Earth

WHAT YOUR SUPPORT CAN DO

Friends of the Earth's campaigns get results
– thanks to our many supporters and the
weight of public opinion. By joining us you
make your voice heard and help us to
continue working towards:

- Stopping the destruction of **tropical rainforests**
- Halting **global warming**
- Protecting the **ozone layer**
- Preventing **air pollution** and **acid rain**
- Promoting **recycling**
- Forcing the clean-up of **rivers** and **drinking water**
- Stopping **hazardous waste** dumping
- Controlling dangerous **chemicals**, including **pesticides**
- Encouraging sustainable **agriculture**
- Ensuring the protection of **wildlife habitats**
- Bringing about a sane and sensible **transport** policy
- Seeing the phase-out of **nuclear power** in the UK
- Promoting **energy efficiency** and **renewable energy**

Friends of the Earth must ensure that this is
the decade of urgent environmental action.
Right now, each one of us **can** make a
difference. The Earth needs all the Friends
it can get.

Isn't it time you joined us?

RECYCLED PAPER

Friends of the Earth

IT'S TIME YOU JOINED US

156

Texts and patterns

In this short final section different varieties and styles of English will be compared and analysed and there will be a summary of the main grammatical features covered in this unit.

ACTIVES, PASSIVES AND TRANSITIVES

Activity

Sentences often express actions, and there are two main ways in which actions can be viewed. What are the contrasts in the way in which the action is expressed in the following sentences?

> Two players chased the referee.
> The referee was chased by two players.

The first sentence uses the **active voice**; the second sentence uses the **passive voice**, which is not as frequent overall. Which of the following sentences are passive and which are active? Write a description of how active sentences are turned into passive sentences.

> The dog attacked the intruder.
> The intruder was attacked by the dog.
> The test tube was heated and the solution was prepared.
> I was informed by the police.
> The police informed me.
> The two substances are mixed in equal proportions.
> We can obtain both these books from the library.
> Both these books can be obtained from the library.
> It is accepted that there is no proper evidence.
> It has been decided.

157

Commentary

Crystal (1995: 225) describes the following steps in making the basic form of the passive voice:

1   Move the subject of the active verb to the end of the sentence, making it the passive agent. Add *by*.
2   Move the object of the active verb to the front of the sentence, making it the passive subject.
3   Replace the active verb phrase by a passive one – usually a form of the auxiliary verb *be* followed by the -ed participle.

Activity

Now examine the following sentences. What are the differences between active and passive sentences in the way in which information is communicated? What is the effect when the by + agent is omitted?

> The port was blockaded by French lorry drivers.
> French lorry drivers blockaded the port.
> The port was blockaded.
>
> An increase in membership fees was suggested.
> I suggested an increase in membership fees.
>
> I was told you have a new job.
> Carol told me you have a new job.

Commentary

In the active sentences the subject is placed first and it is immediately clear who is responsible for the action. In the passive sentences the agent is moved to a less prominent position at the end of the sentence. In the sentences in which the agent is deleted no responsibility at all can be assigned; such a choice allows actions to be described as if the agent is not relevant or cannot be mentioned or is deliberately not revealed.

158

Activity

Different newspapers report events in different ways, and their use of actives and passives can be significant for the point of view given to the reader. In Text: Pit bull attack (1 and 2), newspaper reports from the *Guardian* and the *Daily Star* respectively, the attack on a man by pit bull terriers is described with particular use of the active and passive voice. What are the main differences in their use in the two newspapers? *Why* are there these differences?

Text: Pit bull attack (1)

Man critical after pit bull attack

A man was critically ill in hospital with facial injuries last night after being savaged by two pit bull terriers. Police shot dead one of the dogs.

Frank Tempest, aged 54, of Lincoln was attacked as he walked home from work. Police warned people to stay indoors as 20 police officers, six armed, hunted for the dogs. One animal was shot and the other caught and destroyed.

Describing Mr Tempest's injuries, a police spokesman said: 'You wouldn't recognize it as a human face - it is positively horrendous.'

Police said the owner of the dogs could not be prosecuted as both were dead.

Dame Janet Fookes, Conservative MP for Plymouth Drake, said the Government should introduce compulsory dog registration.

Guardian, 9 May 1991

Text: Pit bull attack (2)

DOGS RIP A MAN'S NOSE OFF

HORROR ATTACK!

By Martin Stote

COPS shot two savage pit bull terriers yesterday after they gored a man's face to shreds.

The escaped devil-dogs tore into shift worker Frank Tempest, 54, as he walked home at dawn.

Shocked witnesses said the hell hounds **RIPPED OFF** his nose, **MAULED** his ear and **TORE** skin off his face.

The dogs ambushed father-of-four Frank, then dragged him screaming along the road as he struggled to fight them off.

Police sealed off the street and warned terrified neighbours to stay indoors as the marauding dogs savaged a cat to death.

Then six police marksmen with automatic rifles blasted the dogs, believed to be a bitch and her pup, with a hail of bullets.

One pit bull was shot dead, the other wounded and trailed for an hour before being killed.

Both had escaped from a house close to despatch loader Frank's home in Monk's Road Lincoln.

Police refused to name the owner last night and said he would NOT face prosecution.

Daily Star, 9 May 1991

It is noticeable that in the *Daily Star* there are many more clauses in which the verbs are *active*. For example:

> Cops shot two savage pit bull terriers
> They gored a man's face to shreds
> The hell hounds ripped off his nose
> > mauled his ear
> > tore skin off his face
> The dogs ... ambushed Frank
> [They] dragged him
> Police sealed off the street
> [They] warned terrified neighbours
> Marauding dogs savaged a cat
> Police marksmen ... blasted the dogs.

And only a few clauses in which there are examples of the *passive* voice:

> One pit bull was shot dead
> The other [was] wounded

In the *Guardian* there are many fewer clauses in which the verbs are active. For example:

> Police shot dead one of the dogs
> Police warned people
> [Police] hunted for the dogs.

And there are more clauses in which there are examples of the passive voice:

> After being savaged by ...
> Frank ... was attacked
> One animal was shot
> The other [was] caught
> > [was] destroyed
> The owner ... could not be prosecuted.

The main difference between the two newspapers is that the *Daily Star* emphasises the actions and the ways in which one person or (animal) does something to another. The report in the *Daily Star* is therefore more instantaneous; it is as if people imagine things being directly enacted before their eyes. Many of the verbs, moreover, are not just 'active'; they are also mainly verbs of violent physical action: shot, gored, ripped off, mauled, tore, dragged, savaged, blasted. Such choices sensationalise the story, involving the reader and giving the story more impact.

Two other features of this use of verbs can be noted. First, the *repetition* of so many verbs of the same type and of the same character. Second, all of the active verbs described above are **transitive** verbs. Verbs which express actions can either be transitive or **intransitive**. For example:

> An hour elapsed
> The wind blew
> The people protested

are all actions, and are in the active voice, but the verbs are intransitive in that they do not transfer their actions onto another object. Thus

> The girl bought the car
> The man hit the intruder

both contain transitive verbs, both in the active voice, which transfer their actions to an object which is affected or changed as a result of the action.

So in the *Daily Star* there is a marked use of repeated, transitive verbs in the active voice.

In the *Guardian* the story is presented less sensationally and in a more balanced way, although there are a good number of active transitive verbs to depict the action of the story. But there is a greater balance between active and passive clauses and the actions are depicted by means of less directly violent verb choices. There is a greater sense of things happening to people and, overall, a calmer, more reflective presentation.

Activity

Write a brief analysis of Text: 'Gloire de Dijon' (1917). In particular, you may wish to consider the following features of the poem:

1   uses of repetition
2   tense
3   sentence length and type
4   nouns (types of noun?) (modifiers?).

Text: 'Gloire de Dijon'

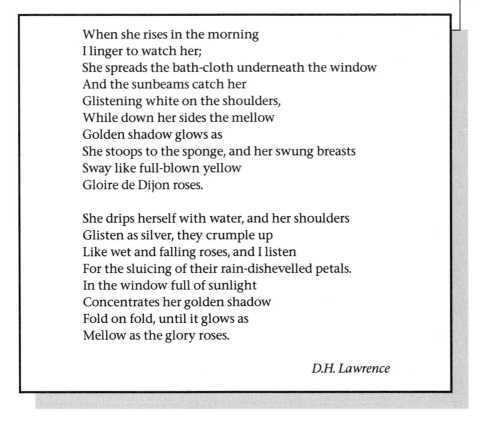

When she rises in the morning
I linger to watch her;
She spreads the bath-cloth underneath the window
And the sunbeams catch her
Glistening white on the shoulders,
While down her sides the mellow
Golden shadow glows as
She stoops to the sponge, and her swung breasts
Sway like full-blown yellow
Gloire de Dijon roses.

She drips herself with water, and her shoulders
Glisten as silver, they crumple up
Like wet and falling roses, and I listen
For the sluicing of their rain-dishevelled petals.
In the window full of sunlight
Concentrates her golden shadow
Fold on fold, until it glows as
Mellow as the glory roses.

D.H. Lawrence

Activity

The following texts are taken from a number of different sources, including jokes, newspaper headlines, slogans, advertisements, and so on. In all cases there are **grammatical ambiguities**. See if you can work out and explain these ambiguities using what you have learned about grammar from this unit.

The first example is done for you.

1   GIANT WAVES DOWN TUNNEL

This is a newspaper headline. There are two meanings to the headline. Either a giant is waving down a tunnel or a tunnel has had giant waves

163

crashing through it. The reason for the ambiguity is that 'giant' can be either a modifier or a noun and that 'waves' can be either a verb or a noun.

2 *Q:* How do you make a Swiss roll?
   A: Push him down a mountain
3 The man opened the door in his pyjamas.
4 Milk drinkers are turning to powder.
5 Stewardess: There's a problem in the cabin.
   Passenger: What is it?
   Stewardess: It's a little room in the front of the plane where the pilot sits but don't worry about that now ...

There are no commentaries on these last two activities. In this instance you should try to come to your conclusions using the guidance provided so far by this unit.

Text and context
Written discourse

Aim of this unit

The aim of this unit is to explore some of the language devices which enable whole written texts to work.

In linguistics, the phrase **discourse analysis** is used to refer to the analysis of both spoken and written texts. In each case, the aim is to analyse the way texts work across the boundaries of single sentences or utterances to form whole stretches of language.

This sounds very simple, but actually the word 'discourse' has had quite a long and complicated history. The situation now is that it means slightly different things inside and outside the academic world; it can also mean different things in different academic subject areas. For these reasons, it's worth spending a bit of time thinking about its variant meanings.

The basic meaning of 'discourse', in modern ordinary usage, is 'talk'.

Originally, the term 'discourse' came from Latin, *discursus*, meaning 'to run', 'to run on', 'to run to and fro'. Historically, it has been applied more to rehearsed forms of spoken language – like speeches, where people 'run on' about a topic – than to spontaneous speech. The modern

165

meaning of 'discourse' as encompassing all forms of talk has evolved because conversations, like formal speeches, 'run'. This means that speakers make an effort to give their interactions shape and coherence – not consciously, but as an integral part of co-operating with another speaker to make meaning. So when people refer to *talk as discourse* they are drawing attention to *the way talk is a crafted medium*. While it has long been understood that this was true of speeches and other aspects of formal oratory, it has only recently been recognised that casual conversation is subtly and skilfully fashioned by speakers as they go along, often at rapid speed. The way different types of talk work will be explored in Unit 5.

Another way of looking at talk-as-discourse is to use the metaphor of weaving. In fact, we use this metaphor very often in our own talk about talk: for example, we talk about 'losing the thread of the conversation', 'cottoning on' to what people mean when they 'spin us a yarn'; teachers often close their lessons by referring to 'tying up loose ends'. We clearly see speakers as engaged together in discourse in the way a group of weavers would be to create a pattern in some fabric.

But it's not only spoken language that 'runs' or gets woven into patterns.

This is also true of written language; and the modern use of the word 'discourse' can also be used to refer to aspects of written texts. This tends to be used much more within the academic world than outside it.

The word **text** itself originally meant 'something woven' (Latin *texere*, *textum* – 'to weave'), and you can see a relationship between text, textile ('capable of being woven') and texture ('having the quality of woven cloth'). Written language is also often referred to as 'material'.

Like speakers, then, writers manipulate different aspects of language in order to weave their texts and give their material 'texture'. So to talk about discourse in written texts is to focus on the way written texts are constructed. This is what this unit is all about.

Contents

Make and mend

This section involves practical activities of reassembling and writing material in order to show you what you already know about the way texts work.

Tracing the patterns

In this section, you will be exploring how you knew what to do in the first section. You will be looking at how texts work in a number of different ways:

1   *Lexical cohesion*
    This looks at the way aspects of vocabulary link parts of texts together.
2   *Grammatical cohesion*
    Here you will be exploring some of the important ways that grammar holds texts together across sentence boundaries.
3   *Information structure*
    This focuses on the role of grammatical features in the ordering and presentation of information within texts.

The textile industry

In this section, the focus is on the way texts operate within contexts. This involves thinking about aspects of culture and representation.

Texts used

- ◎   Advertisements
- ◎   Information leaflets
- ◎   Extracts from novels and short stories
- ◎   Poems
- ◎   Some children's writing
- ◎   A range of notes and memos

If the metaphor of text as weaving is true, then it must be possible to see how the various threads are woven together within written material.

The activities that follow aim to show how some important aspects of language act as the threads that give texts a particular texture.

Make and mend

Activity

Stitching it back together

Our constant and powerful need to understand what's around us leads us to try to make sense of anything that's presented to us as a text. To illustrate this idea, read through Text: Statements.

Text: Statements

Allow the fruit to steam in its own juice for a further 15 minutes.

So she hated it when that infuriating Keith Scott seemed to go out of his way to suggest that her heart wasn't in the affair.

That's why we created 'Portfolio', a brand new concept in saving.

Put them into a fireproof dish with the water, and a tablespoon of the sugar.

She knew that he loved her - in a calm settled way rather than any grand passion - and that he would make her a good, kind husband.

Ensuring that the lid is tightly sealed, put the dish into a preheated oven, Gas Regulo 6.

So that way, you can have your cake and eat it too.

Pour over the top, and serve with double cream.

Melodie Neil and Jed Martin were old friends.

Mix juice with the brandy, mulled wine, and rest of the sugar.

We do, too.

Wash and core the apples, taking care to remove all pips.

In short, when she became engaged to him she knew exactly what she was doing.

Spoon out the cooked apples and arrange them attractively in rounds on a serving plate.

Do you feel that you never get a fair slice of the capital cake?

Slice finely.

Portfolio is a high interest investment account that makes your money work for you, while still giving you instant access to your capital.

Reduce temperature to 3 after 10 minutes.

Could you read any of it in any way that worked and made sense?

If you could, that proves that you were already looking for patterns within the text.

In fact, the text you have just read contains statements in random order from three completely different sources. With your knowledge of this, use any strategies you have in order to put the original texts back together.

Divide up the statements then, within each text, arrange the statements in order, so that they read naturally.

When you have finished your sorting, check your answers by turning to p. 245.

Look particularly at where you didn't get the order right. Can you see what led you astray?

Activity

Discourse consequences

This activity can only be done in groups.

Text: Starter lines consists of the first lines for six different types of writing – different genres.

Each group should take a different line, and add a second line to it in the same genre. They should then fold the paper over so that only the second line is visible, and pass it on to the next group. When all the groups have contributed a line, open up the folded page and read it aloud to the whole group.

As a whole group, assess how far the six different texts follow rules for the various genres (even if the writers have chosen to parody the text, they will be still be using the rules).

Text: Starter lines

1. Once upon a time there was a beautiful princess who lived in a castle high up on a mountainside.
2. Cricket is a game which involves as much psychological nerve as physical strength and dexterity.
3. This week you will need to have your wits about you, as Saturn's influence could lead you to be off guard at a crucial moment.
4. Male, 42, home-owner, recently relocated to Bristol.
5. 'Spacegrazer to Hyperpod, come in.' Zhata feared the worst. The asteroid storm had passed just too close for comfort.
6. To make watercress soup, first sauté a finely chopped onion by melting a knob of butter in a saucepan over a medium heat.

Activity

Twenty-minute texts

Working in groups, each group should write a short text in one of the genres listed below. Each piece of writing must contain the following words:

figure   leaves   dusk

Don't spend any more than twenty minutes on your piece of writing.

Genres

- Epitaph
- Maths textbook
- Tabloid newspaper article
- Romantic fiction
- Advert
- Menu
- Set of instructions
- Estate agent's blurb

When you have finished all your texts, pin them up and read them out.

How has each piece of writing followed the rules for its particular genre?

The sections that follow aim to show you some of the linguistic strategies you have just been using in working with texts.

Tracing the patterns

If a speaker or hearer of English hears or reads a passage of the language which is more than one sentence in length, he or she can normally decide without difficulty whether it forms a unified whole or is just a collection of unrelated sentences. **Cohesion** (or its absence) is what makes the difference between the two.

> Cohesion is what gives a text texture.
>
> (Halliday and Hasan 1976)

LEXICAL COHESION

One of the strategies you used was your understanding of words and phrases in the English language - the vocabulary system. In particular, you used your awareness of *relationships between words*: this is called **lexical cohesion**. There are many different kinds of relationship that could be involved.

Activity

In Text: Links, some of the links that are commonly used between words are outlined, with an example, where possible, from the sorting exercise you did previously (Text: Statements). As you read through these notes, see if you can add to the lists by finding examples from the texts you yourselves have written:

171

Text: Links

Direct repetition (exactly the same word repeated):
Text C: juice ... juice

Synonyms, or near-synonyms (use of words with similar meanings):
Text B: saving ... investment

Superordination (where one word encompasses another in meaning):
Text C: fruit ... apples

Antonyms (opposites):
Text A: loved ... hated
Text C: put [them] *into* ... spoon *out*

Specific-general reference (words referring to the same thing or person, but where one has more detail than the other):
Text C: a fireproof dish ... the dish
Text C (going from general to specific): apples ... cooked apples

Ordered series (words that we know as a set series - for example, the days of the week, months of the year, or the seasons):
Text C: Regulo 6 ... 3; 10 minutes ... 15 minutes

Whole-part (where one term names a part of an item that the other word describes in full):
Text C: apples ... pips

A much more general aspect of lexical cohesion is the use by writers of particular semantic fields (see Unit 2, p. 90): this means referring to a specific area of experience or knowledge. The clearest examples of semantic fields occur in the specialist language of occupations.

Activity

Read through Text: Occupations, which contains the language of ten different occupations. Try to work out what the occupations are, and which particular words and phrases helped you to pinpoint them.

Text: Occupations

The vehicle was seen proceeding down the main street in a westerly direction leading to a spacious and well-appointed residence with considerable potential. She went to work, mixing up the six-ten with two parts of 425, and dabbing the mixture through 6 ezimeshes. 'This one has a fine shaggy nose and a fruity bouquet with a flowery head', she said. He managed to get into a good position, just kissing the cushion. He said 'Just pop up onto the couch and we'll see what we can do'. She pulled down the menu, chose the command by using the cursor, then quit. She said to knead well, roll into a ball and leave overnight to rise. Instead, he mulched well, turned over and left the beds to settle. Good progress made, but concentration sometimes rather poor; more effort required if success is to be expected in the important months ahead.

(Answers on p. 246)

However, semantic fields do not have to contain technical language, or occupational terms. It may be simply that a text uses several words that all refer to the same subject matter, activity or experience: for example, the romantic fiction text in the sorting exercise at the beginning of this unit (p. 169) contained many words associated with love.

Activity

Go through each of the extracts you reassembled in the first activity, and write a list of words and phrases within each text that are in the same semantic field. Make up your own headings for the columns. If you find that you have more than one semantic field in a text, outline each field by listing them in separate columns. For example, for the romantic fiction you might decide on the headings 'words for feelings' and 'words for relationships', in order to make finer distinctions than would be possible with one heading of 'love'.

Text A: romantic fiction	words for feelings	words for relationships

When you have shared and discussed your headings, turn to the texts you wrote yourselves. Can you find any examples of semantic fields that you have employed, in order to construct a particular genre?

Sometimes, writers deliberately weave together different semantic fields in order to foreground a particular idea. **Foregrounding** is a type of highlighting – it means that the writer is drawing attention to something and making the reader view it in a certain way. Look again at Text B (p. 245). Why does the writer of this text use two very different semantic fields – what idea is being foregrounded? How does the writer's use of the two different semantic fields help to shape the text?

Now read through Text: 'The Good, the Bad and the Ugly', which uses vocabulary from two very different types of activity. After you have read it carefully, list the two semantic fields that are used, giving as many examples of the use of each as you can find. Put a ring round any terms that could be included in either field.

Why do you think the writer has chosen to weave together these two different types of vocabulary? Why does the advert not simply use farming terms?

(Note: *The Good, the Bad and the Ugly* is the title of a famous Western film starring Clint Eastwood.)

THE GOOD

Sting CT® Herbicide applied in stubbles or onto land cultivated after harvest, eliminates the problem of volunteers and annual weeds in the following crop.
But good stubble management is only part of the story. Sting CT biodegrades rapidly in the soil. In terms of operator safety, it isn't classified under COSHH. Also, it's much less expensive than paraquat*.
So Sting CT doesn't cost the earth.

THE BAD

Sting CT is active on volunteer cereals, volunteer oilseed rape, annual grasses and broad-leaved weeds at all stages of growth. It penetrates right down to the roots to prevent regrowth. What's more it's rainfast from 1 hour after application, and thanks to this fast absorption it allows you to start drilling within 6 hours of stubble cleaning.

AND THE UGLY
PLUS A WHOLE CAST OF VOLUNTEERS

By removing the "green bridge" you prevent the carry-over of diseases and remove a haven for ugly pests, for instance BYDV carrying aphids, which could otherwise carry virus infection into your next crop.

The Good The Bad and The Ugly is an everyday story of stubble management. With Sting CT, the plot has a happy ending.

*Average rates

For more information on Sting CT and Stubble Management send to:
Monsanto, Freepost, PO Box 61, London NW1 17H.
No stamp required.

Name:

Address:

Tel:

Sting CT

Fast, Thorough and Doesn't Cost the Earth

Another option that a writer has, in using vocabulary from different semantic fields, is to entwine the words and phrases so closely that the two systems are difficult to disentangle. One way of bringing different systems of vocabulary together is to use metaphor: this is where one thing is described as if it were another (see Unit 2). Because metaphor tells us that one thing *is* another, it is a powerful factor in positioning the reader and constructing a particular viewpoint.

Look at Text: 'It's ugly underneath'.

◎ The car is described here as if it were something else: what?
◎ Make a list of the words which carry the metaphor.
◎ Why do you think the advertiser has chosen to use this metaphor?
◎ How does the text – including the image – construct a viewpoint for the reader?

(Notes: The car being described in this advert is called a 'Scirocco Scala'; 'La Scala' is also a famous opera house in Milan. There is a supermodel called Elle MacPherson. The centre of Fiat car production is in Turin.)

Don't worry. It's ugly underneath.

Beneath the unarguable beauty of the Scirocco lurks a beastly mass of unlovely engineering.

Although we're certain that a Volkswagen engineer would beg to differ.

To him, a Macpherson strut can be more alluring than a Monroe wiggle.

The merest glimpse of undersealing can set his pulse a-racing.

The point is that any top model's most coveted possession is her vital statistics.

In this case, 1781, 81, 86.4, 112. (Capacity, bore, stroke and brake horsepower.)

The Scala also offers something else to confound conventional wisdom about the nature of beauty.

Torque. 112.5 pounds per foot of the stuff, to be precise.

It's what makes the car so long-legged. Reaching 60 in just 8.3 seconds, with a top speed of 118 miles per hour.

The interior, too, presents rather more than just a pretty fascia. A multi-function computer is standard equipment.

While, as far as temperament goes, the Scala shares little in common with its namesake in Milan. Let alone its rivals in Turin.

Scirocco

SPECIFICATION AND PERFORMANCE FIGURES APPLY TO SCIROCCO SCALA. FOR PRICES AND BROCHURES CONTACT VOLKSWAGEN INFORMATION SERVICE SC4, YEOMANS DRIVE, BLAKELANDS, MILTON KEYNES MK14 5AN. TEL: (0908) 271616. FLEET SALES: (0908) 60361. EXPORT SALES: 01-986 8411.

Another wide-ranging strategy which you used in writing and handling texts in the first part of this unit was an understanding of levels of formality in vocabulary (see also Unit 2).

We talk about language being more or less formal as a way of describing how we vary our language according to the context we are in: for example, we will all use a relatively informal type of language when we are in the pub, relaxing with friends, compared with the more formal style we are likely to produce in a court of law or in an interview for a job. Formality can also be a reflection of social-group membership, particularly occupation, where some types of occupational language have retained specialist words which can sound very formal in everyday discourse: for example, a financial consultant or solicitor might use the word 'remuneration' where the rest of us would use 'salary' or just 'wages'. Calling a type of language formal or informal refers to more than simply vocabulary, but vocabulary will be an important contributory factor in a reader's impression of the formality of a text. For example, although the words 'home', 'house', 'residence' and 'domicile' might refer to exactly the same building, they vary a great deal in formality and therefore to replace one with another in a text will create a very different effect.

To enable you to see what formality of vocabulary might mean in practical terms, read through Text: Levels of formality. In each text, the level of formality has been disrupted at various points by the insertion of inappropriate vocabulary. Can you pinpoint where this happens, and suggest some vocabulary in each case which would be more in keeping with the style of the passage?

Text: Levels of formality

Letter from a bank manager to a customer

Dear Ms Allen,

Thank you for your letter of 1st September, requesting overdraft facilities of £500. In order that this overdraft facility can be granted we would first need sight of your contract of employment. Would you therefore kindly inform us of the School at which you will now be earning your daily crust.

Yours sincerely,
A. Curtis

Teacher's report

James needs to realise that success is the result of hard work and consistent effort. At present, he is being a real pain because he is so bone idle in class. If he wishes to do well in the examination, and achieve a grade which will do justice to his considerable ability, he must pull his socks up – and sharpish.

Biology exam paper

Q1 As they pass from testis to oviduct during and after mating, mammalian sperms will pass through each of the following structures except the:
(a)   urethra
(b)   vas deferens
(c)   vagina
(d)   bottom

Q2 When the water in which a certain species of frog is living contains 5cm³ of dissolved oxygen per litre the frogs remain totally submerged but, when the oxygen content falls to 3cm³ per litre, they go up to the top for a breather.
    As a result of reading the information above, do you have any inkling about how frogs breathe in water?

Memo from a university professor to his staff

Can I remind you that travel claims must be submitted *promptly*. Other departments, I learn, are not paying claims which are more than two months late. In particular, please remember that the financial year-end is now 31st July. Claims not submitted by 15th August will be substantially delayed by year-end procedures, and screw up our budgeting. Please get your claims in ON TIME.

Extract from a hotel brochure:

Reception of Guests
The Hotel endeavours to have rooms ready to receive guests by noon, and it is hoped that departing guests will courteously assist in making this possible by getting a move on and not hanging about in bedrooms on the day of departure.

The texts in the previous activity come from genres of writing which tend to have a particular level of formality associated with them (although changes in levels of formality can occur as part of the process of language change).

But the operation of formality is actually more complex and subtle than that: for example, a writer, group of writers or members of an occupational group may write about the same subject in different ways according to the audience they are aiming at, and the purpose of their text.

Texts A–D were found in the same local council city planning department. Each text has a different writer/reader relationship, and a different purpose. These differences are not accidental, but rather arise from the different types of communication expected of the city's professional planners. The texts are placed in the order in which they were written, during a specific process: this was the drawing up of a Development Plan for the city of Manchester, specifying the priorities and intentions for city planning over the decade leading up to the turn of the century.

Text A is a piece of national legislation – an extract from the Town and Country Planning Act, 1990. This text, written by lawyers, would be used most often by lawyers and professional planners. Text A is a reference document whose purpose is to establish clear rules and conditions for the planning developments in any community. The extract here describes the powers of the Secretary of State to intervene if a local planning authority does not fulfil certain obligations.

Text B is part of a free newspaper – *City Planning News* – which was delivered to all Manchester households. There were three newspapers altogether; the aim of this one was to encourage members of the public to contribute ideas to the planning department about issues of concern in local communities around the city. It was written by the Head of the Planning and Environmental Health Department.

The two texts here are from different parts of the paper: 'Down Your Street' is an early attempt to summarise some of the material that follows, while 'Can I Extend My Home?' appears later on in the paper.

Text C is an extract from a statement written to support the public inquiry that accompanied the process of devising the Development Plan for Manchester. Written by the same person as Text B, this type of document is officially entitled a 'Proof of Evidence'. The statement was made available to anyone who attended the public inquiry, which was open to all members of the public, and which acted as a follow-up to the public consultation represented by the newspapers. Its purpose was to give readers an idea of the planners' thinking at that stage with regard to policies on city development.

181

Text D, also written by the city's Head of Planning and Environmental Health Department, is an extract from the final Development Plan for the city of Manchester. While Texts B and C were written as part of a process, this text acts as a reference document which would be expected to be understood by anyone making a planning application. Its purpose is to be an agreed statement of policy, to act as a framework within which planning applications can be judged and agreed or rejected. The extract given here sets out some of the rules for house extensions.

When you have read through all the material, try to answer the following questions:

◎ How are the variations in audience and purpose reflected in the *vocabulary* used in these texts? Which of these texts is the most formal, and which the most informal? Can you pick out some contrasting vocabulary, to show differences in formality?

◎ As well as differences in formality, are there variations in vocabulary which relate to an abstract/concrete dimension? If so, how do you explain these differences?

◎ To what extent are other factors (e.g. grammar, layout) responsible for readers' possible impressions of formality/informality in these texts? Find some examples of language features that are *not* related to vocabulary.

Text A: Town and Country Planning Act, 1990

Default powers

25 - (1) Where, by virtue of any of the previous provisions of this Chapter, any unitary development plan or proposals for the alteration or replacement of such a plan are required to be prepared, or steps are required to be taken for the adoption of any such plan or proposals, then –

(a) if at any time the Secretary of State is satisfied, after holding a local inquiry or other hearing, that the local planning authority are not taking the steps necessary to enable them to prepare or adopt such a plan or proposals within a reasonable period; or

(b) in a case where a period is specified for the preparation or adoption of any such plan or proposals, if no such plan or proposals have been prepared or adopted by the local planning authority within that period,

the Secretary of State may prepare and make the plan or any part of it or, as the case may be, alter or replace it, as he thinks fit.

Down Your Street

This is the part of the Plan for Manchester which gets down to the detail. But all we can do in this newspaper is give you an idea of the most important points for your part of the City – we hope it's enough to make you want to find out more.

■ The Plan for Manchester isn't about everything the Council does. It's only really about the way land is used throughout the City – should it be for housing? offices? shops? open space? It has a lot to say about making Manchester a safer and more accessible City for everyone to live, move about and work in – and much to say about transport, too. But you won't find much about education, or street cleaning or libraries and all the rest of the Council's many services.

■ We haven't tried to decide the future of every piece of land and every block of property in the City. That would be an impossible task. Anyway, because we're trying to look ahead till the end of the century, things are bound to change, and the plan would quickly become out of date if there was too much detail in it.

■ Instead, the plan tries to pick out the most important local issues and then makes clear statements ('policies') about them. You may agree or disagree with these policies. Of course, you might also think we've left something out altogether – whatever your view, tell us.

■ Don't forget the City-wide policies summarised on pages 2 and 3 which will be a guide for everyone – residents, landowners, developers, business people and the Council itself. So you must keep them in mind when reading about your own neighbourhood.

■ On page 15 you'll also find another list of suggested policies which are important. They deal with the Council's attitude to a whole range of more detailed things like house extensions, flat conversions, hot food takeaways, amusement arcades and taxi offices. These are matters on which the Council frequently receives applications for planning permission. They are often very controversial locally. The Council needs to make decisions in the light of this local reaction but also taking into account its broad policies for these kinds of activities. Because they are meant to apply throughout the City, we've put them in one place to save space.

■ Lastly – please remember we want everyone in the City to find out as much as they can about our ideas for the next 10 years. Come to the exhibitions. Tell the planners what you think!

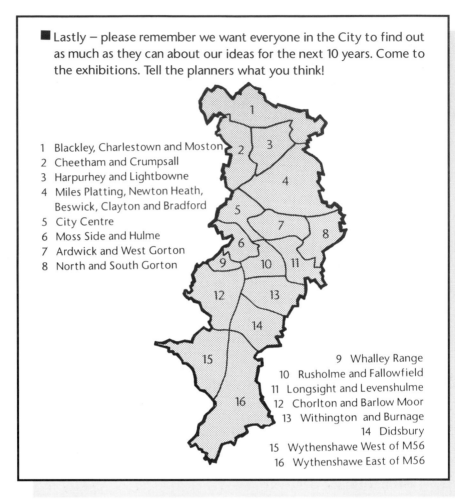

1 Blackley, Charlestown and Moston
2 Cheetham and Crumpsall
3 Harpurhey and Lightbowne
4 Miles Platting, Newton Heath, Beswick, Clayton and Bradford
5 City Centre
6 Moss Side and Hulme
7 Ardwick and West Gorton
8 North and South Gorton

9 Whalley Range
10 Rusholme and Fallowfield
11 Longsight and Levenshulme
12 Chorlton and Barlow Moor
13 Withington and Burnage
14 Didsbury
15 Wythenshawe West of M56
16 Wythenshawe East of M56

CAN I EXTEND MY HOME?

The Council receives many hundreds of applications for quite small-scale proposals every year. To help deal with them in a consistent way, the Plan includes a set of 'development control policies', which cover the most common type of planning application. These are important, because when the Plan is approved, the Council will be able to point to these policies when deciding future applications – and they will also help the Secretary of State for the Environment come to a view if there is an appeal to him.

There's no room to go into any detail in this newspaper – so if you want to know more, ask to see the Plan itself. Copies of the individual policies can also be made available.

The City Council's current practice of consulting widely on planning applications that have a significant impact will not be affected by this and this remains important in helping the Council to reach a view about what local people think the impact of a proposal is going to be. At the same time, the whole point of having clear policies is that it helps everyone to know where they stand, and this means that the Council cannot lightly set aside these policies even where local opinion is strongly against a proposal that is consistent with them. This is why these policies are so important. So let's have a quick look at the most important ones.

House Extensions

These can often cause upset between neighbours, if not handled properly. The Plan sets down some 'groundrules' for dealing with extensions, to try and make sure that they don't cut off too much light, or cause problems of overlooking. They also have to 'fit in' with the rest of the Street – so, for example, two-storey extensions will usually have to have a pitched roof. And you won't usually be able to build a 2-storey extension right up to your neighbour's boundary, or a rear extension which is more than about 12 feet out from the back wall.

As with all kinds of planning application, your local area planner is there to give free advice (whether you are an applicant or a potential objector!).

Text C: 'Proof of Evidence'

8.6 The City's many *parks* are, of course, the responsibility of the City Council. I am aware of the concern which has been expressed in some quarters about the Council's intentions in relation to the future of the parks and am pleased to have this opportunity to provide some reassurance on that score. For the avoidance of doubt, the Council accepts, without reservation, that the City's parks are essential assets for the people of Manchester, and that their main value lies in their being quiet and safe places for informal recreation, particularly for young children and the elderly. They also have immense importance for nature conservation and for their landscape value. Nothing in the UDP seeks to disturb that analysis or that commitment.

Text D: City Development Plan

DC1.3 Notwithstanding the generality of the above policies, the Council will not normally approve:
(a) rearward extensions greater than 3.65m (12 ft) in length;
(b) 2-storey extensions with a flat roof, particularly those which would be visible from the public highway;
(c) 2-storey extensions to terraced properties which occupy the full width of the house;
(d) flat roofed extensions to bungalows;
(e) extensions which conflict with the Council's guidelines on privacy distances (which are published as supplementary guidance).

Activity

Now look back at the texts you were working with in the sorting exercise at the start of this unit (p. 169). How far did the formality or informality of the vocabulary contribute to how the texts worked?

Choose one of the texts and examine the vocabulary closely, then write some notes to record your ideas. If you find it difficult to describe how formal or informal you find the vocabulary, try to think of synonyms for the term you are considering. This will help you to place the term as part of a set of alternative expressions in English to refer to the idea in question.

Activity

Sometimes, writers deliberately manipulate formal and informal styles in order to achieve certain effects.

Text: *Oranges Are Not the Only Fruit* (1987) is an extract from the novel by Jeanette Winterson. In it, the narrator is talking about her experiences as a child in a Lancashire primary school in the 1950s – particularly, the way that the boys and girls taunted and bullied each other.

Can you see how the writer interweaves more and less formal vocabulary in order to suggest two different voices – that of the adult narrator, and that of the child she originally was?

Pick out examples of language features which help to construct each voice.

Text: *Oranges Are Not the Only Fruit*

Country dancing was thirty-three rickety kids in black plimsolls and green knickers trying to keep up with Miss who always danced with Sir anyway and never looked at anybody else. They got engaged soon after, but it didn't do us any good because they started going in for ball-room competitions, which meant they spent all our lessons practising their footwork while we shuffled up and down to the recorded instructions on the gramophone. The threats were the worst; being forced to hold hands with somebody you hated. We flapped along twisting each others' fingers off and promising untold horrors as soon as the lesson was over. Tired of being bullied, I became adept at inventing the most fundamental tortures under the guise of sweet sainthood.

'What me Miss? No Miss. Oh *Miss*, I never did'. But I did, I always did. The most frightening for the girls was the offer of total immersion in the cesspit round the back of Rathbone's Wrought Iron. For the boys, anything that involved their willies. And so, three terms later, I squatted down in the shoebags and got depressed. The shoebag room was dark and smelly, it was always smelly, even at the beginning of terms.

Commentary

The child's voice is suggested by certain vocabulary items, such as 'knickers', 'shoebag', 'willies', 'smelly', 'Miss', 'Sir', as well as by the direct speech, 'What me Miss? No Miss. Oh *Miss*, I never did'. In contrast, the adult's language is considerably more complex and abstract: 'untold horrors', 'adept', 'fundamental tortures', 'sweet sainthood', 'total immersion'. The two styles are woven together very cleverly, with subtle shifts occurring within a short space; this can create humorous effects, as in the anti-climax of lines 'The most frightening . . . their willies'.

GRAMMATICAL COHESION

So far, you have been looking at how you used your lexical knowledge - your knowledge of vocabulary - as a strategy to help you reorganise and write the texts in the first part of this unit. The way lexical items are woven together through a text was referred to as lexical cohesion.

But in working on those texts, you also used your understanding of grammatical structures, and this forms the focus for what follows. The way that grammatical features are woven together across sentence boundaries is called **grammatical cohesion**.

Anyone who can speak and/or write a language knows grammar, as these structural patterns are learnt very early in life as an integral part of learning language; knowing grammar is different from knowing how to label parts of sentences, however. The knowledge you were using in the early part of this unit was your knowledge of grammar in use, and that was all the equipment you needed to do the tasks. But in order to see what you did, this part of the unit will need to go into a bit of detail about some of the structures you were using and matching. This will mean labelling some of the most commonly used grammatical principles and patterns. You may well be looking again at some of the aspects of grammar you studied in Unit 3; the focus here, however, is how grammar works across sentences rather than within them.

Reference

The Penguin *Concise English Dictionary* defines 'to refer' as 'to send for information', 'to seek information'. The principle of **reference** within texts is exactly that: it tells the reader that they can only make complete sense of the word or structure they are looking at if they look elsewhere in the text to get a fuller picture.

There are particular words that are often used for reference purposes. Some details are given below.

Personal pronoun reference

Personal pronouns are words that can substitute for nouns, and are as follows:

I   you (singular)   he   she   it   we   you (plural)   they   one
Note that some of these pronouns can occur in different forms, depending on the role of the word in a particular sentence. Below are the possible variants:

me   him her   us   them

When one of these pronouns occurs in a text, the reader expects to have to link it with something – either an item that has already been mentioned or something that's coming up. The fact that these pronouns are called personal pronouns gives an indication of their reference function – they will mainly be referring to people; however, the words 'it' and 'they'/ 'them' can also be used to refer to non-human animates, inanimate objects and abstract ideas.

If the pronoun is referring back to something, this is called **anaphoric reference**; if the pronoun is referring to something coming later, this is called **cataphoric reference**. Here is an example of each:

Tom said that *he* was going home (anaphoric reference)

I couldn't believe *it – the house was a complete wreck* (cataphoric reference)

Much ambiguity is based on the workings of cohesion in a text – or rather, the lack of cohesion. In the example below (from a member of the public writing to his local council), can you see how the unintentional humour comes from the cohesion problems in the sentence?

> Our kitchen floor is very damp. We have two children and would like a third. Could you please send someone round to do something about it?

But lack of cohesion can also be very useful, in that it can throw reference wide open and make the reader work to locate the meaning: for example, for the word 'it' in the advertising slogan 'COKE IS *IT*' and in the VW advert you studied earlier, '*It's* ugly underneath'.

Making all the pronoun references link up is a skill that it takes children some time to learn. This is as true in speech as it is in writing.

Activity

Look at the two texts that follow.

The first consists of some speech which arose in the context of a teacher sending a 7-year-old pupil on an errand.

The second, The Quard, is a piece of writing by a 7-year-old. (Note: it's uncertain what a 'quard' is – perhaps a beach buggy vehicle?)

Both of these children are struggling with the cohesion demands of the communication. Go through the texts, pointing out where difficulties arise.

> Teacher A (Mrs Curtin): Go and ask Mrs Travis if she can give you the note that your mum wrote for her last week and bring it back here to me now.
> Pupil (to Teacher B, Mrs Travis): Mrs Curtin says please can she give you the note for my mum?

My And Andrews Adventure
With a Quard.

One day Andrew Turner Came
To my house . My Dad
Took us to a beach race .
And my cousin was race.ng
but When He Went of
the jump you Could not
See him So We Went
to the hole and we
went down the hole
and First We Went
to a Forest and
We could not Find
the Quard. The next stop
Was at the Quard Shop.
and We found Him and He
won.

Activity

While pronoun reference can be a challenge for us as we learn language, sometimes writers deliberately disrupt pronoun cohesion in order to achieve certain effects.

Text: Rabbit's speech is a poem by Lewis Carroll. From *Alice in Wonderland*, the poem is a speech delivered by the Rabbit to the court, and is referred to in the book as a set of 'mysterious verses'.

How does Carroll use pronoun reference in order to create an air of mystery?

Text: Rabbit's speech

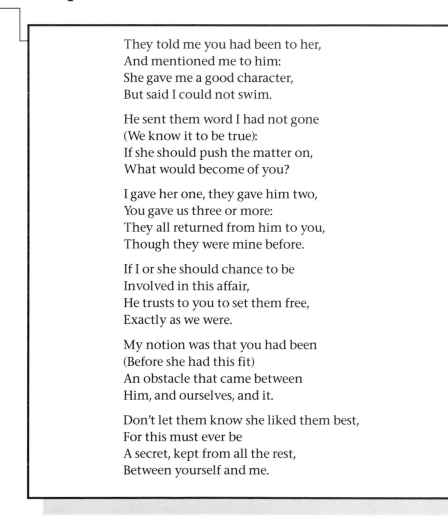

They told me you had been to her,
And mentioned me to him:
She gave me a good character,
But said I could not swim.

He sent them word I had not gone
(We know it to be true):
If she should push the matter on,
What would become of you?

I gave her one, they gave him two,
You gave us three or more:
They all returned from him to you,
Though they were mine before.

If I or she should chance to be
Involved in this affair,
He trusts to you to set them free,
Exactly as we were.

My notion was that you had been
(Before she had this fit)
An obstacle that came between
Him, and ourselves, and it.

Don't let them know she liked them best,
For this must ever be
A secret, kept from all the rest,
Between yourself and me.

Activity

A mysterious atmosphere is also the aim of Text: 'A Haunted House', which is the opening of a short story by Virginia Woolf, published in 1921. How does Woolf's use of personal pronouns help to create this atmosphere?:

Text: 'A Haunted House'

Whatever hour you woke there was a door shutting. From room to room they went, hand in hand, lifting here, opening there, making sure – a ghostly couple.

'Here we left it,' she said. And he added, 'Oh, but here too!' 'It's upstairs,' she murmured. 'And in the garden,' he whispered. 'Quietly,' they said, 'or we shall wake them.'

But it wasn't you that woke us. Oh, no. 'They're looking for it; they're drawing the curtain,' one might say, and so read on a page or two. 'Now they've found it,' one would be certain, stopping the pencil on the margin. And then, tired of reading, one might rise and see for oneself, the house all empty, the doors standing open, only the wood pigeons bubbling with content and the hum of the threshing machine sounding from the farm. 'What did I come in here for? What did I want to find?' My hands were empty. 'Perhaps it's upstairs then?' The apples were in the loft. And so down again, the garden still as ever, only the book had slipped into the grass.

Stevie Smith's poem 'Not Waving But Drowning' (1957) also uses a range of pronouns to refer to a number of different people, and to create specific effects. Map out how these pronouns work, thinking particularly about the following:

◎   Who are the various people in this poem?
◎   Why did Stevie Smith choose to use pronouns to refer to people rather than their names?

193

Text: 'Not Waving But Drowning'

Nobody heard him, the dead man,
But still he lay moaning:
I was much further out than you thought
And not waving but drowning

Poor chap, he always loved larking
And now he's dead
It must have been too cold for him his heart gave way,
They said

Oh no, no, no, it was too cold always
(Still the dead one lay moaning)
I was much too far out all my life
And not waving but drowning.

Commentary

Virginia Woolf extract

A sense of mystery is created in this text partly by the fact that the reader is unsure who is in the story, and this effect results from the range of pronouns used: you, they, we, it, she, he, one, I. At the beginning, it seems that 'you' means 'one' and that 'they' are 'a ghostly couple'. But then it's uncertain who is talking in direct speech in the second paragraph; also, the second use of 'you' (in the final paragraph) appears to mean, not 'one' as before, but 'they' (i.e. the ghosts). Throughout the whole text, it's unclear exactly what 'it' is that everyone seems to be searching for. The language makes the reader behave like the characters, in that it makes the act of reading an act of searching to locate the meaning.

Stevie Smith poem

The poem concerns a tragi-comic misunderstanding — a drowning man was ignored because onlookers thought he was cheerily waving at them, when he was really calling for help. This is taken beyond the literal level of a physical drowning to suggest another reading: that we explain away other people's difficulties in rather simplistic ways because we can't face the implications – our own responsibilities, for example.

The misunderstanding is presented by the use of two sets of voices: the 'I' of the dead man, and the 'they' of the onlookers; these voices are presented by a third voice – that of the narrator, who, unlike the onlookers, can hear the dead man speaking.

In using pronouns rather than individual names, the poem suggests that its message has significance for all of us, whoever we are.

Activity

It should be clear by now that the type of cohesive link involving pronoun reference is an important element in the way many texts work.

Now go back to the texts that you worked on in the 'Make and mend' part of this unit. Find as many examples as you can of grammatical cohesion which uses pronoun reference. Trace how you might have used this system as a supportive strategy in the texts you rearranged and wrote.

The politics of pronouns

Before leaving the personal pronoun system, there are one or two points to note that relate to changes that have occurred through time. Grammar, like other aspects of language, is subject to the processes of language change, and although the personal pronoun system appears to be relatively fixed, there have been important shifts in meaning and use. These shifts will be of particular significance if you are studying older texts, or comparing older texts with modern ones. It's important to realise that grammatical structures are not simply neutral – they are intimately related to power: for example, pronoun reference in a text is all about who is in the picture and how they're being seen, as well as about helping to construct a particular kind of relationship between writer and reader. These are all issues of power, because written texts are a powerful source of information for us about the nature of our world – not just the physical world, but our social, political and emotional 'realities' too.

One difficulty with the personal pronoun system as it exists in English is that there is no neutral way to refer simply to 'a person', without specifying a sex for them: 'one' can carry suggestions of pretension, and is hardly a term in everyday use; 'it' sounds rude when used of a person (think how insulting parents would find it if their newborn baby was referred to as 'it' by a friend peering into the pram on the street). 'They' has had varied fortunes in terms of its acceptability: while it was seen as correct in Shakespeare's time – for example, in *The Winter's Tale*:

> God grant everyone their heart's desire

by the eighteenth century, prescriptive grammars were ruling this type of sentence as incorrect because singular and plural references were being used together. Eighteenth-century grammars ruled that if pieces of communication were intended to refer to people in general, or a person of unspecified sex, the terms 'man' and 'he' should be used, claiming that these uses were **generic** – i.e. referring in a general way. In fact, it is clear from research that we actually understand 'he' and 'man' to refer to 'male person' rather than simply 'person'. This means that the words are not capable of generic reference for modern readers.

Nowadays, in order to get round the clumsiness of using 'he or she' every time we want to refer to 'a person of either sex', we use 'they' very often in speech, and increasingly frequently in writing. For example, this sentence occurred earlier in this sub-section:

> The principle of reference within texts is exactly that: it tells the reader that they can only make complete sense of the word or structure they are looking at if they look elsewhere in the text to get a fuller picture.

It's important to note, though, that people will disagree about whether the above sentence is correct, since eighteenth-century ideas about grammar were still current up to the 1960s. People's opinions about correctness will have been influenced by their age and the type of education they had.

Another personal pronoun that has had a directly political history is 'you'.

Originally, English had two forms of 'you': 'thou'/'thee' was used to one person, and 'ye'/'you' for group address. 'Thou' was used when the person was the subject of the sentence, and 'thee' for the object; similarly, 'ye' was used for the subject, 'you' for the object. An example of each is given below:

> *Thou* hast my heart (thou = singular = subject of sentence)
> I love *thee* (thee = singular = object of sentence)
> *Ye* must go now (ye = plural = subject of sentence)
> I will follow *you* (you = plural = object of sentence)

As well as denoting simply singular or plural address, however, these terms also came to mark relationships between people: if people who were social equals were addressing each other, the plural forms could be used between the individuals (i.e. as singular forms) to signal distance and formality, while the singular forms could signal closeness and intimacy when used reciprocally; if the people were not equals, however, the plural forms could be used in addressing the more powerful person, as a mark of respect and authority, while the singular forms could be used in addressing the less powerful person to mark low status. A diagrammatic representation of these possibilities is given below.

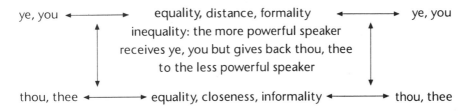

ye, you ⟷ equality, distance, formality ⟷ ye, you
inequality: the more powerful speaker
receives ye, you but gives back thou, thee
to the less powerful speaker
thou, thee ⟷ equality, closeness, informality ⟷ thou, thee

This pattern meant that speakers could signal meanings in a subtle way, simply by using a certain pronoun. While this distinction has been lost in modern usage (although the older forms are sometimes retained in dialect, and much can be expressed via personal names and titles), older texts can present patterns of pronoun reference that say much about social relationships.

The fact that 'thou' and 'thee' died out within standard English usage remains something of a mystery, although it has been put down to the fact that they became associated with the Quaker movement, who wanted the terms to become the universal address forms as markers of equality for all. As Quaker groups were seen as radical, establishment choice favoured 'you' instead.

Although the use of a plural term to denote respect to one individual has died out in the system above, we still have some residue of this idea in the royal 'we' to denote one powerful person in particular.

Stepping out of the text

At the beginning of this sub-section on grammatical cohesion, the idea of reference was defined as 'seeking information from elsewhere'.

Up to now, the focus has been on the reader searching various parts of the text for that information. But reference, particularly involving certain of the personal pronouns, can also involve moving outside the text to find the appropriate locus of information.

For example, the use of 'you' in a text as a direct address to the reader tells that reader to use himself/herself as the reference point; the use of 'I' in a text tells the reader that the writer (or the narrator) is being self-referential. In both these cases, the pronouns are functioning as sign-posts leading out of the text and making us focus on the human agents who are producing and receiving the text.

Where a reference item moves us outside a text, so that we can only make full sense of the text by referring to its context, this is called an **exophoric reference**; where we stay within the text, not needing any support from outside, this is called **endophoric reference**.

Activity

Go back to the texts you worked on in the first part of this unit, and find as many examples as you can of exophoric reference. Are there particular types or 'genres' of text that rely heavily on exophoric reference as part of their written conventions?

Commentary

There are certain types of text that are characterised by their use of exophoric references via the personal pronoun system: for example, many advertisements address the reader directly, using 'you', and companies refer to themselves as 'we'. An example of these pronouns can be seen in the 'Portfolio' advert you reassembled (p. 169), and you may well have found further examples of direct address in the texts you wrote your-selves.

Address forms which take us outside the text are also very charac-teristic of literature, particularly some types of prose fiction. For example, nineteenth-century novelists often addressed the reader directly: at the end of Charlotte Bronte's *Jane Eyre*, the narrator, Jane, talking of her relationship with Mr Rochester, says: 'Reader, I married him'.

The attraction of referring outside a text is that this can leave plenty of room for manoeuvre, as it is unclear who 'you', 'I' and 'we' actually are.

While this could suggest confusion, in fact there is much creative potential in not pinning down exactly who the creators and receivers of a text are, because that then means that readers have to construct their own versions of these figures: for writers of literature and adverts alike (and any other texts that try to work in an interactive way), it means that many possible 'readings' can occur.

Because the type of communication that's described above is potentially very complex, it can be useful to represent diagrammatically how these layers of reference might work.

Look at the BT advert on p. 300 (Unit 5).

In this, the copywriters are the real writers of the advert, but there is an implied writer/speaker constructed through the language that's used to address the reader. The real readers are us, but there are some implied readers, too: ideas about what we might think of as important, ideas about how we live and the attitudes we have are all embedded in the text, constructing 'us' as certain types of people, and not necessarily the people we really are; reference to 'us' as a specific group also varies through the text, from 'you' at the beginning, to 'gentlemen' towards the end.

All this goes to show how a text can create a particular relationship between the real writer and the real reader by constructing a piece of fictional discourse between implied versions of themselves:

real writer — implied writer — TEXT — implied reader — real reader

| advertising copywriter | narrator | | assumptions made about us in the text | the real person |
| novelist | ditto | | ditto | ditto |

etc.

If you have difficulty understanding the difference between the real audience and the implied one, then think about the following analogies: TV adverts for washing powder show women ('implied readers') as people whose lives revolve around the quality of their washing. Is this a true reflection of how women really live their lives (the 'real readers')? TV adverts for aftershave show men ('implied readers') who only have to splash on a little of the product for hordes of women suddenly to appear and look at the men in an admiring and available way. Is this an accurate picture of the everyday lives of men (the 'real readers')?

Demonstrative reference (deictics)

Another type of reference which acts as a cohesive tie is carried by the following terms:

the, this, that, these, those, here, there.

These terms demonstrate where something is; they are **deictic** terms — they are 'verbal pointers'.

As with personal pronouns, demonstrative reference can work backwards (anaphoric) or forwards (cataphoric). Here is an example of each:

I went to *Italy* last year, and I want to go *there* again soon (anaphoric)
But the problem is *this: how can I afford it?* (cataphoric).

The terms above can be categorised according to how they position the writer and reader (or speaker and listener, since the terms are used frequently in speech, too).

'This', 'these', and 'here' all mean 'near the writer/speaker', while 'that', 'those', and 'there' all mean 'away from the writer/speaker'.

While in speech these terms are often used to refer to physical items in the environment, in writing physical proximity can stand metaphorically for attitude as well.

Activity

In Text: Dialogues are some examples of demonstrative reference in speech.

Read through the dialogues and trace how the demonstrative terms work within the conversations to refer to the physical context of the speakers.

Text: Dialogues

Context 1: Speaker A is asking Speaker B to help her disentangle her earring from the telephone handset wire:

> A: Can you help me *here*? I've got my ...
> B: What are you doing *there*?
>   (B moves closer to A)
> A: It's *this* stupid thing ... it's all tangled up ...
> B: Hold on. Keep still a minute. It's *this* clasp *here*. Ah, got it ...

Context 2: Speakers C and D are house decorators discussing the wallpapering of a room:

> C: If you finish off *that* roll in the corner ...
> D: What about *this* end *here*, though?
> C: *That* will do the bit up by the beams over *there*.

Activity

As well as placing aspects of the physical speech context, deictic items can also refer to ideas in another speaker's utterance in order to make links with them. For example, imagine that the following speakers are having a discussion about their favourite meals, but that they are nowhere near any real food:

> *Speaker 1:*   I really like fish and chips.
> *Speaker 2:*   *That's* my favourite dinner, too.
> *Speaker 3:*   What about pasta and pizza?
> *Speaker 4:*   *Those* are nice, too.

Commentary

In the utterances above, the words 'that' and 'those' point, not to any real dinner, but to the words that name the food.

Even more removed from any physical reference is the use that sometimes occurs of the word 'that' to mean 'the thing/person we all know about'. Here are some examples:

I've got *that* Friday feeling.
That Beethoven was a genius.
You've got *that* 'know-it-all' look on your face.

Activity

Because demonstrative reference is all about pointing out, this type of cohesion can be used to strike strong attitudes as well as physical positions. Advertisers, literary authors and writers of all kinds can use our knowledge of demonstrative terms to signal relationships and point of view.

Look at Text: Kellogg's Cornflakes, Text: Quaker Puffed Wheat, and Text: Ovaltine. What part do demonstrative and personal pronoun reference play in positioning the readers of the texts? (There is one commentary, on the 'Ovaltine' advert.)

It may be useful to know that Ovaltine was originally classified as a medical product, being sold in chemists' shops, rather than as a general foodstuff.

Hold on!

He needn't catch the early bus looking like *THIS*

'Half awake and half starved—he's off to a bad start today! That's because he still hasn't really broken his night-long fast with a worthwhile breakfast. Yet he needn't miss the bus if he has Kellogg's with his breakfast!

Send him to work like *THIS*

He's on the beam all right today—he's had a quick, satisfying breakfast that included Kellogg's, top-of-the-milk, and sugar. No chance of indigestion even though he did eat it quickly. Straight from the pack, Kellogg's delicious deep-toasted Corn Flakes contain energy-giving carbohydrates.

Breakfast is the most important meal of the day—doctors and health-experts are agreed on this. They warn you that if you're going to do a hard day's work you've got to give your body the fuel it needs to keep going after a whole night without food.

But this is just what tens of thousands of men and women ignore. They demand too much of their bodies, think they can't prepare and eat breakfast *and* get to work on time—so they skip or skimp what should be the first, good meal of the day.

Get him there early—
with breakfast inside him!
Do you have this problem, too? There's a simple and tasty solution! Give your man his usual breakfast plus a heaped bowlful of crisp, golden-toasted Kellogg's Corn Flakes with sugar, and cream or milk. Kellogg's is best and tastiest because this delicious cereal brings out the full goodness of the rich heart of the finest grains of corn.

A breakfast like this will get anyone to work on time and with a good supply of energy to keep him working happily and *well* till the first break.

There's no preparation, no cooking, no messy washing up of pots and pans. Kellogg's is a breakfast *everyone* can help themselves to in no time at all.

A natural source of energy

Health experts agree that Kellogg's, with milk and sugar, provides energy in a really digestible form. Partly because of the delicious crunchiness, partly because of the perfect, wafer-thin, oven-toasted flakes,

Kellogg's, "go down well" with everyone. Isn't it worth while ensuring that a man goes to work *on time* and feeling *up to it?*

Of course it is!

So just see that he goes to work on Kellogg's.

Go to work on Kellogg's

—*IT'S READY-TO-EAT!*

Text: Quaker Puffed Wheat

An open letter to Mothers of fast-growing children

THOSE children of yours are growing so rapidly. The great concern of every mother must be that the growth shall be normal and regular, and that body, mind and muscle shall develop at the same rate.

Many children show a tendency to outgrow their strength. They become listless and disinclined for play. Their appetites are capricious and they are often weak and ailing.

Healthy and normal development depends almost entirely on correct diet and proper nourishment. Every particle of the material used in creating energy and building up the brain and body is obtained from food.

Growing children need more nourishment than ordinary food supplies. That is why "Ovaltine" should be their daily beverage. This delicious food-drink supplies, in a concentrated, correctly balanced and easily digested form, all the nourishing elements and vitamins that are essential for healthy growth.

"Ovaltine" is prepared from creamy milk, malt extract, and eggs from our own and selected farms. These are Nature's best foods. Eggs supply organic phosphorus— an essential element for building up brain and nerves.

The addition of "Ovaltine" removes the objection many children have to plain milk. "Ovaltine" renders milk more digestible, and therefore more beneficial. The nourishing value of all ordinary foods is increased when "Ovaltine" is the daily beverage.

Give your children "Ovaltine" instead of tea, coffee, etc. They will grow up strong and healthy—with sturdy bodies, sound nerves and alert minds.

"Ovaltine"

"OVALTINE" BUILDS UP BRAIN, NERVE AND BODY

Prices in Gt. Britain and Northern Ireland, 1/3, 2/- and 3/9 per tin.

P677

Commentary

Ovaltine advert

The authoritative voice of the text is immediately established by the phrase 'those children of yours': 'those' sets up a distance from the speaker, and 'yours' locates ownership and therefore responsibility for the potential problem raised by the speaker – that of children who may not grow normally.

The main body of the text uses scientific-sounding discourse in the form of many statements to further establish the expertise of the author of the 'open letter' in talking to the recipients – 'mothers of fast-growing children' (therefore all mothers, since few mothers would acknowledge that they had children who were slow-growing).

At the end, the power of authority is reinforced by a command which reminds the reader whose children are being discussed: 'Give *your* children "Ovaltine" '.

Activity

Rather than referring to the position of the speaker and hearer within a text, the term 'the' is often used to convey different levels of generality or specificity.

For example, it can be used generically in expressions such as the following:

> The snail is a fascinating creature.
> The family is a social institution.
> The heart is a large muscle.

In these examples, the reference is not to one particular animal, family or heart but to a whole species or type of item.

But 'the' can also refer to something very specific, with the suggestion that this item is the one and only example of its kind. In many types of discourse, we often use 'the' to refer anaphorically to something which has already been been introduced by using 'a'. For example, in this introduction to a fairy tale, 'a' becomes 'the' as the story proceeds:

> Once upon a time there was *a* king in *a* foreign land who had a great desire to marry. *The* king looked high and low in *the* land, but all in vain ...

Now look at the use of 'the' in Text: Names. What message is this term conveying? (In the first example, it might be useful to know that there are two universities in Manchester – the other one is called 'The University of Manchester', and its logo is given here, for information:

Comparative reference

Comparative reference tells the reader not just to 'look elsewhere for information', but to look elsewhere with a particular aim in mind – to *compare* the items that are being linked.

The most common way in English to mark grammatically that two items are being compared is to add 'er' to an adjective: for example, taller, nicer, healthier. It's also possible to suggest comparison with more than one item, by adding 'est': for example, tallest, nicest, healthiest.

Comparison can involve ideas about quantity and number: these meanings are carried by words like 'more', 'fewer', 'less', 'another'.

In many cases, we are given the reference point for the comparison being made, for example:

> Annie is taller than Sue.
> This sweater is nicer than that one.
> Salad is healthier than fried bread.

But it is also possible to omit the reference point – leaving out the aspect that the mentioned item is being compared with.

Activity

Look at Text: Slogans, all of which have been taken from advertising texts. In each case, the comparative reference is incomplete. Try to explain in each case what the effect is of not completing the reference.

Text: Slogans

MORE CATS PREFER IT

GET YOUR CLOTHES WHITER

THE MILDER TOBACCO

FOR A TASTIER MEAL

BE HEALTHIER - LIVE LONGER

A CLEANER FUEL - FOR CLEANER AIR

KINDER TO THE ENVIRONMENT

McVITIES BAKE A BETTER BISCUIT

MORE POKE, LESS SMOKE: MOBIL DIESEL PLUS

When you have finished, read through the Quaker Puffed Wheat advert again (p. 204), locating the comparative references and explaining their effects.

Substitution and ellipsis

Alongside reference, **substitution** and **ellipsis** are also both powerful ingredients in textual cohesion.

Substitution means what it suggests — the writer or speaker has substituted one item for another in the text. This can often involve long phrases, replaced by useful smaller items such as the single words 'do' or 'so', and is very characteristic of spontaneous spoken discourse. One important function of this type of substitution is to make texts more economic by avoiding tedious repetition. The examples below show how, while 'do' is used to replace verbs, 'so' is more often used as a substitute for whole clauses. In each case, the phrase that is being substituted by 'do' or 'so' is in italics. The dialogue is between two friends, and they are discussing A's intended house sale.

> *A:* Has the agent for your house *put it in the local paper*?
> *B:* I think he must have *done*, because Terry saw it advertised around his chips from the chip shop.
> *A:* *That must have been a bit of a shock* if you hadn't told him.
> *B:* I think *so*.

Substitution can also involve nouns, and here we often make a substitution in order to redefine the original item. For example:

> He looked at the potatoes, and picked out *the large ones*.
> Please read through the contracts, and sign *the duplicate one*.

While substitution is about swapping elements, ellipsis involves omitting elements altogether. Speakers who know each other well often use ellipsis because they have many shared meanings and references that do not need stating explicitly. As a result, when measured against writing, speech can appear to have gaps and incompleteness: for example, minor sentences (sentences without a verb) are very common in speech (for a fuller treatment of ellipsis, see Unit 5).

In some types of written texts, ellipsis can be used deliberately in order to create an illusion of closeness between writer and reader. The reader is forced to adopt the same position towards the writer that a speaker would adopt to a close friend in conversation. Rather than obscuring meaning or loosening the cohesion in a text, ellipsis is a binding factor because ties between writer and reader are strengthened through the work that the reader has to do to fill the gaps.

Activity

Look at Text: Subaru, and identify places where there are omissions — ideas left incompletely stated, apparent gaps in sense or structure.

◎ To what extent does ellipsis contribute to the feel of this text as spoken language?

◎ What advantage do you think there might be for the advertiser in creating this illusion?

AT LAST,
THE SUBARU OF
SUPERMINIS.

JUSTY. THE WORLD'S FIRST 1.2 4WD SUPERMINI.

A solitary cat. In a street of its own.

A poetic little mover. Precise. Instinctively sure-footed.

Subaru four-wheel drive. Gripping stuff.

On good roads. Rotten roads. No roads at all. Bad weather or not.

Drive quality, superb. You feel in safe hands.

With a sinewy little Subaru of an engine.

Clean burn. Sweet torque. Pulls like a dream.

Feels right. Superbly comfortable fit. Everything to hand or foot.

Good with numbers. 5-speed box. 3 valves per cylinder. And a choice of 3 or 5 doors.

And of course four-wheel drive.

Justy. The Subaru of superminis.

Please send me more information on the Subaru Justy.

Name

Address

Post Code

SUBARU

SUBARU (UK) LIMITED, RYDER STREET, WEST BROMWICH, WEST MIDLANDS B70 0EJ. TELEPHONE: (021) 557 6200. A SUBSIDIARY OF INTERNATIONAL MOTORS LIMITED.

THE WORLD'S FAVOURITE FOUR-WHEEL DRIVES.

Commentary

The text uses ellipsis in the form of many minor sentences, including single words ('Justy', 'Precise'), two-word sequences ('Gripping stuff', 'Rotten roads', 'Clean burn', 'Sweet torque', 'Feels right'), and longer sentences where certain elements have been omitted: for example, verbs ('A solitary cat'), and nouns that stand for the subject ('Pulls like a dream'). This, along with other features — notably the fast turnover of items, as if imitating a person's unplanned thoughts, including after-thoughts signalled by 'and' — suggests spoken language rather than writing. On the other hand, the text is set out to resemble a poem visually, with the language arranged in 'stanza' form, fitting in with the idea of the car as 'a poetic little mover'. The text as a whole, including the visual aspects, calls up elements of the detective genre in its suggestions of the loneliness and threat of city meanstreets; the verbal commentary also has the staccato rhythm and dramatic tension of a detective film's narrator. The message of the text, though, is one of reassurance: the car is solid, reliable and secure. The hand in the picture inset is female, with carefully painted nails. This is a vehicle which will protect a genteel woman driver in a man's world: its engine, though little, will growl if necessary; the car is a comfortable outfit; 'Justy' is good with numbers even if its driver isn't.

The text's imitation of spoken language brings the narrator close to the reader, calling up a frisson of fear in order then to be able to dispel it.

Activity

Look back at the texts you worked with in the 'Make and mend' part of this unit (both those you reassembled and those you wrote), and try to find examples of substitution and ellipsis. Then, keeping the same focus, look again at any of the further texts you have studied in this unit. Where you find examples, assess how far the written texts you are looking at are trying to convey the feel of spoken language.

Conjunction

The term **conjunction** means 'joining'.

In a sense, all the aspects of cohesion are about joining or linking items together, but conjunction refers specifically to words and phrases which express *how* items should be linked. An example from the sentence you have just read is the word 'but': this tells the reader that what is to follow will revise, limit or re-focus the first part of the sentence.

Different types of writing tend to use different types of connecting word.

This is not just about conventions that have developed – it is often very much to do with the purpose of the piece of writing (see also 'Information structure', later in this unit). So, for example, a story may well concentrate on the way one event followed another in time. If this is so, then conjunctions such as 'first', 'then', 'after that', 'in the end' are likely to appear. On the other hand, an information text may be more interested in showing how an idea or theme is made up of different inter-relating elements, and phrases such as 'on the other hand' may be more relevant here (as at the beginning of this sentence).

Activity

To look at this idea more practically, read through Text: High Peak, which is the front page of an information leaflet on conservation areas from the High Peak Borough Council.

In the text, the conjunctions have been underlined for you. Decide how they link together the various parts of the text – what instructions do they give the reader on how to put elements of the text together?

When you have finished, look for any more cohesive links, based on the types you have covered so far: for example, uses of 'this' and 'these'.

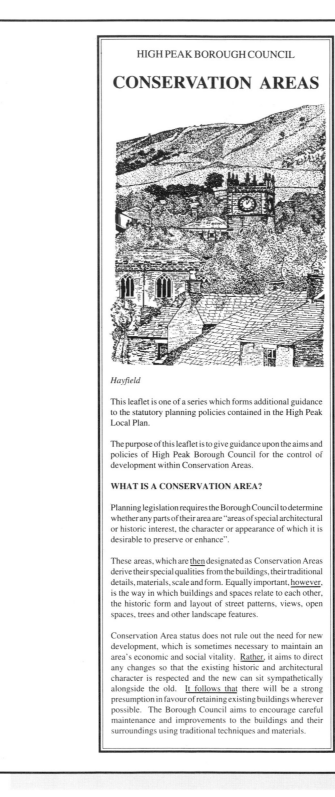

HIGH PEAK BOROUGH COUNCIL

CONSERVATION AREAS

Hayfield

This leaflet is one of a series which forms additional guidance to the statutory planning policies contained in the High Peak Local Plan.

The purpose of this leaflet is to give guidance upon the aims and policies of High Peak Borough Council for the control of development within Conservation Areas.

WHAT IS A CONSERVATION AREA?

Planning legislation requires the Borough Council to determine whether any parts of their area are "areas of special architectural or historic interest, the character or appearance of which it is desirable to preserve or enhance".

These areas, which are <u>then</u> designated as Conservation Areas derive their special qualities from the buildings, their traditional details, materials, scale and form. Equally important, <u>however</u>, is the way in which buildings and spaces relate to each other, the historic form and layout of street patterns, views, open spaces, trees and other landscape features.

Conservation Area status does not rule out the need for new development, which is sometimes necessary to maintain an area's economic and social vitality. <u>Rather</u>, it aims to direct any changes so that the existing historic and architectural character is respected and the new can sit sympathetically alongside the old. <u>It follows that</u> there will be a strong presumption in favour of retaining existing buildings wherever possible. The Borough Council aims to encourage careful maintenance and improvements to the buildings and their surroundings using traditional techniques and materials.

Here are some more conjunctions, with a brief explanation for each group of what they are telling the reader to do. (Note that some conjunctions can occur in more than one category.) Read through the notes, add any further examples you can think of, then specify the types of text (e.g. stories) that tend to use the various types of conjunction.

Type of conjunction	Meaning	Examples
additives/ alternatives	add/give an alternative	and, or, furthermore, in addition, likewise, in other words
adversative	contradict, concede	but, yet, though, however, on the contrary
causal	one idea/event causes another	so, then, for this reason, consequently, it follows that, as a result
temporal	one event follows another in time	one day, then, finally, up to now, the next day
continuatives	please continue to follow the text	well, now, of course, anyway, surely, after all

INFORMATION STRUCTURE

So far, attention has been focused on the way vocabulary and certain grammatical structures act as binding agents in texts. This sub-section looks at further aspects of both these areas, but with a focus on how particular types of text are connected with the internal ordering of information within them.

Different texts follow different rules which dictate to a certain extent the shape of the text produced: to return to the metaphor of weaving, you could say that texts come in different shapes in the same way that fabric is made into different garments.

But texts also have internal patterns in the same way that fabric has particular designs. The equivalent of a fabric design for a text is the pattern which results from how information and ideas are organised. For example, in the High Peak Borough Council leaflet, there are certain features that mark it out as belonging to the genre we might call 'information text', and some of these are to do with its directly visual shape: the title, in upper-case letters, the illustration, the boxed nature of the text, the way the text is broken up into spatially distinct sections. This is the equivalent of recognising a garment as a shirt or a dress. But there are also features of a more narrowly linguistic kind that relate to the way the text chooses to present its information and to foreground certain parts of it: this is more like the designs we see printed on a piece of material. These features are also part of the way we recognise and typify a genre, and they form the focus for the work that follows.

Sentence functions

Different sentences can perform very different functions, and, for this reason, the kind of sentence chosen often relates directly to what the text is trying to do.

Here are the four main functions sentences in English can perform:

◎ *Questioning:* Question sentences ask the reader to look for information.
◎ *Stating:* Statement sentences offer the reader a description of the state of things.
◎ *Commanding:* Command sentences (sometimes called 'imperatives') tell the reader to do something.
◎ *Exclaiming:* Exclamations express emotion directly.

To illustrate the differences in these functions, look at the High Peak Borough Council leaflet again.

The writers of this leaflet have chosen to use a question–answer format as a way of presenting information, so they have a question sentence as the heading:

WHAT IS A CONSERVATION AREA?

The effect of this is to justify the text that follows, in the sense that the text 'pretends' the reader has asked this question in the first place, so the writer is therefore doing the reader a favour by answering it. This in turn makes the text seem less authoritative than if the question had been a statement sentence:

CONSERVATION AREAS EXPLAINED

218

The other possible sentence functions – command and exclamation – would have had different effects again: a command sentence would increase the distance between writer and reader by giving the reader an order to be carried out:

FIND OUT ABOUT CONSERVATION AREAS – READ THIS LEAFLET

while an exclamation would have suggested that the whole subject of conservation was highly emotive and controversial (which it may well be, but the council is unlikely to want to suggest this):

CONSERVATION AREAS!

To summarise: information texts are known to be difficult texts to read because they demand a lot of information-processing skills from the reader. They are also likely to seem remote and authoritative, since explaining something to someone suggests that the giver of information is more powerful (because more knowledgeable) than the receiver. In this particular leaflet, the writer has tried to remove this distance by using a question sentence to introduce the information.

Activity

Go back again to the texts you worked with in the 'Make and mend' part of this unit.

◉ Do the different genres of the texts use different kinds of sentences?
◉ What are the effects of the different kinds of sentence they use?

When you have finished, look at Text: Gap.
This illustrates how sentence functions can be manipulated in order to create multi-layered readings. The text is an advertisement for a chain store called 'The Gap'. The advert came out around Christmas time in a variety of forms – on flyers and cards in the shop itself, as well as on hoardings and buses. Explain how the advert uses the idea of different sentence functions to create more than one level of meaning. (You might also consider why the advertisers chose to use lower-case letters on the word 'what', and why they positioned the text in a certain way, used a variety of typefaces, and chose the term 'certificates'.)

219

Text: Gap

what to give.

what to get.

Gap gift certificates.

Gap gift certificates are good at
all Gap and GapKids stores. They are
available in any denomination, and
come in a great little bag.

GAP

PATRICK DEMARCHELIER © GAP 1993

The lines 'what to give', 'what to get' could be read as two different types of sentence structure: as questions, or as statements. The fact that question marks are missing doesn't stop us from reading a possible question structure into the text. We would perhaps have been more 'worried' about the lack of question marks if the sentences had been full ones, with main verbs, and if they had had capital letters at the beginning in each case. As they stand, the sentences suggest spoken language as much as written and, as such, we are likely to be more ambivalent about whether they need formal punctuation.

The advertisers are clearly hoping to call up both question and statement structure: readers will then understand the statements as answers to the questions:

Q: what shall I give? what shall I get (buy/receive)?
A: (Gap is) what to give and get.

There are gaps in the text in a number of ways: grammatically, as above, in the statement reading of the sentences; in the visual space left in the text as a result of moving the second sentence to the right; and at the bottom, where a large space has been filled by the word 'Gap' stretched out vertically.

In its italicised form and decorative typeface, the official answer – 'Gap gift certificates' – supplies a solution which appears speech-like, gentle and friendly. The text below this is laid out as if on a commemorative plaque – the kind of layout seen on a certificate, a word which connotes achievement and reward rather than the financial transaction suggested by the word 'voucher'.

Another way we learn to recognise different genres of writing is by looking at the verbs used, particularly **tense** and **voice** (see Unit 3).

Tense

Tense refers to the way verbs are used to signal time: for example, a verb can be marked to show that an action happened in the past. This is done mainly by adding 'ed', but a minority of verbs change their internal structure. Here is an example of each type of marking: talk → talked (regular verb); speak → spoke (irregular verb). Certain types of writing tend to use particular verb tenses as part of their convention, and this in turn is related to what the text is trying to do. As an illustration of possible differences in what texts are concerned with, it is useful to think in terms of broad categories – for example, prose fiction compared with non-fiction information texts. Because information texts are intended to tell the reader about 'the nature of things' or 'how things are', these types of text tend to use present-tense verb forms couched in statements about present 'reality'. While prose fiction may equally give messages about the nature of the world, it tends to do this by looking back and giving an account of a series of events that happened to a set of fictional characters. It is therefore more likely that prose fiction will employ past-tense verb forms. Note that these statements are referring to norms or tendencies, not absolutes – so exceptions are always possible. In particular, it can be a very useful scene-setting strategy in fiction to 'stop the clock' and give a description of a place or person which uses present-tense verbs to convey the idea 'this is how things usually are in this place/with this person'.

Activity

Compare the verb tenses in the High Peak Borough Council leaflet with those in Text: *K is for Killer*, which is from a detective novel by Sue Grafton. How far do the verb tenses bear out the picture given in these notes?

Text: *K is for Killer*

I drove east along Cabana, the wide boulevard that parallels the beach. When the moon is full, the darkness has the quality of a film scene shot day for night. The landscape is so highly illuminated that the trees actually cast shadows. Tonight the moon was in its final quarter, rising low in the sky. From the road I couldn't see the ocean, but I could hear the reverberating rumble of the tide rolling in. There was just enough wind to set the palm trees in motion, shaggy heads nodding together in some secret communication. A car passed me, going in the opposite direction, but there were no pedestrians in sight. I'm not often out at such an hour, and it was curiously exhilarating.

By day, Santa Teresa seems like any small southern California town. Churches and businesses hug the ground against the threat of earthquakes. The rooflines are low, and the architectural influence is largely Spanish. There's something solid and reassuring about all the white adobe and the red tile roofs. Lawns are manicured, and the shrubs are crisply trimmed. By night the same features seem stark and dramatic, full of black and white contrasts that lend intensity to the hardscape. The sky at night isn't really black at all. It's a soft charcoal gray, nearly chalky with light pollution, the trees like ink stains on a darkened carpet. Even the wind has a different feel to it, as light as a feather quilt against the skin.

The real name for CC's is the Caliente Cafe, a low rent establishment housed in an abandoned service station near the railroad tracks. The original gasoline pumps and the storage tanks below had been removed years before, and the contaminated soil had been paved over with asphalt. Now, on hot days the blacktop tends to soften and a toxic syrup seeps out, a tarry liquid quickly converted into wisps of smoke, suggesting that the tarmac is on the verge of bursting into flames. Winters, the pavement cracks from dry cold, and a sulfurous smell wafts across the parking lot. CC's is not the kind of place to encourage bare feet.

I parked out in front beneath a sizzling red neon sign. Outside, the air smelled like corn tortillas fried in lard; inside, like salsa and recirculated cigarette smoke. I could hear the high-pitched whine of a blender working overtime, whipping ice and tequila into the margarita mix.

Voice

Verb voice is also something that tends to vary according to the genre of the writing. Voice refers to the way different emphases can be given to sentences (see Unit 3, p. 158).

There are two types of voice: active and passive.

If a verb takes an object (a thing or person affected by the action of the verb) as well as a subject (the thing or person doing the action) then it can be changed from active to passive. In the sentences below, the elements in italics form the object of the verb in each case:

She sold *the car.*
He kept *the pictures.*

223

These sentences are in an active form at present. Each can be expressed in a different way, however:

> The car was sold by her.
> The pictures were kept by him.

Now the sentences are passive: the object of the previously active sentence has moved to the front, to subject position; the verb has changed its form (to the form that it would take with 'have') and has added the verb 'to be'; the previous subject has moved to the end of the sentence, becoming a phrase (called the 'agent phrase'). In fact, this phrase could be left out altogether:

> The car was sold.
> The pictures were kept.

The fact that this phrase could be left out is a crucial factor in why the passive construction is favoured in some types of writing. Passives are often a way of depersonalising a text, because in removing agent phrases, the people and forces behind actions can be downplayed, leaving the process itself as the major focus – above, the selling of the car, the keeping of the pictures. It follows that any written genre wanting to highlight, for example, institutional procedures rather than individual concerns – such as legal documents or scientific reports – will tend to choose passive structures rather than active ones. In the High Peak Borough Council leaflet, the italicised parts of the text below are passives:

> These areas, which *are* then *designated* as Conservation areas ...
> Rather, it aims to direct any changes so that the existing historic and architectural character *is respected* ...

Passives are not simply an alternative form of expression, however. The fact that the agent behind the process can be removed from a passive construction can also mean that a text can appear to have a veneer of neutrality, scientific 'truth' or newsworthy 'fact' when, expressed in another way, it seems to be nothing more than personal dogma or ideological bias.

Activity

In Text: Voice are three brief texts written entirely in the active voice.

Turn them into the passive throughout, leaving out, wherever possible, the agent phrases. Possible rewrites are given on p. 246.

Text: Voice

> They drove the car quickly away from the scene of the crime. They had blown open the safe, shot the security guard and left him for dead. A bystander called the emergency services and a passing motorist comforted the guard until they arrived.
>
> I took a group of 40 people and surveyed their attitudes to alcohol. I found that most of the people surveyed drank more alcohol per week than the level that the government recommends.
>
> If you take out a mortgage, the building society will repossess your house if you do not keep up the monthly payments. You must let the building society know if you are going to make late or reduced payments at any time.

When you have finished changing the texts around, think about the following:

◎   What differences in meaning or emphasis have resulted from your rewriting?

◎   What advantages might there be for writers, in using the passive voice?

◎   What types of text, in your experience, are likely to use passive structures?

◎   Are there valid reasons for using passives, as well as dubious reasons?

Theme

Another important aspect of textual cohesion is the way in which the feature we call **theme** works across sentence boundaries.

Theme refers to the first part of a sentence, which is where the subject matter of the sentence is usually laid out for the reader. It covers all the material before the main verb. When sentences are woven tightly together, the end of one sentence (called the 'focus') can become the theme of the next. But themes have to have some continuity across sentences, otherwise a text that *looks* tightly knit can make complete nonsense.

Activity

The text below is tightly knit in that the end of each sentence (focus) is linked with the start of the next (theme). But there are no links between themes (which have been italicised). As a result, the text reads as somewhat bizarre:

> *I* got up early and fed my cat. *Cats* like cream. *Cream* is a popular colour for paint. *Famous painters* include Michelangelo, who painted the Sistine Chapel in the Vatican. *The Vatican* is where the Pope lives.

Do a short piece of writing like the one above, where there is no thematic continuity, but where the end of each sentence links with the start of the next.

Activity

Although the text you have just written would be considered faulty if judged by the rules of normal discourse, you might be able to find a text written in this way in some types of prose fiction – particularly where the writer is trying to imitate a kind of free-wheeling consciousness, where a character's thought process is being presented. Such texts are often described as using a 'stream of consciousness' technique. Text: Student's writing is an example. Can you see any cohesion in this text, or is it composed of entirely random sentences?

Text: Student's writing

Must take the dog for a walk this morning. Washing waving about. Wonder what he might think of me if I don't phone. Blue sky, blue sky. Helen never said, did she? Bloke over there, sitting on the wall. Where's my coat? Thought I left it somewhere else. Funny how old towns speak about their past. To swim, or not to swim, that is the question. Nicer on a Greek beach, body brown and oily, cheap novels in abundance. Don't need many clothes in some parts of the world. On then.

Deborah Freeman

Activity

Text: *The Shepherd* (an extract from the novel by Frederick Forsyth) shows how sentence themes can be controlled very carefully in order to give the reader a sense of place and time. Read it through and plot the way in which the themes construct a particular spatial and temporal orientation for the reader as the text proceeds.

Text: *The Shepherd*

For a brief moment, while waiting for the control tower to clear me for takeoff, I glanced out through the Perspex cockpit canopy at the surrounding German countryside. It lay white and crisp beneath the crackling December moon.

Behind me lay the boundary fence of the Royal Air Force base, and beyond the fence, as I had seen while swinging my little fighter into line with the takeoff runway, the sheet of snow covering the flat farmland stretched away to the line of the pine trees, two miles distant in the night yet so clear I could almost see the shapes of the trees themselves.

227

Ahead of me, as I waited for the voice of the controller to come through the headphones, was the runway itself, a slick black ribbon of tarmac, flanked by twin rows of bright-burning lights, illuminating the solid path cut earlier by the snowplows. Behind the lights were the humped banks of the morning's snow, frozen hard once again where the snowplow blades had pushed them. Far away to my right, the airfield tower stood up like a single glowing candle amid the brilliant hangars where the muffled aircraftmen were even now closing down the station for the night.

Inside the control tower, I knew, all was warmth and merriment, the staff waiting only for my departure to close down also, jump into the waiting cars, and head back to the parties in the mess. Within minutes of my going, the lights would die out, leaving only the huddled hangars, seeming hunched against the bitter night, the shrouded fighter planes, the sleeping fuel-bowser trucks, and, above them all, the single flickering station light, brilliant red above the black-and-white airfield, beating out in Morse code the name of the station – CELLE – to an unheeding sky. For tonight there would be no wandering aviators to look down and check their bearings; tonight was Christmas Eve, in the year of grace 1957, and I was a young pilot trying to get home to Blighty for his Christmas leave.

Commentary

This text gives an acute sense of a moment suspended in time as the pilot waits to take off; during this moment, he appears to have a heightened perception of his surroundings while looking out through the cockpit canopy. There are several sentence themes that specify spatial orientation: behind me; ahead of me; behind the lights; far away to my right; inside the control tower. At the end, we are brought back to the idea of time passing as the waiting pilot thinks ahead to 'within minutes of my going', at which point we view with him how the surroundings will appear as he takes off. We are brought back down to earth when we are told there would be no 'wandering aviators' that night; finally we are given factual details of time and direction – Christmas Eve 1957, a flight back to Britain. These details bring us back inside the plane, ready for take off.

The textile industry

The title of this whole unit is '*Text and context*'.

So far, the focus has been on how texts work internally, in how they are put together. This section examines another level at which texts operate, in the sense of the context that surrounds them.

The word 'context' contains the word 'text': it refers to the factors that work alongside or with the text to create meaning. 'Con' means 'with', and in Latin, the verb *contexere* means 'to weave together with'; the word 'con' in contemporary Italian and Spanish still means 'with', and you can see its operation in phrases such as the Spanish 'chili con carne' ('chili with meat').

So the context for any text is the larger culture which surrounds it, and the reading of any text results from the interplay of the text itself and the cultural framework that the reader brings to it.

The word 'culture', however, is not a straightforward term to define.

One use of the term refers to being part of an elite group: when we say someone is 'cultured', the suggestion is that they know about such areas of artistic expression as classical literature and music, and that they go to such venues as the theatre or art galleries as part of their social life. This is also what is meant by 'high culture', which was a phrase coined by Matthew Arnold to describe, in his opinion, 'the best that has been thought and said in the world'. In contrast, Arnold would have considered such pastimes as going to football matches, watching TV, viewing mass-circulation films or reading popular fiction or magazines as examples of 'low culture'.

This elitist view of culture, however, is not the whole story.

In sociology, culture has a much wider meaning: it refers to all the factors that bind groups together in all aspects of social life:

Culture refers to the ways of life of members of a society, or of groups within a society. It includes how they dress, their marriage customs and family life, their patterns of work, religious ceremonies and leisure pursuits. It also covers the goods they create and which become meaningful for them: bows and arrows, ploughs, factories and machines, computers, books, dwellings ...

(Giddens 1993)

Activity

In the quote above, culture is defined as *the ways of life of members of a society, or of groups within a society*.

Text: The Phone Book and Text: Leatherland contain references to aspects of culture. For each advertisement, identify these references and explain how the references form part of the way the text works.

When you have done this, consider the following questions:

◉ Would these references be understood by everyone in society, and by people from outside the culture that produced them?

◉ In the italicised quote above, culture is seen as referring to smaller groups within society, as well as society as a whole. Do the advertisements highlight the culture of some groups, but not others? If so, how?

◉ Why would advertisers want to refer to the culture of some groups in society rather than others?

Boldly go.

Kirk B, 96 South St, Sandstone..Ledbrooks 98689
Kirk B.A ,19 New Road, Bington...Wilkston 05792
Kirk C, 256 Lansdowne Pl...Ashtree 99892
Kirk C, 42 The Drive, Bascom..Brandyarce 28990
KIRK CAPTAIN JAMES T, Spc Expir
                    Trek Ho, High St................Sherby 30106
Kirk Charles, 84 First Ave, Blandover..Padluck 71103
Kirk, Cyril, 29 Wilbury Rd, Spindleton...Bepen 21710
Kirl D, Caburn Road...Long Deaton 93678
Kirk D.P, 61 Palmeria Av, Lobyton...Kirksworth 42147
Kirk Emil, 88 High St, Balsover..Sherby 51883

Superboldly go.

Kirk A, 20 & 2 Rd, Balsover...Padluck 43689
Kirk A, 22 Embankment Rd, Chadderton.......................................Bepen 50217
Kirk A, 68 Newbury Rd, Penbrook.......................................Long Deaton 99892
Kirk A.B, 84 Marine Dr..Kirksworth 28990
KIRK ADMIRAL JAMES T,
        Astro Conslt—
     Dunbeamin, 16 Rivermeed Rd........................Sherby 30106
Kirk Alan, 46 Goodwins Cres, Chellerham ....Bepen 53689
Kirk, A.R, I, 61 Cambridge Rd, Horton ....Padluck 24750
Kirl B, 88 Skipton Road..Sherby 01821

Every enterprise needs a little assistence. Because a business needs its customers and it's important to help them find you easily. A Simple solution is to beef up your entry in the Phone Book. For a small charge, we'll print your name, address and number in big bold type.

For just a little more, we'll make them even bigger and easier to find. The number of phone calls made every week in business after referring to Phone Books is a staggering twenty seven milion.

It only takes one, though, to find out how to get your fair share of them. Just dial 100 and ask for Freefone Phone Books.

The better you stand out, the easier it will be for your customers to find you. And the more likely it is you'll grow where no business has grown before.

THE *phone* **BOOK**

British
TELECOM

Text: Leatherland

Leatherland presents a new masterpiece.
The Mona Lisa.

If society is made up of many groups, it follows that any text may encode the culture of one group but not another. More than that, a text may, in giving voice to one group's culture, misrepresent another group or depict it in a negative way. In other words, any text adopts a point of view or position as a result of whose culture is being represented and how this is done. Such decisions are very much bound up with what is meant by the 'textile industry' in the title of this section: texts in the public domain such as advertisements, newspapers and forms of literature serve purposes which are often to do with the commercial profit margins of the most powerful groups in society, and they form a system which constructs ways of thinking for all of us.

Texts don't always hide their ideologies, however. Advertisements in particular can use ideas about representation as part of their persuasive message.

Look at Text: Daewoo, which contains a message about how other car adverts have sometimes sold their products (you might compare the car advertisement here with the VW one on p. 178). In Unit 1, the way in which one text can use or refer to another was termed **intertextuality**.

Explain how Text: Daewoo uses intertextuality in order to construct its message.

Text: Daewoo

**EVERY NEW DAEWOO COMES
WITH A RATHER ATTRACTIVE EXTRA.**

Tempted? So you should be because all our models come with three years free servicing. No small print, no disclaimers, just free servicing including all labour and parts. (Apart from the tyres that is, they come with their own guarantee.) Unlike other car manufacturers this offer isn't for a limited period, nor is it an extra, hidden in the hiked up cost of the car. Our offer is the same right across the Daewoo range and is included in the fixed price you see on the cars in the showroom. Those prices range from £8,445 to £12,895 for the 3, 4 and 5 door Nexia and the Espero saloon. As if this isn't enough of an offer, we'll even telephone and arrange your car's service, then collect it from your doorstep leaving you with a courtesy car until yours is returned, if you wish. But what happens in between servicing? That's covered too. Every new Daewoo comes with a three year comprehensive warranty, three years Daewoo Total AA Cover and a six year anti-corrosion warranty. In fact, the only thing you do pay for is insurance and petrol. Take a look at the list and see for yourself. 1). 3 year/60,000 mile free servicing including parts and labour. 2). 3 year/60,000 mile comprehensive warranty. 3). 3 year Total AA Cover. 4). 6 year anti-corrosion warranty.

5). 30 day/1,000 mile money back or exchange guarantee. 6). Free courtesy car. 7). Pick up and return of your car for service if needed. Mainland UK only. 8). Fixed purchase price with no hidden extras. 9). Delivery included. 10). Number plates included. 11). 12 months road tax included. 12). Full tank of fuel. 13). Metallic paint included. 14). Electronic ABS. 15). Driver's airbag. 16). Side impact protection. 17). Power steering. 18). Engine immobiliser. 19). Security glass etching. 20). Mobile phone. 21). Free customer helpline. If you were glad to hear all this we'd be glad to tell you more, so please call us on 0800 666 222.

A car where the extras aren't extra? That'll be the Daewoo.

DAEWOO

234

Activity

One of the problems of looking at culture is that it is difficult to distance yourself from the culture you are living in. This means that you cannot always see your own cultural frameworks because they just seem 'normal'. It's only 'other' cultures that appear odd or unusual.

To explore this idea, read through Text: Body ritual, which is an anthropologist's description of an aspect of Western culture. Do you recognise the ritual being described? How does this text resemble the way in which we often picture other cultures?

Text: Body ritual

The daily body ritual performed by everyone includes a mouth-rite. Despite the fact that these people are so punctilious about care of the mouth, this rite involves a practice which strikes the uninitiated stranger as revolting. It was reported to me that the ritual consists of inserting a small bundle of hog hairs into the mouth, along with certain magical powders, and then moving the bundle in a highly formalised series of gestures.

In addition to the private mouth-rite, the people seek out a holy-mouth-man once or twice a year. These practitioners have an impressive set of paraphernalia, consisting of a variety of augers, awls, probes and prods. The use of these objects in the exorcism of the evils of the mouth involves almost unbelievable ritual torture of the client. The holy-mouth-man opens the client's mouth and, using the above mentioned tools, enlarges any holes which decay may have created in the teeth. Magic materials are put into these holes. If there are no naturally occurring holes in the teeth, large sections of one or more teeth are gouged out so that the natural substance can be applied. In the client's view, the purpose of these ministrations is to arrest decay and to draw fiends. The extremely sacred and traditional character of the rite is evident in the fact that the natives return to the holy-mouth-men year after year, despite the fact that their teeth continue to decay.

(From H. Miner, *Body Ritual Among the Nacirema*)

(Answer on p. 246)

Activity

Text: Raleigh is advertising a bicycle, but it is also presenting quite a lot of information about cultural ideas and values. Imagine that you are an anthropologist from a foreign culture where there is no such thing as a bicycle. Decide on the following:

◎ What is a bicycle and what experience might you have if you rode one?
◎ How might this text be different if the bicycle was being sold as a fitness item, or a form of city transport?

Text: Raleigh

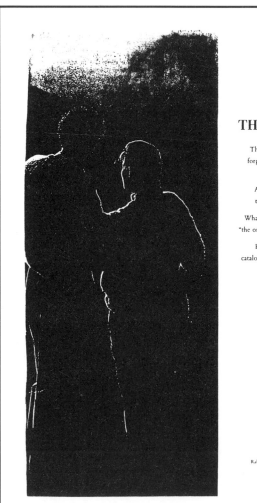

**FREE FROM
THE MADDING CROWD**

There comes a time to leave the world behind,
forget life's pressures and rediscover the freedom
of the great outdoors.

A country village, a secluded lane, a wooded
track – all are waiting to reveal new secrets.

What better way to share those pleasures than with
"the one you love" and a Pioneer bicycle from Raleigh.

Ring 0898 100712* for your colour Pioneer
catalogue and details of your nearest Raleigh Stockist.

PIONEER

OUR WHEELS ARE YOUR WINGS

Raleigh Industries Ltd., Triumph Road, Nottingham NG7 2DD.
*A call costs 36p per min. (cheap rate)
and 48p at all other times.

Collect some written texts in order to explore a particular dimension you have found interesting in this unit.

Here are some starting points, to get you thinking:

◎ intertextuality – texts that refer explicitly to other texts
◎ the representation of groups – e.g. gender, age, ethnicity, social class, region
◎ different types of writing on a common theme. These could include:

food: recipes, menus, adverts, food labels, poems ...
drink: beer mats, wine labels, wine reviews, adverts ...
relationships: greetings cards, lonely hearts columns, fiction ...
travel: holiday brochures, travel writing, travel guides ...

When you have collected a range of material, focus on an overall question for language analysis which will enable you to contrast a small number of texts for a specific reason. For example, within the area of food, the following contrasts might yield interesting results:

Language change: comparing an older text with a contemporary one from the same genre, what has changed, and why?

Spoken compared with written discourse: spoken (i.e. TV or radio) recipe compared with a written one. You could even compare texts from the same person, as several professional cooks have produced books to accompany their TV series.

The functions and features of different genres: how might the purposes of two types of writing – for example, a persuasive advert compared with an informative food label – be reflected in their language use? Are they more similar or more distinctive than we might think?

Texts specifically aimed at different audiences: how do recipes or menus aimed at children vary from those aimed at adults? Do adverts for food target male and female audiences differently? Do menus aimed at different regional and social-class groups encode ideas about the supposed audience?

Activity

To enable you to explore the usefulness of contrasting two different texts within the same genre, read through Text: Menu A and Text: Menu B. They are from very different establishments: A is from a roadside café in the Manchester area; B is from a large chain hotel in Newcastle.

What ideas about its target audience are suggested by each of the menus?

Text: Menu A

WAYFARER CAFE

ALL DAY FULL B/FAST WITH B/B
OR TOAST, INC POT TEA
HOMEMADE + 2 VEG, POTS
STEAK + KIDNEY, ALL IN
HOT-POT
HAM SHANK, CHIPS OR JACKET
LIVER + ONIONS
YORKSHIRES/MUSHY PEAS/BLACK PUD EXTRA

APPLE PIE + CUSTARD
BAKEWELL TART
PARKIN

VARIOUS SNACKS
SAUSAGE MUFFIN
BACON BARM
SCOLLOPS + GRAVY
CHIPS + GRAVY/CURRY SAUCE
OR TO ORDER

Text: Menu B

THE RAVENSCROFT SUITE:
GOURMET DINNER DANCE

An interesting warm salad of smoked bacon, wild mushrooms and duck, quickly cooked and abound with a melange of winter leaves sprinkled in a walnut dressing

*

Peeled prawns bound in a tomato enhanced mayonnaise with diced pineapple and walnuts, nestled on a meli-melo of lettuce served in a glass

*

A collection of cured meats and poultry, nestled on a rustic salad and doused in a warm raspberry dressing

*

A terrine of fresh vegetables, sliced onto a coulis of tomato and fresh herbs

***

Supreme of fresh salmon attentively grilled, presented on a cushion of homemade noodles with a champagne sauce

***

Fillets of fresh monkfish spread with a mousse of scampi caressed in cabbage and poached, sliced onto a dry vermouth and avocado sauce

***

Medallions of pork pan-fried and masked in a pink peppercorn sauce accompanied by caramelized kumquats

***

Escalope of turkey folded with cranberry sauce, dusted in breadcrumbs and baked, escorted by a rich Madeira sauce

***

Rounds of venison quickly pan-fried and masked with a sharp blackcurrant sauce with just a suspicion of Juniper berry

***

A tournedos of beef topped with a liver parfait, enrobed in crepinette and oven-baked, served with a Madeira and truffle fondue

Commentary

Graphology/phonology

These two texts represent variations within the menu genre in terms of their layout and organisation. Menu A groups its items in three sections, separated by space: the first section lists main meals, the second lists sweet dishes, while the third offers snacks. Menu B is laid out differently: all the items are equally spaced, but the number of asterisks denotes whether the food described is a starter or main course item. In each case, it is assumed that the reader knows about the organisation of the text as part of his/her reading skills within English-speaking cultural groups: a reader of Menu A would therefore not expect to have to select an item from each of the sections, while a reader of Menu B would not expect the items framed by three asterisks to be snacks.

Menu A uses upper-case letters in a plain typeface, suggesting clarity and straightforwardness, while the italic lower-case script of Menu B carries connotations of artistic purpose.

Menu A uses a range of abbreviations and symbols: b/fast, b/b, inc, veg, homemade, steak + kidney, pots, jacket, yorkshires, pud, 2, +, /. Again, there is an assumption here of shared understanding: there is no need for the text to spell out in any detail what is being referred to. The resulting economy of language suggests little use for the decorative, aesthetic aspect of communication. In contrast, the language of Menu B strives to expand rather than contract: for example, where Menu A uses a plus sign, Menu B renders additive meaning by phrases such as 'accompanied by' and 'escorted by'. Menu B also foregrounds its own language by imitating an artistic construct in its use of sound symbolism – peeled prawns, meli-melo, fillets of fresh monkfish, caressed in cabbage, pork pan-fried ... pink peppercorn, accompanied ... caramelized kumquats. The reader could be forgiven for thinking that some of the ingredients are included as much for their alliterative as for their culinary value.

Vocabulary

Menu A contains a large proportion of regional dialect terms, labelling regional food from the Lancashire/Yorkshire area: 'homemade' (a steak pie), 'hot-pot', 'ham shank' (leg of boiled ham), 'Yorkshires' (Yorkshire pudding), 'mushy peas' (baked marrowfat peas), 'black pudding', 'Bakewell tart' (from Bakewell, Derbyshire), 'parkin' (a cake made with black treacle), 'muffin' and 'barm' (both dialect terms for bread rolls), 'scollops' (potato slices dipped in batter and fried). While neither chips nor gravy are regional items, their combination on the same plate is much favoured in the North.

Menu B contains many terms derived from French, including some which are still given French pronunciation – for example: 'melange', 'coulis', 'mousse', 'parfait'. French terms are used to describe particular cuts of meat or fish – 'supreme', 'fillets', 'medallions', 'escalope', 'tournedos'; and the French-derived term, 'poultry', is preferred to the Anglo-Saxon alternative, 'chicken'. Dressings and coverings of various kinds – 'mayonnaise', 'coulis', 'mousse', 'parfait', 'sauce' – are of French derivation. French terms also refer to arrangements of food – for example, 'melange', 'meli-melo' (French for 'topsy-turvy'), or particular dishes and items – 'terrine', 'fondue', 'crepinette'.

Beyond the terms related specifically to food, many other terms within the text are French/Latin-based, and have connotations of formality and high status: for example, 'enhanced', 'presented', 'accompanied'. Some terms also suggest sensuality – 'nestled', 'cushion', 'caressed' – while others almost raise the food items to a level of human animacy: the warm salad is 'interesting', the salmon is '*attentively* grilled', the venison carries a 'suspicion' of Juniper, while the turkey is 'escorted', and the beef is 'enrobed'. The picture constructed is one where the food is a sensual experience, but of a high aesthetic level, unfolding within a world of good manners and delicacy, not within an animalistic world of base appetites.

The connotations of the names of the respective establishments provide revealing semantic contrasts: the 'Wayfarer' represents a transport-type cafe, appearing to suggest a travelling clientele, but offering a very localised fare which needs no explanation, therefore constructing readers who are known and familiar customers; the 'Ravenscroft', on the other hand, suggests ample provision in offering itself as a 'suite', and constructs an audience of sophisticated food experts – 'gourmets' – who have the leisure time to dance as well as eat. The food appears to be explained in some detail, but is couched in language which is not everyday and familiar, and which, in many cases, would need some knowledge in order to pronounce as well as understand.

Grammar

While both texts are lists of a kind, Menu A presents nouns with occasional modification: for example, 'full b/fast', 'ham shank', 'mushy peas', 'Bakewell tart', 'various snacks', 'sausage muffin', 'bacon barm'. In contrast, Menu B presents nouns or noun phrases which are heavily modified, with complex sets of dependencies: for example 'peeled prawns' is qualified by 'bound in a tomato enhanced mayonnaise', which is in turn qualified by 'with diced pineapple and walnuts'; the whole of this structure is then qualified by 'nestled on a meli-melo of lettuce', which is in turn qualified by 'served in a glass'. The effect is of layers of structure where the relationships between the parts of the utterance have to be unravelled; this effect is repeated in each description. The grammar is a linguistic simulation of the food it describes.

One or two aspects of the grammar of Menu B are deviant: for example, 'abound with', 'sprinkled in'. By the time the reader reaches the possibility of being 'caressed in cabbage', there is the distinct feeling that the writer has been overcome by the excesses of his/her own verbiage.

Discourse

The functions of the two texts are clearly different. Menu A offers information, while Menu B is more of a persuasive text resembling an advertisement. Menu A constructs an audience which is a known clientele who expect straightforward food with few trimmings; Menu B offers food which is dressed up via a text which simulates that elaboration. The audience constructed by Menu B is passing trade rather than regular patrons; such patrons may not actually be sophisticated, but the text suggests that they like to think they are – receptive to and impressed by the high-status connotations of French cuisine, rather than Anglo-Saxon cookery.

Activity

If your data is rich in interesting language features, then you don't need very much material in order to do a useful analysis. For example, Text: InterCity (an advert for British Rail's 'InterCity' service) itself sets up two contrasting texts as part of its message – one text basing itself on notions of speech, and the other on written language.

Explain how the two parts of this advert work. Note: the original advert included two images: above 'Flat out on the outside' was a drawing of a train rushing through landscape; in the middle of 'Laid back on the inside' was a drawing of a dozing female face.

There is no commentary on this activity, but working on this text will form a good bridge between this unit and the one on spoken discourse that follows.

Text: InterCity

Flat out on the outside.

London 2.55pm you've got to get to Edinburgh in a hurry so you board the new InterCity 225 at Kings Cross and Britain's fastest train races out of the station and the grey of North London becomes the green of Hertfordshire and surely this can't be Peterborough already but yes it is or rather yes it was because you're off again and this is your driver speaking we are now flying at a height of 6 feet above the ground at speeds up to 125 mph and countryside rushes past a blur of green and gold fast forward to York don't blink or you'll miss the historic Minster all aboard and once again you're going flat-out across Yorkshire's hills and dales with no roadworks radar-traps or flashing blue lights to stop you and the cars in the fast lane on a motorway race past you backwards coming soon to a window near you Newcastle phew its a wonder you don't need seat belts on this train and the Northumberland coast is clear and you sprint along beside the sea to picturesque Berwick and one day you decide you'd like to stay here longer but not today and you're in Scotland now don't take the high road or the low road take the railway and you'll be there before anyone because time waits for no man except you travelling on the InterCity 225 it's now three hours fifty nine minutes since you left today this must be a record welcome to Edinburgh.

Laid back on the inside.

London, 2.55pm.

You have to get to Edinburgh, but you want to enjoy travelling there as much as arriving there.

So you board the new InterCity 225 at Kings Cross.

The whistle goes and Britain's most comfortable train glides effortlessly out of the station.

(Do trains still run on rails, you wonder, or cushions of air?)

You sink slowly back into your seat (ahh bliss) and look around.

While the world rushes past outside, it feels unusually tranquil inside.

The effect of the soft lighting, muted colours and tinted glass.

Even the electronic doors at either end slide to and fro with a soothing shhhhhh.

What was it you were worrying about just a few minutes ago?

Funny, you can't remember.

Time to wander along to the buffet, perhaps.

Relax, the buffet comes to you, courtesy of a steward with a trolley.

Coffee? Tea? Orange Juice?

Sandwiches? Friendly repartee?

A sense of well-being now begins to fill you and you start to unwind, as if you were starting a holiday.

Here in the sanctuary of the InterCity 225, you have plenty of something that normally you have precious little of.

Time to yourself and peace and quiet in which to enjoy it.

You can read the paper from cover to cover, for once.

Compose a long overdue letter to Auntie Mary in New Zealand.

Practise transcendental meditation.

Or just sit back and enjoy the view, while we change the scenery.

Here, life seems wonderful indeed.

At some point you must have passed Peterborough, York, Newcastle and Berwick.

Because you arrive at your destination, three hours fifty nine minutes after you left Kings Cross.

Far too soon.

Oh, if only you were travelling further than Edinburgh.

INTERCITY

Answers to activities

Statements (p. 169)

Texts: A = romantic fiction book 'blurb'; B = advert; C = recipe.

A

Melodie Neil and Jed Martin were old friends.
She knew that he loved her − in a calm settled way rather than any grand passion − and that he would make her a good, kind husband.
In short, when she became engaged to him she knew exactly what she was doing.
So she hated it when that infuriating Keith Scott seemed to go out of his way to suggest that her heart wasn't in the affair.

B

Do you feel that you never get a fair slice of the capital cake?
We do, too.
That's why we created 'Portfolio', a brand new concept in saving.
Portfolio is a high interest investment account that makes your money work for you, while still giving you instant access to your capital.
So that way, you can have your cake and eat it too.

C

Wash and core the apples, taking care to remove all pips.
Slice finely.
Put them into a fireproof dish with the water, and a tablespoon of the sugar.
Ensuring that the lid is tightly sealed, put the dish into a preheated oven, Gas Regulo 6.
Reduce temperature to 3 after 10 minutes.
Allow the fruit to steam in its own juice for a further 15 minutes.
Spoon out the cooked apples and arrange them attractively in rounds on a serving plate.
Mix juice with the brandy, mulled wine, and rest of the sugar.
Pour over the top, and serve with double cream.

Occupations (p. 173)

The vehicle was seen proceeding down the main street in a westerly direction = police force.

Leading to a spacious and well appointed residence with considerable potential = estate agency

She went to work, mixing up the six-ten with two parts of 425, and dabbing the mixture through 6 ezimeshes = hairdressing

'This one has a fine shaggy nose and a fruity bouquet with a flowery head', she said = winetasting

He managed to get into a good position, just kissing the cushion = snooker

He said 'Just pop up onto the couch and we'll see what we can do' = medical profession

She pulled down the menu, chose the command by using the cursor, then quit = computers

She said to knead well, roll into a ball and leave overnight to rise = baking

Instead, he mulched well, turned over and left the beds to settle = gardening

Good progress made, but concentration sometimes rather poor; more effort required if success is to be expected in the important months ahead = teaching

Voice (p. 225)

Possible rewrites:

The car was driven quickly away from the scene of the crime. The safe had been blown open, the security guard had been shot and left for dead. Emergency services were called and the guard was comforted until their arrival.

A group of 40 people were surveyed on their attitudes to alcohol. Most of the people surveyed were found to drink more than the recommended level of alcohol per week.

If a mortgage is taken out, the house will be repossessed if monthly payments are not kept up. The building society must be informed if late or reduced payments are going to be made at any time.

Body ritual (p. 235)

Going to the dentist.

Text and context
Spoken discourse

The aim of this unit is to demonstrate that, just as written discourse has rules which govern its form and help convey meaning, so too does spoken discourse have rules which we follow. These rules have one major difference, however, from the rules which govern written texts, and that is that we are largely unaware of them. In fact in two-way conversations we are unconsciously taking part in a script which hasn't been written yet. As we improvise our way to sharing an experience, explaining ourselves, getting information, telling a joke or even spreading gossip we are negotiating time with our respondent in which to speak, knowing when we have a signal to take a turn in speaking and supporting the other speaker during her/his turn.

Spoken discourse exists within a social context, and this unit aims to use everyday **speech events** as a starting point from which to recognise that while we may not speak in words, sentences and paragraphs, we do have rules to follow, though they can be broken just as the rules of syntax can be. It's important to realise that spoken discourse should not be judged using the rules of written English: terms such as 'word', 'sentence'

247

and 'paragraph' above, all come from the study of writing. The written form is not an appropriate medium for oral language but, of course, in order to properly analyse speech we need to see it on paper.

Having signposted some of the features of speech events, this unit will then consider one-way discourse such as storytelling and speeches; it will go on to explore the features of dialogue, and will conclude with an examination of how the speech of some social groups is represented on the page.

Contents

1   Speech events
2   Storytelling
3   Speeches
4   Conversation: some ground rules
5   Conversation in practice
6   The representation of talk

Texts used

◎   Some personal writing
◎   Three oral narratives
◎   Two political speeches
◎   A script from a language work book
◎   An extract from a play
◎   Three conversations

Speech events

Imagine how the conversation might go as you take your leave of some-one after having had dinner at their house. You might signal your intention of leaving by some line such as 'I must be going', you might express gratitude for the meal, you might say thank you, you might praise the excellence of the food, you might suggest a return visit to your place, the conversation might drift back to an earlier topic or even start a completely new one, you might say thank you again, and then you embark on the 'goodbyes' and 'goodnights' before finally going. In such a situation or speech event as this English speakers will be unconsciously following rules whose purpose is to express thanks, reinforce relationships, leave on good terms and allow a suitable length of time between first suggesting you must go and actually going. Saying you must go and then immediately fleeing the house would be considered inappropriate and rude - certainly in British culture. Conversation, then, exists within a social context and this context determines the purpose and shapes the discourse.

Activity

Consider possible interactions in the following speech events. What do you think the rules are that govern discourse here? And what would break the rules?

◎ Customer–hairdresser conversation
◎ Introductions
◎ Answering the phone and signing off
◎ Recording answerphone messages – both outgoing and incoming
◎ Phoning for an appointment at the doctor's

Conversation, however, is not always clear-cut, and sometimes a breakdown in communication occurs because intention is misunderstood. What the speaker intends but what the listener hears has informed much of Deborah Tannen's work on gender and conversation (1992). She cites, for example, the case of the woman who had just undergone surgery to have a lump removed from her breast. She tells her female friends that she found it upsetting to have been cut into, and that the operation had left a scar and changed the shape of her breast. Her friends replied: 'I know.

249

It's as if your body has been violated.' But when she told her husband, he replied: 'You can have plastic surgery to cover up the scar and restore the shape of your breast.'

She felt comforted by her friends' comments, but upset by what her husband said. Her friends gave her *understanding* but her husband reacted to her complaint by giving *advice*. His intention was to offer help, but what his wife heard was him telling her to undergo even more surgery.

Intention lies behind a range of specific utterances called **speech acts**. When someone says, for example:

> I apologise
> I promise
> I do (at a wedding)

s/he is doing something *beyond* what's being said. By saying 'I apologise', for instance, s/he has performed an apology; there has been a change in the state of things, an act has been carried out. Speech acts are particularly prevalent and important in the language associated with ritual and ceremony. Here speech acts may contribute to the accepted rules or code of conduct or order that a ceremony has to follow; they often also have legal status. Saying 'I *do*' at the appropriate moment in a wedding ceremony – assuming you meet all the other criteria, being the bride or groom, for example; the choir boy or organist shouting out 'I do!' doesn't count – will get you married in the eyes of the law. The minister also confers legal status when s/he announces 'I *name* this child . . .'; the judge when s/he declares 'I *sentence* you to two years' imprisonment'.

Saying, then, is doing and doing is performing. Speech acts are involved in lots of everyday conversation and a simple test to check if an utterance *is* a speech act is to put the words 'I hereby' in front and see if it makes sense. So:

> I hereby apologise
> I hereby promise
> I hereby do take

make sense, but 'I hereby know you' doesn't.

Several attempts have been made to classify the thousands of possible speech acts in everyday occurrence. Perhaps the most useful has been made by Searle (1969) who has suggested five groups:

Representatives: the speaker is committed, in varying degrees, to the *truth* of a proposition, e.g. 'affirm', 'believe', 'conclude', 'report'.

250

Directives: the speaker tries to get the hearer to *do* something, e.g. 'ask', 'challenge', 'command', 'request'.

Commissives: the speaker is committed, in varying degrees, to a certain *course of action*, e.g. 'bet', 'guarantee', 'pledge', 'promise', 'swear'.

Expressives: the speaker expresses an *attitude* about a state of affairs, e.g. 'apologise', 'deplore', 'thank', 'welcome'.

Declarations: the speaker alters the *status quo* by making the utterance, e.g. 'I resign', 'you're offside', 'I name this child', 'you're nicked', 'you're busted punk'.

Activity

Look at the following examples: which group does each belong to?

> insist
> congratulate
> I now pronounce you man and wife
> vow
> deny

Commentary

◎   'Waiter, I *insist* on seeing the manager' is an example of a directive.
◎   'I'd like to *congratulate* everyone involved in making the show such a success' is an expressive.
◎   'I now *pronounce* you man and wife' is a declarative.
◎   'I *vow* to obey the rules of the Black Hand Gang' is a commissive.
◎   'I *deny* all knowledge of the facts' is a representative.

In reality, in everyday discourse, many speech acts do not directly address the listener. For many reasons – because we might be obeying the politeness principle, for example, and don't wish to impose – we may ask for something to be done *indirectly*. 'Can you pass the salt?' for instance, is not really a question but a directive; an answer of 'Yes' without any

251

attempt to actually *pass* it would seem totally inappropriate. Forms, then, such as 'Can you pass the salt?' in preference to the more direct 'I command that you pass the salt' are known as **indirect speech acts**.

It's possible, of course, to phrase speech acts in various ways – you can, for instance apologise *without* actually using the term 'apologise', as in 'OK I was wrong'; have a bet with someone by saying 'You're on'. Directives can be especially interesting in the gradient they take from direct order to humble question. Imagine that you've got a fly in your soup in a restaurant; a gradient might go something like this:

- Waiter, get the manager immediately
- Waiter, I insist on seeing the manager.
- Waiter, I want to see the manager.
- Waiter, I'd like to see the manager, please.
- Waiter, if it's not too much trouble I'd like to see the manager.
- Waiter, I don't suppose I could see the manager, could I?

Activity

Try a similar gradient from direct to indirect speech act:

1   *Asking* someone out on a date
2   *Requesting* someone to stop talking in the cinema.

Extension

1   Exploring the style and pattern of everyday speech events can prove valuable, fruitful and interesting. Consider also whether different ethnic groups follow different rules in some situations. Also can gender or age play a part in what happens? How does gender play a part on the phone, for instance? These questions are taken up in the final section of this unit.

2   Alternatively consider examining the ritualistic language of ceremonies such as weddings, baptisms, funerals. Oscar, Britpop, Booker Prize or similar award-winning ceremonies or the language of the courts are also areas fertile for investigation.

Storytelling

SPOKEN VERSUS WRITTEN

This section will draw on two real spoken stories in order to highlight some of the common features of the oral narrative. Jonathan's story is about a car crash on the M4; Esther's is about travelling in a plane which is struck by lightning. Text: Jonathan's story (1) gives the openings of his story, one the spoken version and the other a written version. Which is which? (To make them appear the same on the page slashes have been used instead of conventional punctuation.)

Text: Jonathan's story (1)

Extract 1

sometimes I think I'm lucky to be alive / I can't help enjoying really simple things because all the time I'm telling myself that I could be dead instead / once for instance I could have died on the motorway / it was the beginning of my second term of my second year at university / I had spent Christmas with my parents / dad took me to the railway station in Kidderminster / I had to go to Birmingham and then change for Reading / as he shook my hand a yellow Ford drew up / my friend Paul was in it / he smiled roundly and said he had the day off so he'd drive me back to university / I accepted

Extract 2

right well um the whole thing happened er as a result of going back to university one day / this was when I was about nineteen in January 1983 er a friend of mine suddenly turned up er at a railway station my best friend just as I was about to get on the train / back to Reading and said I'll drive you back er I was delighted er partly as it was company and an adventure through half the country / so we started driving back and got desperately lost / we were trying to get back to Reading from just above Worcester we ended up near Bristol

Jonathan Timbers

253

Activity

Having spotted which is the spoken version take a few minutes to jot down some of the ways it differs from the written one.

Commentary

You might have noted the use of words like 'um' and 'er' in the transcription of the spoken version. 'Ums', 'ers', 'erms' are **fillers**. Very common in spoken discourse, they act as pauses, or very often, as in extract 2, they accompany pauses and in effect lengthen the gap between words. In spontaneous speech we are 'thinking on our feet' and the use of fillers allows us to do some forward planning on what to say next. They help to cement ideas together in conversation. Also fillers are often added to the common conjunctions 'and' and 'but'; the pause is then effectively lengthened.

The spoken version seems unnecessarily repetitive, e.g. 'a friend of mine . . . my best friend' and 'I'll drive you back . . . we started driving back'.

The two extracts are reproduced in Text: Jonathan's story (2) in their punctuated and transcribed versions.

Text: Jonathan's story (2)

Extract 1

Sometimes I think I'm lucky to be alive. I can't help enjoying really simple things because all the time I'm telling myself that I could be dead instead. Once, for instance, I could have died on the motorway. It was the beginning of my second term of my second year at university. I had spent Christmas with my parents. Dad took me to the railway station in Kidderminster. I had to go to Birmingham and then change for Reading. As he shook my hand a yellow Ford drew up. My friend Paul was in it. He smiled roundly and said he had the day off, so he'd drive me back to university. I accepted.

Extract 2

right well um the whole thing happened er as a result of going back to
university one day (.) this was when I was about nineteen in January
1983 er a friend of mine suddenly turned up er at a railway station my
best friend just as I was about to get on the train (.) back to Reading and
said I'll drive you back er I was delighted er partly as it was company
and an adventure through half the country (.) so we started driving
back and got desperately lost (.) we were trying to get back to Reading
from just above Worcester we ended up near Bristol

The use of a full-stop, in brackets, in a transcription indicates a pause —
conventionally of about a half-second duration. Longer pauses of one
second, two seconds, three seconds, etc., would be conveyed as: (1), (2),
(3), etc.

LABOV'S NARRATIVE CATEGORIES

A comparison of spoken and written forms of the same narrative can be
very useful in highlighting some of the ways in which oral narratives
work. We expect stories to have a beginning, a middle and an end. Oral
stories, however, operate in a different context from that of written
forms: attention may have to be attracted from potential listeners and,
once attracted, kept. William Labov (1972), in an essay entitled 'The transformation of experience in narrative syntax', posited a six-part structure
for a fully-formed oral narrative, based on work he had done on
collecting real narratives from New York Black English vernacular
culture.

Abstract: signals that a story is about to begin, gets the listener's attention, might ask for permission to tell a story, gives some indication of
what the story is about.

Orientation: puts the story into a context, gives the time, place,
person(s) involved and situation/activity; the 'when, where, who and
what?' of the story.

Complicating action: the main narrative body providing the 'what happened' element of the story.

Resolution: the final events, the 'what finally happened' element.

Evaluation: makes the point of the story clear, suggests why it's worth being told, why it's of interest.

Coda: signals that the story has finished, can also link back to the beginning or return to the present time frame.

With the exception of evaluation, the categories are listed above in the order they would be expected in a typical fully-formed narrative. Of course, though, many narratives may lack one or more components or may justifiably have elements which seem to do the work of two components. For example, non-fully-formed narratives may have openings which seem to be both abstract and orientation; or, where stories have been invited by the listener or interviewer, then an abstract would seem to be irrelevant, or even silly. Evaluation can appear at any point in the story and this is represented graphically in the diagram below:

```
e        v       a       l       u       a        t        i        o        n
abstract     orientation          complicating    resolution         coda
                                  action
```

Activity

Now look back at the very start of each extract in Text: Jonathan's story (2). What do you think extract 1 is doing that extract 2 doesn't attempt?

Commentary

The opening of extract 1 seems to be justifying its existence; it's saying why it's being written, why it's worth reading. Finally, it's giving some idea of what the story is going to be about: almost dying in a motorway crash. The oral narrative of extract 2 jumps straight into the story and refers to the incident with no specific detail as 'the whole thing happened'. This is the abstract of the narrative.

The next part of each extract seeks to establish the *time* that the incident took place; e.g. extract 1: 'the beginning of my second term of my second year at university . . . [at] Christmas'; and extract 2: 'going back to university one day . . . when I was about nineteen in January 1983'. Also the *place*; extract 1: 'the railway station in Kidderminster . . . had to go to Birmingham . . . then change for Reading'; extract 2: 'a railway station . . . the train back to Reading'. We learn about the *persons* involved; extract 1: 'parents . . . dad . . . my friend Paul'; extract 2: 'a friend of mine . . . my best friend'. Finally we are told of the circumstances, the *situation*, i.e. being driven back to university. All these details help to place the story in context and can be labelled orientation.

The story proper, the 'what happened' element, known as the complicating action, only gets going in extract 2: 'so we started driving back . . . ', etc.

Activity

Now have a look at another oral narrative, Text: Esther's story, and decide which elements could be constituted as abstract, orientation and complicating action. It may help to discuss this in small groups. This time the complete story is reproduced but for the moment limit yourself to the first nine lines (up to 'strapped in').

Text: Esther's story

Extract 3

I remember being on an aircraft (.) when I was about five (.) and I was with my parents coming back from a holiday in Greece (.) and would you believe I mean it sounds ridiculous now but the aeroplane was being hit by lightning and um there was an aircraft above and an aircraft below and we were coming back and it was a massive storm and I can't remember a lot of it (.) I was sat with my mum and my father was sat with my sister behind (.) the lights went off and the air hostesses went absolutely wild everyone was strapped in (.)

the pilot explained what was going on but don't panic and there was um a lot of Muslims coming back and they were all saying their prayers and going (.) aiee aiee and I remember a lady standing up and saying we're all gonna die we're all gonna die and this lady stood up and smacked her across the face and said if we're all gonna die we don't want to listen to you and um afterwards I mean 'cos I was really young I didn't realise (.) I realised there was panic going on in the plane and when we actually landed and the pilot came out and said you were very lucky um (.)

it was frightening though very frightening (.) but it doesn't (.) I think it was because I was so young that I've never been frightened of flying (.) never I mean even when I get on an aeroplane now I'm not bothered

Esther Gosnay

It's often possible to note a pattern in the form that some of Labov's categories take. Orientation, for example, is often marked by *past progressive verb* forms:

we *were staying* in a Howard Johnson Inn at Hollywood Beach …
I *was coming* back from a holiday in Greece
the aeroplane *was being hit* by lightning
most of us *were staying* in a hostel which was to the west of the city.

Orientation also makes use of *adverbial modifiers* of *time* and *place*. For example:

as a result of going back to university *one day*
when I went *to Hornsea*.

Complicating action is normally told through a series of narrative clauses, ordered chronologically, with verbs in the *simple past*. This section, also, may well be the longest as the events of the story are related until the resolution is reached. For example, from later in Jonathan's story:

at that point Paul *woke up* and he then *corrected* but he *over-corrected* and so instead of going over the hard shoulder we *headed* towards the central barrier of the M4 at 70 miles per hour er we *hit* that.

The rest of Jonathan's dicing with death is given in Text: Jonathan's story (3) with Labov's labels. A full discussion follows.

most of this is the main body of the story: the *complicating action*

on the way we managed to park for five minutes er it was a queue of traffic lights (.) and we also tested y'know one or two of the beers of the local area er y'know we found a really good one called Wadsworth Six erm

on the way on the M4 we eventually managed to find the M4 to drive up to Reading again having driven about 100 miles out of our way (.) er Paul managed to switch the heating on the car really high (.) er

and we were travelling about 70 and I suddenly noticed we were beginning to creep onto the hard shoulder (.) *and I couldn't actually believe that I mean I couldn't drive my dad had always driven me nearly everywhere basically apart from a couple of wild nights when I was 17* (.)

and the idea that cars weren't on rails somehow suddenly struck me as unbelievable (.) and er I suddenly realised we were coming off the road (.) and at that point Paul woke up and he then corrected but he over-corrected and so instead of going over the hard shoulder we headed towards the central barrier of the M4 at 70 miles per hour (.) er we hit that (.) er we then proceeded to flip over it (.) into the fast lane of the other carriageway (.) erm

I remember thinking (.) oh shit and having this mental image of y'know steps up to heaven and I think I remember thinking oh shit this is really unoriginal (.) and as we flipped over the central barrier my head went out to the side window and I wasn't wearing a seat belt *as the seat belt rules hadn't quite come in yet* er we then (.) the top of the car hit the fast lane of the other carriageway and I was sort of half way out and half way in the car (.)

it was really interesting when you go outside the window because the air pressure suddenly changes in your ears and I went through so hard it really didn't do too much damage to my face er but I managed to sort of bang the back of my head on the hard shoulder as we flipped over at 70 miles per hour (.)

I also recognised that the car was about to roll on top of me (.) and sort of sever my head (.) so I managed to push myself out and sort of my arms suddenly developed this incredible strength and just pushed myself out the side window (.)

erm I couldn't really see at all *and had there been any traffic coming immediately on the hard shoulder course I'd be knocked over and crushed but* erm er I was in a complete daze and started looking for my glasses which had

complicating action = series of narrative clauses, ordered chronologically, with verbs in the simple past

except: *embedded speech* = the classic form might be: 'this is it!'

except: *evaluative commentary* = a comment by the speaker on the events been flung in the middle of the motorway (.) the first car that came was a staff nurse off duty and she bundled me into the back of the car and took me to the nearest hospital (.) which er turned out to be a sort of rather nice cottage hospital but I got put in the senile ward (.) so I kept on getting well the few times I managed to get to sleep getting woken up at like midnight by *somebody shouting bring the pisspot nurse or no not the injection I know what those injections are for* (.)

dramatized re-enctments = acting out a story, giving a performance

er I did actually manage to get to sleep for I think for about half an hour that night and as soon as more or less after half an hour some nurse came through and shone a bright light in my eyes to see y'know to see if my vision was working (.) *by that night it had come back* and a very strong image even now of being wheeled through on casualty not really being able to see anything but *thinking well at least I'm alive even if my eyesight's like this for the rest of my life*

resolution = the final event

coda = signals that the story has ended, may also include *evaluation*

Commentary

Evaluation covers anything which is not strictly narrative, anything above and beyond the 'blow-by-blow' account of what happened; it's anything which is not strictly necessary in relating the events, the 'we did this and then we did that and this happened and then that happened'. It is of course pervasive in most narratives (and sometimes the most interesting element) and it takes many forms. The two broad areas most useful for us to consider can be labelled evaluative commentary and embedded speech.

Perhaps the most common form, evaluative commentary, as the term suggests, is a comment by the speaker on the events. An example of this occurs early in Esther's narrative even before the story proper starts:

and would you believe I mean it sounds ridiculous now

where she takes momentary time off from the story proper to underline her assertion that the aeroplane she was travelling in was being hit by lightning and she also uses this comment to deflect any doubting listeners. It's as if she's saying 'Yes I know all this sounds a bit far-fetched or exaggerated, but it really happened!'

Jonathan does something similar in his car-crash story. With the car in which he was travelling drifting out of control, he offers the frank admission that

> the idea that cars weren't on rails suddenly struck me as unbeliev-able.

Evaluative commentary can also add extra interesting information. As Jonathan crashes and is forced through the car window, he comments:

> it was really interesting when you go outside the window because the air pressure suddenly changes in your ears.

Also under this heading you might find comments such as:

> I really thought my number was up

or any other idiomatic expression meaning impending death. Any comment, too, which aims to underline the seriousness of the situation, such as:

> we were very lucky; or
> two seconds later and it would have hit us

can be considered as evaluative commentary.

Another form of these 'time outs' from the bare bones of the story is embedded speech; this may well add interest too, and heighten the dramatic presentation of the story. The classic form would be:

> I said to myself, 'This is it!'

Of course in reality such clichéd responses are rare. But any words articulated as direct speech, indirect speech or even left as thoughts would count as evaluation. We find an example at the end of Esther's story:

> when we actually landed and the pilot came out and said you were very lucky,

and, on collision course at 70 miles per hour for the central barrier, Jonathan tells us:

> I remember thinking (.) oh shit and having this mental image of
> y'know steps up to heaven and I think I remember thinking oh shit
> this is really unoriginal.

A further point on embedded speech is worth making. Labov does not
regard speech as part of the narrative core; he only counts what is done
rather than what is said. This may be problematic, however. It
may well be difficult, if not impossible, to divorce some speech from
the narrative flow as if it just doesn't contribute to 'what happens'. Obviously the pilot's comment above *is* outside of what is essentially happening:
the plane being hit by lightning; the events would have happened anyway.
But there will be cases when the speech *is* part of what happens and does
precipitate events, bring things to a head, or whatever; we may be driven
to action by what someone says. To take a well-known example from the
world of film, surely Dirty Harry's taunt to the gunman he's facing of 'Make
my day, punk!' *does* influence the action and cannot, therefore, be considered extraneous or unnecessary to the plot. It seems, then, sensible to
differentiate between speech which is central to the core of the story and
speech which is not. Dirty Harry's speech, therefore, would be complicating
action, and the pilot's comment would be classed as evaluation.

Relevant to this, it seems sensible, too, to consider at this point
the work done by Wolfson (1982) on storytelling as dramatised
re-enactments. She writes:

> When a speaker acts out a story, as if to give his audience the oppor-
> tunity to experience the event and his evaluation of it, he may be
> said to be giving a performance.

Wolfson also draws attention to dramatised categories which seek to
provide a more vivid and involving experience of that story, while
exploiting special performance features as resources for highlighting the
story's main point. Further examples from Esther's story seem more
accurately described as dramatised re-enactments rather than the more
general term embedded speech:

> the pilot explained what was going on but don't panic; and
> a lady stood up and said we're all gonna die we're all gonna die.

The highlight of her storytelling performance:

> they were all saying their prayers and going ... aiee aiee

illustrates two more of Wolfson's categories: expressive sounds, and
motions and gestures.

1   Write a linguistic analysis of the narrative in Text: Jessica's story. In the process consider how helpful Labov's categories are; and imagine how much of a story would be left without the speech.

2   The narratives given by Jonathan and Esther were in response to the question: 'Can you tell me of a time when you were in a life-threatening situation?' Jessica's story, on the other hand, centres around a friend's discomfiture. Collect a range of narratives – e.g. when someone's life was in danger, a story about someone you know, a funny story. Do they follow the same structure? Does the nature of the narrative influence the relative importance of each category?

3   Compare spoken and written versions of the same narratives. It's better to ask for a spoken version first; then having got that on tape ask your informant if s/he would give you a written version. It's also more interesting to choose informants from different backgrounds and of different ages.

One word of warning

Transcribing spoken discourse is very time-consuming, and potential informants can be very unpredictable. It's essential, therefore, that you are present during the recording, and if things aren't going to plan don't worry; move on to new informants and when you're fairly sure you've got something useful, *then* write up a transcription.

Text: Jessica's story

well Gabriel (.) who's a little on the impulsive side (.) met this bloke when she was sixteen (.) moved in with him the next day but that's beside the point (.) she met this bloke on Saturday night (.) he said ooooh come out to the pub like on Sunday lunchtime (.) so she went out (.) started drinking with this sort of rugger-bugger type (.)

so eight pints later she was in the curry house like this (.) and she funnily enough she slumped over her chicken tikka or whatever (.) and erm what they did all these ten blokes hid round the corner like in the kitchen of the curry house and they got the manager to come and wake her up and say all your mates have gone (.) you've got a hundred quid bill (.) you've got to pay (1) she'd only met this bloke the night before (1) and she was going like (.) oh my God I haven't got anything here (.) take my jewellery (.) take my watch (.) I'll (.) I'll come back with the money as soon as I've been to the bank later (.) he was going no no I'm not going to let you leave the premises (.) I'm going to call the police (.) all this sort of stuff (1)

anyway they waited till she was on the point of hysterics and they all came out going ha ha what a good joke (.) like this (.) it's not a very nice story is it (.) she's still with him (.) that's four years later (.) and that's his bloody nicest feature (.) that's the nicest story she can tell about him

Jessica Gardner

Speeches

Scripted speech, like the oral narrative, is normally 'one way', that is once the speaker has the floor s/he continues until the end of the speech is reached and the normal rules of co-operation in conversation don't apply or, at least, don't operate in the same way. Of course this is not to say that speakers aren't interrupted, supported or even heckled; indeed in some contexts audience response is expected or even encouraged. The stand-up comic may thrive on feedback or incorporate it into her/his routine; the Prime Minister needs to deal with it at Question Time. That notwithstanding, the scripted speech is composed before delivery and skilful speakers, or their speech writers, use certain rhetorical structures to help them in what is normally the prime aim of a speech and that is to convey a message and convince the audience of a point of view.

Look at these three examples. Try and say what makes them memorable.

> 1   that's one small step for a man
>   one giant leap for mankind
> 2   to be or not to be
>   that is the question
> 3   I came
>   I saw
>   I conquered

The quotability of a speech can be very important, and speakers may make great efforts to construct what we now term as 'soundbites', short, pithy, sometimes witty chunks of language which catch the ear and the imagination of the media and, through them, the attention and memory of the public.

1   Neil Armstrong's classic two-liner – 'that's one small step for a man / one giant leap for mankind' – as he became the first human to walk on the moon has a balanced structure where the second line mirrors the first. There are three clear links between the lines: small–giant, step–leap, man–mankind. This rhetorical structure where two groups of words are closely related to each other – in meaning and form – is called a contrasting pair.
2   Hamlet's lines 'to be or not to be that is the question', are perhaps a more obvious example of another contrasting pair. Here the contrast is more black and white and the two key words 'to be' are actually repeated, giving almost total symmetry to the line.
3   The structure of 'I came, I saw, I conquered' is known as a three-part list. They are very common in speeches.

Of course what works in language which is meant to be *heard* sometimes also works in language which is meant to be *read*. For example, the previous sentence has the form of a contrasting pair. And the second sentence of this section contains a three-part list:

1   interrupted
2   supported
3   or even heckled.

Look at Text: Portillo (1), the opening of a speech given by Michael Portillo at the Conservative Party Conference in 1994, and note any contrasting pairs and three-part lists.

Text: Portillo (1)

Madam Chairman, ladies and gentleman.
There are two kinds of politician.
Those who try to fool the electors.
And those who tell the truth.
Here is the truth about unemployment.
It's a waste.
Individuals suffer. Families suffer. The nation suffers.
That is the first truth.
Here is another.
Politicians don't create jobs. Businessmen do.
Madam Chairman, unemployment is still far too high.
Young people, sixteen, no qualifications, never had a job.
Graduates with lots of qualifications, still can't get a job.
Professionals, 45, never been out of work, suddenly made redundant.

Commentary

The traditional opening of the speech is in itself a three-part list and then Portillo employs a contrasting pair *within* another three-part list:

1   There are two kinds of politician.
2   (a)   Those who try to fool the electors.
3   (b)   And those who tell the truth.

Perhaps not always easily spotted, combinations of contrasting pairs and three-part lists have structured some memorable lines. Winston Churchill's speech in 1940 in praise of the Battle of Britain fighter pilots concludes with a three-part list, the third item of which contrasts with the first two:

			Never in the field of human conflict has
1	(a)	{	so much been owed by
2			so many to
3	(b)		so few.

Such combinations can make for powerful rhetorical effects. Portillo's speech uses another contrasting pair:

(a) Politicians don't create jobs.
(b) Businessmen do.

Two well-remembered quotations of John F. Kennedy are also structured as contrasts. First, from his inaugural address as US president in 1961:

(a) Ask not what your country can do for you.
(b) Ask what you can do for your country.

And then in West Berlin, 1963:

(a) Two thousand years ago the proudest boast was 'Civis Romanus sum'.
(b) Today, in the world of freedom, the proudest boast is 'Ich bin ein Berliner'.

When you start to look for them you'll find contrasting pairs performing as a common but very effective rhetorical device. Of course they are not always as short and pithy as the 'Politicians don't create jobs. Businessmen do' variety of Portillo's speech, which, as mentioned earlier, is on the lookout for easily-remembered soundbites. Sometimes they can be used to pattern wonderfully moving speeches. Martin Luther King's famous 'I have a dream' speech from the Lincoln Memorial, Washington in 1963 involved many contrasts, the most quoted of which is:

(a) {
I have a dream that one day
my four little children will not be judged
by the colour of their skin
(b) but by the content of their character.

The opening of Portillo's speech also features two examples of three-part lists. The first, 'Individuals suffer. Families suffer. The nation suffers' repeats the same tight structure of subject—verb, with the force of the list being emphasised by the use of the same verb. The second example is more varied but still mimics the same form of person—experience—job status. The use of three-part lists seems to fulfil a sense of completeness. Two items aren't enough to make a point; four items are too many. Three, then, seems to be both the minimum and maximum necessary to make a point effective. Everywhere we find items in threes:

ready, steady, go
abc
123
blah, blah, blah
Maggie, Maggie, Maggie - out, out, out!

and even:

in the name of the Father and of the Son and of the Holy Ghost.

And 100 years before Kennedy's Berlin speech, Abraham Lincoln in the Gettysburg Address delivered this memorable three-part list:

1   Government of the people
2   by the people
3   for the people.

Of course, not every message can be delivered in a neat three-part list. Sometimes, in order to make a point, a list of like items may well be much longer than three, or a key word, like 'truth' in Portillo's speech, might be a constant reference point. These would be examples of general repetition, another feature of speech to underline emphasis. Also fairly typical in political speeches are favourable references to 'us' and unfavourable references to 'them'. Indeed the main brunt of a politician's speech might be an attack on the opposition.

Activity

Look at Text: Portillo (2), an edited version of the rest of Portillo's speech. What features can you find?

Text: Portillo (2)

Madam Chairman, Europe isn't working.
We've got to get Europe back to work.
Mr Blair is busy creating a wasteland of what was once a principled political party. A land of left-over ideas. A political desert, littered with discarded policies and previous convictions, cast away like empty beer cans.
Welcome to Blair country.

A government led by Tony Blair would be tough on wealth and tough on the causes of wealth.
Oh yes, he may be busy casting all Labour's principles aside.
Stripping off the layers, like peeling an onion.
But like peeling an onion, it will all end in tears.
It's a gigantic con and we are going to go out of this hall and strip the Labour Party of its new pretensions. We're going to tear it apart, limb from limb, speech by speech, soundbite after soundbite until everyone can see it for what it really is:
Empty of philosophy.
Empty of inspiration.
Empty of beliefs.

I want to see a Britain worthy of its history. We are the heirs of Pitt, Disraeli, Salisbury and Churchill.
We are the greatest parliamentary democracy on earth.
We are an inventive, responsible, resolute, self-confident people.
We are listened to in the counsels of the world.

Our policies are forged by experience, tailored to our times, shaped by the future.
We are members of one of the most successful governing parties the world has ever known.
Never did I feel more certain of being a Conservative.
Never was it more important to be a Conservative.
Never have I felt more proud to be a Conservative.

Commentary

Among the many features present you might have noted that Michael Portillo in his speech not only attacks the 'them' of the Labour Party, accusing them of (being)

> Empty of philosophy.
> Empty of inspiration.
> Empty of beliefs.

but he goes on to launch a personal attack on Tony Blair, the leader of the Labour Party, ending with a quotable soundbite:

> Mr Blair is busy creating a wasteland of what was once a principled political party. A land of left-over ideas. A political desert, littered with discarded policies and previous convictions, cast away like empty beer cans.
> Welcome to Blair country.

And as Portillo builds to the climax of his speech he switches back to favourable references to 'us'. First 'us' means Britain and its people:

> We are the greatest parliamentary democracy on earth.
> We are an inventive, responsible, resolute, self-confident people.
> We are listened to in the counsels of the world.

Then, 'us' becomes the Conservative Party:

> Our policies are forged by experience, tailored to our times, shaped by the future.

and, in another three-part list, he ends with a flourish:

> Never did I feel more certain of being a Conservative.
> Never was it more important to be a Conservative.
> Never have I felt more proud to be a Conservative.

Politicians sometimes borrow a trick used in advertisements and that is to use one word that has two different meanings which, however, are still appropriate in context. This use of language is referred to as lexical ambiguity.

When Portillo says 'Europe isn't working' he is playing on the two meanings that:

1   Europe as a concept or political market isn't being successful; and
2   Many Europeans are unemployed.

Once alerted to this use of language you may be surprised to see how extensively it is employed in advertisements, billboard slogans and popular newspaper headlines.

Before we leave the issue of speeches in front of live audiences two further points can be made. First, in order to keep the attention of the audience and help convey the message, the language used is normally simple: jargon and even facts and figures are kept to a minimum. Not only that, but ideas or arguments — if there any — are also kept simple and conveyed in simple clauses. And, second, attention is given to attracting applause; after all there's nothing like a burst of applause to give your words credibility when featured on the national news. There's a suggestion on how to explore this at the end of this section (p. 274).

THE FIRESIDE CHAT SPEECH

Unlike the cut and thrust of the debating chamber or the frisson of the conference hall, the speech delivered in the cosy 'fireside chat' style, so beloved of former US President Ronald Reagan, does allow for a more developed argument.

Activity

Read Text: Reagan, the opening section of a television broadcast made by President Reagan to the American public in 1987 in which he discusses the controversial arms-for-hostages deal with Iran. Note what features already discussed above are present and also attempt to trace his argument, in particular his shift from the first person — 'I'/'my' — to the second person — 'you'/'your'.

Text: Reagan

My fellow Americans, I've spoken to you from this historic office on many occasions and about many things. The power of the presidency is often thought to reside within this Oval office. Yet it doesn't rest here; it rests in you, the American people, and in your trust.

Your trust is what gives a president his powers of leadership and his personal strength, and it's what I want to talk to you about this evening.

For the past three months, I've been silent on the revelations about Iran. You must have been thinking: 'Well, why doesn't he tell us what's happening? Why doesn't he just speak to us as he has in the past when we've faced troubles or tragedies?' Others of you, I guess, were thinking: 'What's he doing hiding out in the White House?' The reason I haven't spoken to you before now is this: You deserved the truth. And, as frustrating as the waiting has been, I felt it was improper to come to you with sketchy reports, or possibly even erroneous statements, which would then have to be corrected, creating even more doubt and confusion.

There's been enough of that. I've paid a price for my silence in terms of your trust and confidence. But I have had to wait, as have you, for the complete story. That's why I appointed Ambassador David Abshire as my special counsellor to help get out the thousands of documents to the various investigations. And I appointed a special review board, the Tower Board, which took on the chore of pulling the truth together for me and getting to the bottom of things. It has now issued its findings.

I've studied the Board's report. Its findings are honest, convincing and highly critical, and I accept them. Tonight I want to share with you my thoughts on these findings and report to you on the actions I'm taking to implement the Board's recommendations.

First, let me say I take full responsibility for my own actions and for those of my administration. As angry as I may be about activities undertaken without my knowledge, I am still accountable for those activities. As disappointed as I may be in some who served me, I am still the one who must answer to the American people for this behaviour. And as personally distasteful as I find secret bank accounts and diverted funds, as the Navy would say, this happened on my watch.

Reagan cleverly suggests that power, far from being his, actually belongs to the people. He does this by a shift from 'my'/'I' to a continual reference to the 'you' of the American people, and ends the first paragraph reinforcing this idea with a three-part list of

> you
> the American people
> your trust.

His speech develops along the same structure by shifting from 'me' to 'you', implicating the 'you' of the American people in any responsibility and suggesting that if they don't trust him then American power will fail or weaken. He mentions, for instance:

> spoken to you
> come to you
> share with you
> report to you.

Before admitting responsibility he prepares the ground with this implication of the American people.

Other features typical of this kind of speech are the colloquial forms, such as 'I guess' and 'this happened on my watch', as well as the dramatic use of imagined speech in the third paragraph. The informality of the tone used helps to convey the idea that the President is talking directly to the listener. In the final paragraph, where the continual reference point of 'I' helps to assume liability, Reagan still manages, however, to distance himself slightly from those *really* responsible by talking about being 'angry', 'disappointed', and finding secret bank accounts and diverted funds 'personally distasteful'.

Notice also the repetition of 'your trust', which runs as a cohesive link throughout the speech, and the euphemistic use of 'this happened on my watch' instead of 'I'm guilty'.

Although this core book is divided into apparently discrete units, the nature of language and its implied audience – reader or listener – is such that there will be cross-over and reference points which can usefully be made between the different sections. Some of these discussion points on the use of pronouns in Reagan's speech, for instance, complement fuller discussion in the units on grammar and written discourse.

Extension

1 Political speeches are readily available from political party head-quarters. Analyse them from the page or, if they are being broadcast on radio or TV, consider the speaker's sense of timing and response to applause.

2 Consider how the audience affects the nature of the speech: for example, examine transcripts of speeches made just for broadcast. These include the Queen's Christmas speech and party political broadcasts. Speeches given by authority figures forced into resignation can also be very interesting, mixing the personal with the public voice.

SOME GUIDELINES FOR THE TAPING OF SPOKEN DISCOURSE

◉ You need to get permission before taping potential informants.

◉ Having got this, and having established the best site for the tape recorder, don't be disheartened if your subjects seem unduly conscious of being recorded, making the early exchanges seem unnatural as spontaneous conversation.

◉ Treat the first few minutes as a 'warm up'; most people will soon forget that a tape recorder or dictaphone is present and relax into 'normal' conversation.

◉ We can never be entirely sure, however, what is 'normal' conversation because once we start to observe or record it we encounter what's known as the 'observer's paradox', that is, how far does the act of observing conversation influence its outcome? Does conversation perform for the observer? Only by recording surreptitiously can we get close to what may be natural conversation.

◉ Having said that, should you inadvertently record someone without him/her knowing beforehand - if, for example, s/he happens to join a group after recording has started - then ask that person's permission to use the material gathered when the recording is over.

◉ Finally, always preserve the anonymity of your informants and change the names.

SOME GUIDELINES FOR
THE TRANSCRIBING OF SPOKEN DISCOURSE

- ◎ Normal punctuation doesn't apply.
- ◎ Use full stops, in round brackets, to indicate a pause of half a second – this will suffice for the most commonly occurring pauses.
- ◎ Longer pauses can be indicated by numbers in brackets, e.g. (1) = 1 second, (2) = 2 seconds, and so on.
- ◎ Only use capital letters for proper nouns and to indicate stress or emphasis, e.g. I SAID no thank you.
- ◎ Also don't be afraid to acknowledge anything that isn't clear from a tape, and bracket it, e.g. 'that's one small (inaudible speech) for a man'.
- ◎ And indicate simultaneous speech with a square bracket, e.g.

  A: but didn't you ⌈ think about that
  B:　　　　　　　 ⌊ I knew what I was doing
  A: that makes a change.

Conversation: some ground rules

THE PRINCIPLE OF AGREEMENT

Attempts have been made to sort out the ground rules at work in the 'game' that we call conversation. It will be clear that far from being random and shapeless, our engagement in conversation with others follows rules and conventions, which may be influenced by age, gender, status and context. The first 'rule' to be considered here can be termed the **agreement principle**.

Imagine the following conversation between two friends out jogging one Sunday morning:

Wayne: I've done a lot of exercise this week (.) *I didn't plan* it beforehand (.) that way I find I actually do a lot
Mike: yes

But the next week, while out jogging again, the conversation goes like this:

Wayne: I've done a lot of exercise this week (.) I *planned* it all beforehand (.) that way I find I actually do a lot
Mike: yes

So what's going on? Assuming that Mike is actually listening to what Wayne's saying and that he's being sincere, then it shows a form of co-operation at work, without which much everyday conversation would falter. Mike's answer, 'yes', is a signal to show:

1   he's listening
2   agreement with the comment
3   support for the subject matter.

Wayne has, with Mike's co-operation, been given the green light to comment further on the pros or cons of planning to do exercise, or to elaborate on just what exercise he *has* done.

To make the point further, just imagine if the conversation had gone like this:

Wayne: I've done a lot of exercise this week (.) I didn't plan it beforehand (.) that way I find I actually do a lot
Mike: actually I find the reverse (.) I need to plan everything beforehand

Now Mike is obviously expressing disagreement with the comment and effectively:

1   stopping the flow of opinion
2   setting up an argument.

In short, it could be argued that he's not returning the ball properly. It must be stressed, by the way, that we're dealing with everyday, casual, social dialogue. On those occasions where we are happy for someone to take the lead in a conversation, where we have no particular strong opinion on the subject matter and where we are not seeking to exercise our ego, then tacit agreement is the norm. It may take other forms, of course, for example, murmurs of assent such as 'hm', short grunts or nods of approval.

It needs also to be stressed that, of course, there are occasions and with particular people that this agreement principle is deliberately flouted. It may well be the norm, for instance, that one *never* ever agrees with one's older brother, younger sister, parent, or whatever. If you suddenly started agreeing with your younger sister's taste in music or clothes or football team, your motives would be suspected. This behaviour only serves to prove the normality of agreement and support in everyday exchanges.

Activity

In pairs, try continuing this conversation where Mike disagrees with Wayne's comment:

> *Wayne:* I've done a lot of exercise this week (.) I didn't plan it beforehand (.) that way I find I actually do a lot
> *Mike:* actually I find the reverse(.) I need to plan everything beforehand

Commentary

Several things might happen:

1 Perhaps Wayne loses 'control' of the subject matter.
2 Perhaps that topic dies and either party initiates a new subject to talk about.
3 The worst-case scenario would be an argument where neither party gives way.

One more point needs to be made: although referred to as the agreement principle, the kind of response we're looking at here doesn't necessarily mean that the responder *agrees* with the first speaker's comment; the respondent is supporting the first speaker. Without this kind of response much social discourse would falter and the general expression of one's thoughts, feelings and opinions would be frustrated.

THE PRINCIPLE OF POLITENESS

There are also other, unwritten rules which help to smooth interaction and also add to the quality of human relationships. In her book, *Language and Woman's Place* (1973), Robin Lakoff draws attention to three rules or maxims which we may follow which she terms the **politeness principle**. They are:

1   Don't impose.
2   Give options.
3   Make your receiver feel good.

They explain and describe many utterances which smooth social inter-action, yet of themselves carry no information. For example:

I'm sorry to trouble you but could you move your car

is a typical way of prefacing a request (maxim 1).

do you want to go first or shall I (maxim 2)
can I pick your brains about something (maxim 3).

Activity

Construct further examples of all three maxims.

278

THE CO-OPERATIVE PRINCIPLE

Generally, for conversation to work, we co-operate with each other. As the ball is returned in a game of tennis, so we endeavour to make a return to the sender of language, even if it's only a grunt of approval or the acknowledgement of the agreement principle. As stated earlier, the 'game' of conversation in which we engage every day is more complex than we might realise. We also play the game with a sophisticated intuitive understanding of the 'rules'. These unwritten 'rules' which underpin conversation have been formulated by Paul Grice (1975) as the **co-operative principle**. This states that we interpret language on the assumption that the speaker is obeying the four maxims of:

1   **quality** (being true)
2   **quantity** (being brief)
3   **relation** (being relevant)
4   **manner** (being clear).

This helps to explain expressions such as:

> well to cut a long story short …
> I'll spare you the grisly details

which demonstrate the maxim of quantity at work. When it comes to delivering facts we sometimes choose not to appear too blunt or dogmatic. We may say, for example:

> I think the bus is late

when we are 99 per cent certain that it *is* late, or

> I feel that our relationship is going nowhere

when, again, we probably mean that it definitely *is* going nowhere. Qualifying verbs like 'think' and 'feel' show that we don't wish to fall foul of the maxim of quality. To put it another way, if you categorically state, for example, that 'the bus is late' then you run the risk of having to prove it, or, if it suddenly turns the corner and your watch is fast, you run the risk of being proved wrong. Other expressions which show our concern for not being untruthful are:

279

as far as I know ...
now correct me if I'm wrong, but ...
I'm not absolutely sure, but ...

Excuses come into this category. Students can be very inventive when it comes to giving reasons for not handing assignments in on time, and they might preface their excuses with lines such as:

I know you're not going to believe me, but ...
now look right I know this sounds a bit far fetched, but ...

Incidentally, there might be a clash between obeying both the politeness principle *and* the co-operative principle. For example, when confronted by your friend's dramatic new haircut or pierced eyebrow and being asked 'what d'ya think', your answer of 'yeh really suits you', while observing the maxim of making your receiver feel good, might yet be transgressing the maxim of quality. Think for a moment when you have had recourse to these white lies.

Activity

Can you explain how the utterances below fulfil all four maxims?

help!
fire!

Conversation in practice

Activity

Some of the features typical of conversation in practice can be illustrated by a comparison between two texts both concerned with making or confirming an appointment at the doctors. The first, Text: Scripted dialogue, is taken from a textbook devised for the purposes of language teaching, while the second, Text: Authentic dalogue (1) is a naturally occurring conversation.

P = patient; R = receptionist

Text: Scripted dialogue

(telephone rings)

P: Could I make an appointment to see the doctor please?

R: Certainly. Who do you usually see?

P: Doctor Cullen

R: I'm sorry but Dr Cullen has got patients all day. Would Dr Maley do?

P: Sure

R: OK then. When would you like to come?

P: Could I come at four o'clock?

R: Four o'clock? Fine. Could I have your name please?

(Nunan and Lockwood 1991)

Text: Authentic dialogue (1)

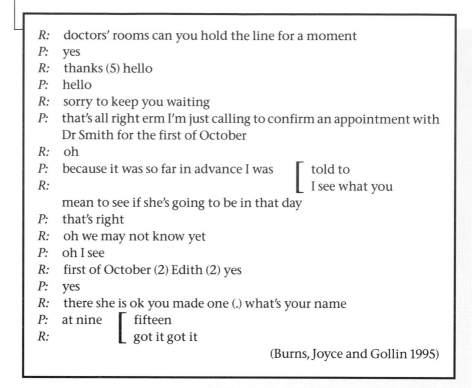

R: doctors' rooms can you hold the line for a moment
P: yes
R: thanks (5) hello
P: hello
R: sorry to keep you waiting
P: that's all right erm I'm just calling to confirm an appointment with Dr Smith for the first of October
R: oh
P: because it was so far in advance I was ⌈ told to
R: ⌊ I see what you
      mean to see if she's going to be in that day
P: that's right
R: oh we may not know yet
P: oh I see
R: first of October (2) Edith (2) yes
P: yes
R: there she is ok you made one (.) what's your name
P: at nine ⌈ fifteen
R: ⌊ got it got it

(Burns, Joyce and Gollin 1995)

Commentary

The second text contains a number of features which mark it off as a piece of naturally occurring dialogue. There are interruptions – the receptionist interrupts the patient twice – unpredicted sequences, utterances completed by the other person, and the conversation ends without the usual polite closing sequences. By contrast the scripted text represents a 'can do' society in which interaction is generally smooth and trouble free, the speakers co-operate with each other, the conversation is neat, tidy and predictable, utterances are almost as complete as sentences and no-one interrupts anyone else.

Look at Text: Authentic dialogue (2), another example of actual dialogue. Jot down any features which now strike you as being typical of the way conversation works.

Text: Authentic dialogue (2)

Dee: I'll tell you something

Joe: yeh

Dee: if your brother's meant to be giving me that camera 'cos Amy
wants it ⌈ and I haven't got it

Joe: ⌊ give it a rest mate give it a rest look right I mean I
talked to Sime about it

Dee: yeh

Joe: I talked to Sime about it ok and he's he's just not happy

Dee: well I told him I'd give him fifty quid for it what's his problem

Joe: well you know it's stolen innit

Dee: yeh well he always

Joe: I mean you know it's not KOSHER

Dee: he's always doing that he's always doing that I don't understand
why he don't just he don't give it to me free I mean he's got plenty of
them anyway I offered him fifty nicker for it don't even want it does he

Joe: well you know I mean the GUY'S HARD UP all right I mean he's
trying to get rid of the thing but what you supposed to do

Tracy Isles

Joe interrupts Dee early in the conversation – at 'and I haven't got it'/ 'give it a rest' – and Dee gives way, gives up her turn at talking. Perhaps surprisingly, studies in conversation show that interruptions are infrequent. We seem to be very skilled at knowing when we can take the turn in conversation. There is a tendency for speakers to look at the person they are addressing when they are completing their turn. Yet we also seem to know when a turn has been completed on the phone which suggests that a fall in the voice is also significant. For the most part, we wait

283

for this completion point, which may be signalled by a question or by a pause at what seems to be the natural end of a statement. (You might consider, at this point, how people manage to keep the turn.) In Text: Authentic dialogue (2) we find examples of completion points signalled by the end of a statement:

> I talked to Sime about it ok and he's he's just not happy
> I mean you know it's not KOSHER

signalled by a question:

> what's his problem

and signalled by **tag questions**, questions literally tagged on the end:

> well you know it's stolen *innit*
> don't even want it *does he.*

Repetition is a very common feature of spontaneous speech, which simply reflects the fact that we are making up what we say as we go along, and there are several examples in this extract: 'give it a rest mate give it a rest', 'he's always doing that he's always doing that' and 'I talked to Sime about it I talked to Sime about it'. **False starts** also feature; they may be corrected, the speaker may hesitate or s/he might have another attempt. Here, Dee starts with 'yeh well he always' then hesitates and starts again with 'he's always doing that'.

This extract also features **reinforcers**: the two single utterances of 'yeh'. In both instances the listener is showing support for the other speaker. Unlike the agreement principle, the listener here isn't responding to an opinion and agreeing with it — in fact opinions aren't being expressed here. But the listener *is* showing that s/he's listening and is giving support for the speaker's turn to continue; consequently these sorts of responses often occur at completion points. Other examples of reinforcers would be 'mm', laughter, or whatever is the current word to express approval.

Hedges is a term which covers many common words and expressions in conversation and they may have different functions.

1   As the term suggests, some words will express uncertainty, be vague or qualify what is being said, for example: 'well', 'like', 'sort of'/'sorta', 'kind of'/'kinda'.
2   On other occasions, however, the speaker may well be certain about

the facts but wishes not to appear assertive. Conversation is, in fact, peppered with such expressions and would be pedantic otherwise. So we get statements prefaced with 'I think' and 'I guess'. As such they are another way of describing the maxim of quality.

3   Finally, they may function to get the listener to share in the speaker's point of view. Terms from (1) do this plus expressions like 'isn't it'/ 'innit', 'I mean', 'you know'/'y'know'.

It's important not to memorise a list of words and feel you can necessarily label them; words with the same form may well have different functions. For instance 'you know' and fillers, like 'er' and 'um', can also function to *keep the turn* in speaking. Both Dee and Joe use 'I mean' in a dual function: to engage the listener's sympathy *and* to keep the turn. Take time to work out what words are doing.

Activity

Look at Text: *Lucky Sods*, an extract from John Godber's play about a couple who keep winning the National Lottery. In what ways does it mimic real conversation and in what ways is it different? The punctuation, of course, follows written convention, which attempts to give some clues about how this dialogue should be spoken: ! = emphasis and . . . = words which trail off.

Text: *Lucky Sods*

> *Jean:*   Oh, by the way, before I forget, I changed your numbers.
> *Morris:*   Eh?
> *Jean:*   I changed your numbers.
> *Morris:*   What for?
> *Jean:*   Because they were wrong.
> *Morris:*   Wrong?
> *Jean:*   Yeh.
> *Morris:*   Wrong?
> *Jean:*   Yes!
> *Morris:*   How can my numbers be wrong?
> *Jean:*   Well, they were.

285

> *Morris:* I picked 'em, how could they have been wrong?
> *Jean:* Well, I looked and ...
> *Morris:* I don't believe this.
> *Jean:* Well, I ...
> *Morris:* You changed my numbers ...
> *Jean:* You never have twenty-six.
> *Morris:* How could you?
> *Jean:* You had twenty-six.
> *Morris:* I've spent all week working out that bloody sequence.
> *Jean:* Well, I thought ...
> *Morris:* I've been working out a sequence all week, I've been listening to the dogs bark, counting bloody magpies, looking how many pieces of scrap are stacked in one square yard just to get my numbers. And you've changed the buggers!
> *Jean:* I thought it was a mistake.
> *Morris:* It is now!
> *Jean:* You always have eighteen, don't you?
> *Morris:* It's my birthday.
> *Jean:* But on your list, you didn't have eighteen, you had twenty-six.
> *Morris:* I know.
> *Jean:* And I thought, oh, he's made a mistake, he's forgotten his birthday.
> *Morris:* How would I forget my own birthday?
> *Jean:* Well, you forget nearly everything else.
> *Morris:* Do I change yours?
> *Jean:* No.
> *Morris:* Do I fiddle about with yours?
> *Jean:* No.
> *Morris:* So don't change mine.
> *Jean:* All right, well, I'm sorry.
> *Morris:* Yeh, what if twenty-six comes up?
> *Jean:* Sorry.

Commentary

Most of the lines are short, sharp and tight without any of the hedges or reinforcers found in real dialogue. Each character's words are more obviously 'lines', and generally completion points are reached before the turn changes hands. There is some mimicking of naturally occurring dialogue, however, in the suggestion of repetition, but this is tightly structured as in the quick-fire interchange involving the word 'wrong'. There is also the suggestion of a false start as in 'Well, I . . . Well, I'.

The main difference, though, between a comically scripted extract such as this and real dialogue is in its structure and cohesive links. Godber's piece is carefully crafted in contrast to the apparently chaotic and structureless conversation of Dee and Joe in Text: Authentic Dialogue (2) who are thinking as they go along, negotiating control of the turn and subject matter in time. The extract from *Lucky Sods* is tightly shaped by cohesion:

change – wrong – sequence – birthday – change

and this helps make it what it sets out to be: humorous.

Some other features to be aware of

1 Adjacency pairs

Analyses of conversation in practice have revealed certain structures whereby a particular kind of opening is likely to get a certain response. A greeting is likely to be followed by another greeting, a summons by an answer, a question by an answer:

A: hello
B: hi there.

Some adjacency pairs can elicit *one* of *two* responses. Blame is likely to be answered by admission or denial, for example, or a request is likely to be answered by agreement or refusal, as in:

Father: I want you to wash the car
Son: oh dad please no.

An adjacency pair can also be inserted inside another:

Father: I want you to wash the car
Son: if you pay me
Father: ok
Son: all right I'll do it

287

2   Three-part exchanges

In reality real conversations are not simply neat question and answer exchanges but often have a follow-up move in which the questioner offers a comment or evaluation on the response. For example:

> *A:* what's the time
> *B:* half past three
> *A:* oh I didn't think it was as late as that

> *A:* going away this year
> *B:* New York for a week
> *A:* sounds good.

3   Ellipsis and substitution

If we can take short cuts in conversation we do. When what we say is clear then spelling out something in full detail would seem pedantic, inappropriate and also take up time. Ellipsis is the *omission* of words unnecessary in everyday discourse; substitution, as the term suggests, describes the feature of *substituting* a word for a longer sequence of words. Both features are so common that we are not really conscious of their operation; it's only when they are *not* used that we suddenly notice them.

Examples of ellipsis are: 'Drink?' instead of 'Do you want a drink?' and 'What next?' for 'I wonder what's going to happen next?' in a situation where what is being referred to is obvious.

Substitution occurs in this next example where Jenny substitutes *it* for *that programme*:

> *Elizabeth:* I heard Dave talking about that programme earlier
> *Jenny:* yeah he went on and on about it

And in the north of England there is a custom that when ordering fish and chips it's enough to say 'Twice and a fish' when you want three portions of fish and two portions of chips, where 'twice' means 'fish and chips twice'.

4   Heads and tails

Heads perform a basically orienting function, serving to pack in information which a speaker considers relevant to their listener and attempting to do so as economically as possible. Heads also establish a shared knowledge in the form of people and places in particular so that listeners can respond without having to seek further clarification.

Examples drawn from a recent study in Nottingham include:

the women they all shouted
that chap over there he said it was ok
this friend of ours her daughter Carol she bought one.

While heads are principally concerned with the structure and organisation of the message, tails are more concerned with an expression of an attitude towards the message and allow speakers to add emphasis as well as provide orientation for the listener. These examples all involve some kind of recapitulation, by means of either a pronoun or a clarifying noun:

I'm thick me
she's a case is Sheila
it's too hectic for me London
it was good that film.

Extension

1   Bearing in mind the guidelines given about taping and transcribing conversation, then the opportunities for investigation are as adventurous as you can make them.
Interesting small-scale studies have been done on:

- ◎   the patter of market traders
- ◎   bar-room talk
- ◎   workers' tea break conversation
- ◎   committee meetings
- ◎   children at play
- ◎   single- and mixed-sex groups in conversation
- ◎   teacher–classroom talk
- ◎   driving instructor–pupil talk
- ◎   radio DJ patter.

The list is endless.

2   It can be a time-consuming business of course. If you want to test what you have learnt and to hone your skills further then do an analysis of the actually occurring dialogue in Text: Students talking in Yorkshire.

289

Text: Students talking in Yorkshire

Arf: we were in Carleton last night and er he says I went to this hotel somewhere (.) someplace (.) didn't we (.) and he just goes Hotel Samoa (.) I goes how the chuffing hell did you remember that (.) he goes I wouldn't have remembered if ⌈ you hadn't have said

Chris: ⌊ this hotel

Kath: what's Hotel Samoa

Chris: where he went on holiday about ten years ago weren't it
(laughter)

Kath: where is it

Chris: but like I say though (.) cos he used to sit in class and he used to be sat for ten minutes and he'd say Hotel Samoa

Ben: BOLLOCK load of shit
(laughter)

Chris: he just said it

Ben: he makes it out as though I used to just sit there saying Hotel Samoa

Chris: you did though
(laughter)

Ben: bollocks
(laughter)

Chris: he used he ⌈ used to say it

Arf: ⌊ what I couldn't understand

Ben: it's like that bloke walking through Cambridge yesterday we just walked past him and he was going mm mm mm (.) like that weren't he (.) that's all he did (.) he just stood there going mm mm mm

Arf: you know when you ⌈ know when

Chris: ⌊ I thought it was an alarm

Arf: you know when I pulled up at that petrol station today and you went in for half an hour to discuss bloke (.) directions with memory bloke

Kath: memory bloke
(laughter)

Arf: met bloke with world's greatest memory tonight (.) anyway that's beside the point (.) there was this woman outside do you remember and she was hobbling like this and she felt

Chris: yeah

Arf: sorry for her and I were taking piss

Ben: what as she walked past

Jules: all her hair was matted up and stuff

Arf: she decide she was homeless

Daniel Pearson

Text: Pub sign

The representation of talk

So far, this unit has concentrated on what talk is really like when we engage in it on an everyday basis. But talk is also represented to us in mediated form - artificially constructed in film and TV texts, and 'written up' on the page in written texts of all kinds, from adverts, literature and newspapers to comics and the Bible.

The aim of this part of the unit is to consider briefly some of the important issues about the relationship between real and represented talk.

Re-presentation

The first issue to consider is the fact that whenever talk is represented, it is *re-presented* - that is, someone has re-worked it. As soon as this happens, effects which are the result of the author's viewpoint and intentions come into play. These intentions may be conscious - the result of deliberate individual decisions - or unconscious - the result of an individual being a member of a certain social group within the larger culture, and learning a particular set of beliefs as part of their socialisation process.

Social groups

The issue of our social-group membership is particularly important when it comes to looking at the representation of talk, because use of language is one of the ways in which we mark out our social groups, and because we all have strong attitudes to the language of the social groups we define as 'other'. At the same time, the people who have had the opportunity to get their ideas into print and onto the screen have traditionally belonged to the more powerful groups, so their versions of what 'other people's talk' is like may come to be accepted wisdom within the wider culture. Exploration of real talk is relatively recent and, while there is still ignorance about what real talk is like, any artificial representations constructed by more powerful social groups can stand unchallenged, as the truth.

In this section, you will be looking at how the spoken language of certain social groups is often represented. These groups are based on the following dimensions: gender; region (and social class); ethnicity. In each case, you will be considering questions about whose viewpoint may be behind representations of spoken language.

GENDERISED TALK: REAL AND REPRESENTED

Studies on language and gender have sought to cast light on people's real experiences of how men and women converse, both in single-sex and mixed-sex groups, in order to investigate the stereotypes we have in our culture – stereotypes such as the trivial, chattering, nagging woman and the strong, silent, long-suffering man. These stereotypes are constantly shored up by a whole range of representations, exemplified by Text: Pub sign and by jokes such as Text: Matchbox jokes.

Text: Matchbox jokes

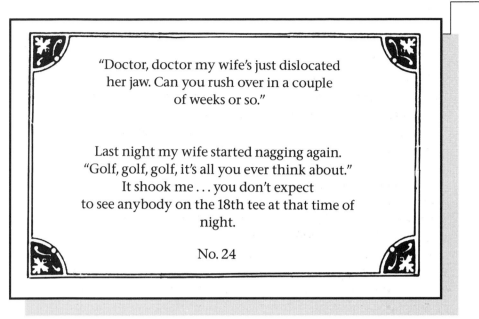

"Doctor, doctor my wife's just dislocated her jaw. Can you rush over in a couple of weeks or so."

Last night my wife started nagging again. "Golf, golf, golf, it's all you ever think about." It shook me . . . you don't expect to see anybody on the 18th tee at that time of night.

No. 24

Such representations are part of a larger picture we have in our culture about how men and women behave: language is one form of behaviour, and we have all sorts of ideas about other forms of behaviour, too. But whose viewpoint is encoded by such stories about the sexes?

Activity

Look back at the pub sign and the jokes, and turn the viewpoint around in them by substituting a male figure for the female in the first, and switching the roles of the male and female figures around in the second: what would be the difference in effect?

Commentary

Turning the texts round reveals the ideology lying behind them.
    If the pub sign had been a male figure, surrounded by the words 'soft words turneth away wrath' and QUIET MAN, the effect would have

293

been very different. In its original version, the pub sign acts as a picture of how women should be: it is an exhortation to women to be meek and mild, with the unstated assumption that women are usually garrulous and strident – so the 'quiet woman' is an impossible ideal, achievable only by cutting a woman's head off; as a male figure, the sign would not act in the same way at all. Because men are not normally seen as talkative (male speech is often seen as the 'norm' from which female talk deviates), the idea of a quiet man suggests something rather unremarkable – although, accompanied by a particular image such as a mysterious cloaked figure, this could call up the idea of a spy or other dubious character.

Turning the jokes around produces some interesting effects, where the idea of female talkativeness is also at the centre of the texts in their original form. Female talk is constructed as verbal harassment, so the idea of the husband capitalising on his wife's enforced silence in the 'doctor, doctor' joke (with the implication that she brought the dislocation on herself, by endless talking) is seen as a form of just revenge by a hen-pecked man. Because men are not supposed to be talkative, the reversed form of this joke loses its point, and leaving the husband with a dis-located jaw appears simply as an act of cruelty.

The 'golf' joke appears comical when reversed, for different reasons than in the original. In reversed form, the comedy is to do with the unlikeliness of the picture created: a woman on the golf course, at dead of night, her husband leaving the kids at home to go looking for her, fretting and getting frustrated by her obsession with a hobby that takes her attention away from him.

Ideologies lying behind common cultural stories are hard to spot because we learn them as part of early socialisation, and they then just seem 'normal' and 'natural'. But when you stand back from them, you can expose the hidden messages that tell us, as men and women, how to behave.

Activity

So far, we have suggested that in our culture we have ideas about the sexes that are constructed around stereotypes, and that these stereotypes often encode the point of view of those who are in a position to get their meanings publicised. The focus now needs to turn to what our own experiences have been about male and female talk, and how this accords with research on real speech.

Discuss your experiences of the following:

◎   Do females talk more than males, and, if so, when?
◎   Do you think men and women follow different rules when they have conversations?

If so, can you give some examples?

Commentary

Contrary to the stereotype of the female as the 'overtalkative' sex who 'gossips' and 'talks a lot' (as reported by Kramer (1977) who surveyed attitudes in the USA), many studies have now been carried out in Britain and the USA which show that, in a variety of contexts, it is men who talk more. Obviously, age, status and context will affect the amount of talk a participant delivers and how much dominance s/he has. Because of the value of access to talk for achievement in education, and because data is arguably easier to collect, many studies in this area have been carried out in educational contexts, and here boys have been shown to speak more than girls. A typical study by Sadker and Sadker (1985) of over a hundred classes in both arts and science subjects found boys talking on average three times more than the girls. One reason for this seems to be the role played by the teacher: there is evidence, for example, that teachers pay more attention to boys, giving them both disapproval and more encouragement and praise.

Another reason for the stereotype of the talkative woman is advanced by Deborah Tannen in *You Just Don't Understand: Men and women in conversation*, where it is claimed that men are trained to become familiar with talking in *public* situations, learning how to hold centre stage through verbal performance such as storytelling, joking and imparting information. Women, on the other hand, are more comfortable with *private* speaking: for them, the language of conversation is more about establishing connections and negotiating relationships. Males might therefore *think* females talk a lot because they hear them talking in situations where men would not, for example on the telephone or in social situations with friends.

This means that the idea of the talkative woman may be a view which encodes male perceptions of how women behave in private, personal contexts. If, in contrast, women were able to express their perceptions of men in the workplace and other public situations, this view might well be of men as 'the overtalkative sex'.

Activity

Contemporary research on language and gender does not suggest that male talk is 'normal' while female talk is 'deviant', nor does it indicate that there is anything intrinsically powerful or powerless about male and female talk, respectively.

What is does suggest is that men and women adopt different conversational *styles* because they are trained to understand and operate spoken discourse differently as a part of being socialised for different roles in society. This approach sees male and female groups as different cultures which, when they are brought together in mixed-sex situations, can clash and cause misunderstandings because the participants are operating different rules.

Below are some examples of the misunderstandings that, according to Deborah Tannen's work (1992), often arise in mixed-sex conversations as a result of men and women following different rules. Read through the examples given, and discuss whether similar examples have occurred in your own experience.

Information and consultation

Tannen suggests that many male–female conversations result in difficulty because men think they are simply exchanging information, while women think they are negotiating. As an example, she quotes a couple who are driving home, when the following conversation takes place:

Sue: Would you like to stop for a drink?
John: No.

They don't stop, but when they get home, they have an argument: Sue says John never consults her feelings, while John says he never knows what Sue really wants because she doesn't tell him – instead, she expects him to guess.

Tannen suggests that, while John thought he was just being asked for information about his needs, Sue thought her question would be the opening move in a conversational sequence where they each went through the various pros and cons of stopping and not stopping. A negotiated decision would then arise at the end.

Topic raising, interrupting and reinforcing

Much research has suggested that women do more work in conversation than men to raise topics and to get others to take them up; also that women maintain others' contributions by using reinforcers (saying 'yeah', 'mm', and so on) more than men do. At the same time, men appear to interrupt women more than the other way round.

Tannen suggests that because women are trained to look for connection in their interactions, they make an effort to get others to talk and to equalise speakers' turns, even downplaying their own subject knowledge in the process; in contrast, because men are trained to look for power in their interactions, they compete to control topics – interrupting if necessary – and they work to hold their turn against others' interruptions, even when their own subject knowledge is poor.

When these different discourse rules are operating together, women's contributions are likely to be heard less than men's because men will be trying to take the floor and women will be encouraging them to do it. Neither side is deliberately dominating or giving way – each is simply doing what it has been trained to do within its own gender group.

Reporting and rapporting

According to Tannen, one of the biggest complaints women have about men as talkers is that they don't give enough information when they recount incidents – they leave out all the 'juicy bits' of any story, giving just the bare bones; in contrast, men complain that women give too much information when they tell stories – they go on and on when they could really sum up the content of their discourse in one sentence.

Tannen's explanation of these complaints is that men and women think they are doing different things when they relay information: men concentrate on the information content alone (the 'message') because they see the recounting of incidents as reporting, while women pay more attention to the 'metamessage' – recounting experiences is a way to relate to the listener. Such an approach is termed rapporting.

Problem-solving or problem-sharing?

It seems that men and women also respond differently in conversations when a problem is presented. Because men are trained to be active and find solutions to problems, it is argued, they adopt a problem–solution approach when someone articulates personal difficulties; in contrast, women are encouraged to think of themselves as listeners. While listening is certainly not a passive activity, it doesn't necessarily involve making suggestions about how to change situations or take action. In female 'troubles-talk' women often take turns in comparing difficulties and in finding likenesses between their respective situations; when men share difficulties, they appear to be reassured by their male friend's making light of or dismissing their worries as insignificant.

An example of a male 'problem—solution' approach is given at the start of this unit (see 'Speech events', p. 247), where a man responds with a suggested course of action when his female partner says she feels disfigured after breast surgery.

Now here is an example which presents a male perspective: a man expresses a problem to his female partner. The man expects problem-solution, but receives — to his intense annoyance — problem-sharing:

Peter: I'm really tired. I didn't sleep well last night.
Alison: I didn't sleep well either.
Peter: Why are you always trying to belittle me?
Alison: I'm not! I'm just trying to tell you that I understand how you feel!

Commentary

If you found that you recognised some of the ways that men and women were talking in these examples, it means that you have learnt the rules of talk that society has deemed appropriate for your sex. These different approaches to talk are sometimes called 'scripts'. No-one sits a child down and tells them what their 'script' should be; instead, ways of talking are modelled for children by adults and by countless messages in the culture that surrounds them.

Activity

One type of message is carried in the fictional world of media representation. We are all familiar with the old type of sexist joke considered earlier — so what do some of our more modern advertising texts say about male and female talk? Have things changed very much?

Look at Text: Nibz cartoon, then read through Text: BT advert.

◎ What messages are given in the BT text about male and female talk?
◎ How are these messages conveyed by the way the whole text works? (Consider some of the aspects of language you have studied earlier in this book.)

Text: Nibz cartoon

'It would be cheaper if we bought our own communications satellite..'

Cartoon by 'Nibz', *Daily Mirror*

299

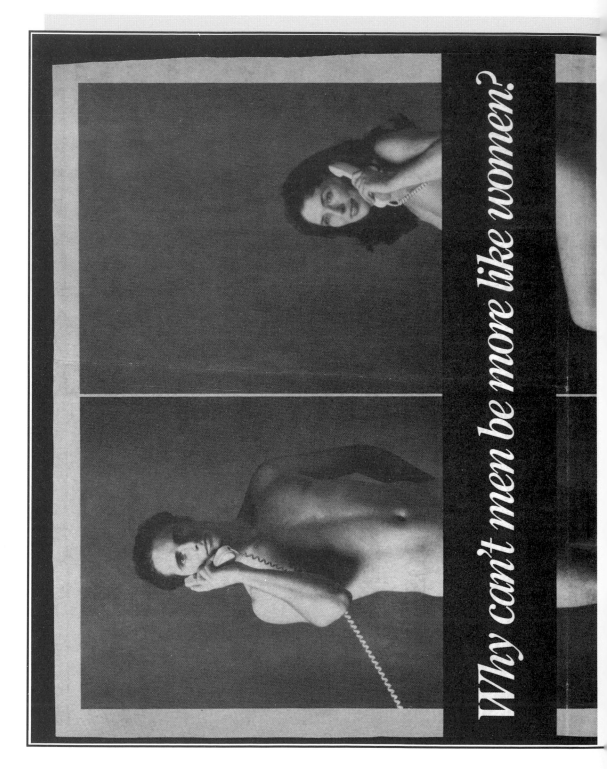

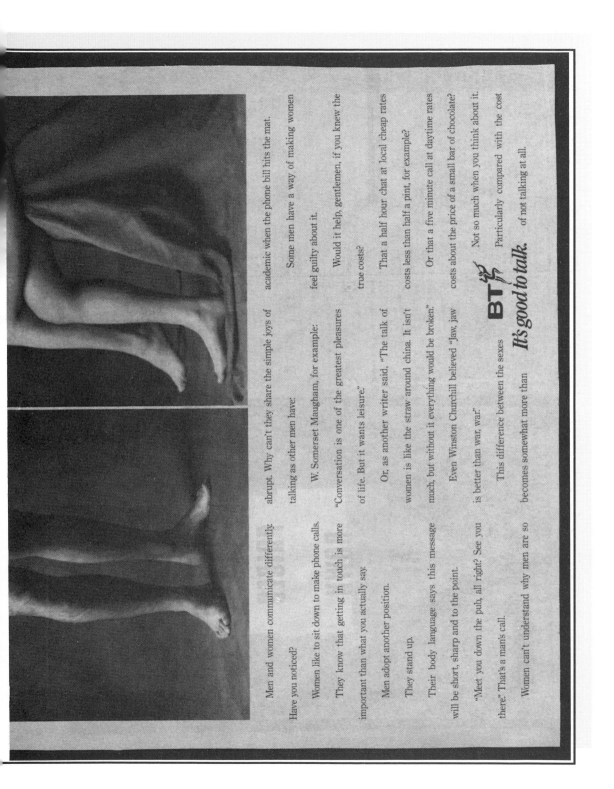

Men and women communicate differently. Have you noticed?

Women like to sit down to make phone calls.

They know that getting in touch is more important than what you actually say.

Men adopt another position.

They stand up.

Their body language says this message will be short, sharp and to the point.

"Meet you down the pub, all right? See you there." That's a man's call.

Women can't understand why men are so abrupt. Why can't they share the simple joys of talking as other men have:

W. Somerset Maugham, for example: "Conversation is one of the greatest pleasures of life. But it wants leisure."

Or, as another writer said, "The talk of women is like the straw around china. It isn't much, but without it everything would be broken."

Even Winston Churchill believed "Jaw, jaw is better than war, war."

This difference between the sexes becomes somewhat more than academic when the phone bill hits the mat.

Some men have a way of making women feel guilty about it.

Would it help, gentlemen, if you knew the true costs?

That a half hour chat at local cheap rates costs less than half a pint, for example?

Or that a five minute call at daytime rates costs about the price of a small bar of chocolate?

Not so much when you think about it. Particularly compared with the cost of not talking at all.

BT

It's good to talk.

301

Commentary

Graphology

The image used in the BT advert takes up two-thirds of the advertising space, and is a very arresting one, for a number of reasons:

1   It resembles pruriently 'censored' soft-porn pictures, where the most offensive parts are blocked out, but leaving enough of the image to titillate the reader/viewer.

2   The 'blocked' question, placed where it is, looks as if it is suggesting that the male body could be adapted to become more 'female'. This is a possible reading because of the use of the word 'be' in the question, rather than 'talk'.

3   There are strong contrasts between the way the man and woman are pictured. The man is standing in a comically regimental posture, with a serious and rather pompous facial expression; he is in the act of listening, rather than speaking. The woman, in contrast, is seated in the style of a model from classical art. This idea is reinforced by the drapery that she is sitting on, by her long, flowing hair, by the voluptuousness of her body, and by the serenity of her expression. Her mouth is a generous one. She could either be speaking or, if listening, she is responding to her interlocutor positively and warmly. It is unclear whether these two figures are speaking to each other, but the oppositions outlined so far are further stressed by the line down the middle of the page – familiar to modern viewers from TV advertising's split-screen contrasts of, for example, the effect of two types of washing powder on clothes, or one housewife racing another to clean the kitchen floor with different products. The centre line here could suggest a broken relationship. These two figures are Adam and Eve-like; but the question running across the page offers the startling proposition that there is something wrong with men rather than women.

4   The intriguing question posed by the blocked text carries echoes of the song sung by Rex Harrison in *My Fair Lady*, where one of the lyrical lines was 'Why can't a woman be more like a man?' Traditionally, 'maleness' has been the norm, from which 'femaleness' has been seen as a deviation. The blocked text therefore challenges received wisdom; the italic type and the use of a question suggests a spoken voice here. Italics are used again for the BT slogan: *It's good to talk*. Since the subject of the slogan is talk itself, it seems appropriate that the spoken medium should be suggested.

The layout of the written text underneath the image is unconventional: neither side of each column is justified, leaving a shape that looks rather loosely organised. Within this, some very short sentences stand alone, for dramatic effect: for example, 'They stand up.'

Vocabulary

The main semantic field in the text concerns communication itself, and terms related to this subject are frequent: communicate, getting in touch, body language, talking, jaw, jaw, chat, call, conversation.

The text itself is an 'argument' in the discursive sense, putting forward the idea that women are good at talk, and men are bad.

Vocabulary items reflect this line of argument, with male talk being characterised as oppositional and aggressive: men adopt a *position*, are *abrupt*, their talk is *short*, *sharp* and *to the point*; female talk is associated with relationship and emotional bonding: women get in *touch*, *share* the joys of talking, without female talk *everything would be broken*.

This 'argument' offers a crude and partial rendition of what recent academic research in male and female talk has suggested. The use of the word 'academic' in the third column shows the text trying to substantiate its assertions while also suggesting that sex differences in talk behaviour have real outcomes in terms of cost. The word 'cost' itself refers to two different areas: money (associated with men); and emotional wellbeing (associated with women).

The text contains a number of informal terms which help to create the idea that this text, although an academic 'argument', is speech-like: for example, 'getting in touch', 'when the phone bill hits the mat','have a way of', 'a half hour chat', 'half a pint', 'about the price of'. The persona created by these vocabulary choices, plus certain grammatical structures (see below) is someone who is offering friendly exposition. The voice has a degree of irony: for example, the self-conscious double meaning of 'men adopt another position', with an effect of anticlimax as the text descends from this phrase to the bald and literal 'they stand up'; the use of the word 'gentlemen' is also an ironic selection, being over-formal for the rest of the discourse, and occurring straight after the accusation that some men are mean, being an over-polite description of such tight-fisted men.

Grammar and discourse

Much of this text is written in the form of statements, or assertions, giving the effect of authority and knowledge. Since these statements are written in the present tense, they suggest ongoing timeless truths that pertain to all speakers.

The questions in the text all ask the reader about the extent of his/ her knowledge, making it appear that the reader has a particular need of the so-called 'facts' being offered.

Some of the grammatical structures suggest spoken language rather than written: for example, the sentences that begin with 'or' and 'that'; the last two sentences, both of which show an ellipsis of thought that often characterises speech. This, coupled with the semantic choices helps to establish closeness with the implied reader, who is being cajoled into a point of view by a 'knowledgeable friend'.

There is a shift in terms of address, moving from an implied general reader of either sex (with 'you') to an implied male reader ('would it help, gentlemen . . . ?). The text then finally addresses the part of the audience who are thought to pay the phone bill.

Cohesive ties within the text appear to establish the 'argument' by a system of reference: for example, the 'men' who are ungenerous talkers in the first section are contrasted with 'other men' in the second part of the argument. These 'other men' are not the men who are typically the partners of the women mentioned, but are exemplified initially by two writers who appreciated talk. In the face of such artistic figures, whom male readers might find it difficult to identify with, Winston Churchill provides a reassuringly macho figure. Finally, we are asked to focus, not on 'other men' but on 'some men' – those unpleasant individuals who complain at the size of the phone bill run up by their female partners.

'It', 'that' and 'this' are also used as cohesive ties, and are usefully unspecific for texts which do not want the logic of their arguments scrutinised: the reader is encouraged to make links and therefore help construct the argument. For example: 'that's a man's call'; 'this difference between the sexes'; 'some men have a way of making women feel guilty about it'.

The piece as a whole imitates an academic, discursive text where a point of view is put forward and supported. Quotation is used within discursive writing of this type; here, we are offered two literary figures (one unnamed) and a famous statesman who are used to endorse the idea that, as the BT slogan asserts, 'It's good to talk'. While imitating a piece of discursive writing, this text departs from this genre in a number of important ways: the image used interacts with the verbal text, to give veracity to apparently self-evident assertions about male and female talk; the layout allows for a looser organisation than the usual thematically arranged paragraphs, making the text appear more relaxed, and making it possible for some statements to stand alone, accruing a dramatic timing more usually associated with spoken delivery in speeches; style choices of vocabulary and grammar work together to create a spoken voice for the implied writer/speaker to deliver the 'argument' to the implied reader/listener, who turns out to be male. The assumption is that men pay the bill; so it is in the interest of BT to encourage men to do more talking, as well as to 'allow' their female companions to carry on talking themselves. In the end, arguing that women are good at talking turns out to be neither the subject of an academic enquiry, nor any compliment to women; instead, female talk is seen as exploitable, like any other form of consumer behaviour.

Extension

1   *Represented talk:* Collect as many representations as you can find of male and female talk – for example, in literary texts, adverts, TV programmes – and analyse whether the sexes are seen as talking in different ways.

2   *Real talk:* Compare the way men and women (or boys and girls) conduct single-sex conversations in a particular context – e.g. on the phone, at the hairdresser's, playing a game, solving a problem, running a business meeting. If you want to take this further, you could then go on to compare your findings with what happens in an equivalent mixed-sex context – e.g. girls working together on a computer, compared with boys and girls engaged in the same activity.

THE REPRESENTATION OF REGION, SOCIAL CLASS AND ETHNICITY

It should be clear from Unit 1, 'Signs and Sounds', that speech and writing are very different systems, and that it is very difficult to represent spoken language on the page by using a conventional written alphabet. However, writers of literature often try to do just that, in order to construct the idea of a character from a certain region, social class or ethnic group.

305

Activity

Read through Text: *Silas Marner* (1861), which is from the novel by George Eliot.

It features a confrontation between an upper-class landowner, Godfrey Cass, and a weaver, Silas Marner, who lives on his estate. Many years previously, Silas Marner had found an abandoned baby, and had brought up the child, Eppie, as his own daughter. The baby was illegitimate – fathered by Godfrey Cass as a result of an affair with a local servant girl, who died from illness and poverty as a result of Godfrey's abandonment. Now that Godfrey and his wife are unable to have any children of their own, Godfrey has decided to come and claim his child, now a teenager.

How does the writer convey the spoken language of Silas Marner and Godfrey Cass? Think particularly about the following:

◎   How are their social class differences marked in the language they use?
◎   What region do you think the book is set in?
◎   How do the spoken language features help create the tension in the dialogue, and establish a point of view for the reader?

Text: *Silas Marner*

'But I've a claim on you, Eppie - the strongest of all claims. It's my duty, Marner, to own Eppie as my child, and provide for her. She's my own child: her mother was my wife. I've a natural claim on her that must stand before every other.'

Eppie had given a violent start, and turned quite pale. Silas, on the contrary, who had been relieved, by Eppie's answer, from the dread lest his mind should be in opposition to hers, felt the spirit of resistance in him set free, not without a touch of parental fierceness. 'Then, sir,' he answered, with an accent of bitterness that had been silent in him since the memorable day when his youthful hope had perished - 'then, sir, why didn't you say so sixteen year ago, and claim her before I'd come to love her, i'stead o' coming to take her from me now, when you might as well take the heart out o' my body? God gave her to me because you turned your back upon her, and He looks upon her as mine: you've no right to her! When a man turns a blessing from his door, it falls to them as take it in.'

'I know that, Marner. I was wrong. I've repented of my conduct in that matter,' said Godfrey, who could not help feeling the edge of Silas's words.

'I'm glad to hear it, sir,' said Marner, with gathering excitement; 'but repentance doesn't alter what's been going on for sixteen years. Your coming now and saying . . . "I'm her father . . ." doesn't alter the feelings inside us. It's me she's been calling her father ever since she could say the word.'

'But I think you might look at the thing more reasonably, Marner,' said Godfrey, unexpectedly awed by the weaver's direct truth-speaking. 'It isn't as if she was to be taken quite away from you, so that you'd never see her again. She'll be very near you, and come to see you very often. She'll feel just the same towards you.'

'Just the same?' said Marner, more bitterly than ever. 'How'll she feel just the same for me as she does now, when we eat o' the same bit, and drink o' the same cup, and think o' the same things from one day's end to another? Just the same? that's idle talk. You'd cut us i' two.'

Commentary

Godfrey Cass speaks in Standard English, while Silas Marner uses regional forms of language. While it is never explicitly stated where the book is set, the physical descriptions suggest the newly industrialised cities of the north Midlands. There is nothing in the actual language of the characters that tells us this – the alterations of the spellings and the various pieces of vocabulary and grammar could represent a number of different regional accents and dialects:

> i'stead o', out o', o' the, i' two
> sixteen *year,* the same *bit,* it falls to *them as* take it in.

What the reader does when reading this type of material is to create an appropriate voice in their own head, to fit the region where the book is set and the social class of the respective characters. For Godfrey Cass, this would probably involve the reader creating an RP-sounding voice, since this is associated with middle- and upper-class speakers. Beyond specifically regional features of language, George Eliot has also chosen a particular style of speaking for the two characters: where Silas's language involves many expressions which describe or connote emotion

307

– for example, 'turned your back on her', 'take the heart out o' my body', 'cut us i' two', 'blessing', 'love' – Godfrey Cass's language relates more to ownership and responsibility – 'claim', 'own', 'duty' – and is more formal and politely euphemistic: 'I've repented of my conduct in that matter'. As a result, where Silas Marner is constructed as a warm, straightforward man, Godfrey Cass appears very cold and shifty. These ideas very much support our stereotypes of regional speakers as warm-hearted, while RP-speaking, Standard English users are often constructed as cold and untrustworthy, despite the status accorded them as speakers of a prestige language variety.

The reader is clearly expected to be on Silas Marner's side – there's nothing quite like the honest, working-class hero standing up to the forces of capitalist hypocrisy to raise a cheer from modern readers. The plot therefore positions the reader to a large extent; but the dramatic tension in this particular scene owes much to the language spoken by the characters, given even more force by George Eliot's 'stage directions'.

Extension

George Eliot was doing something rather revolutionary in presenting a working-class figure who uses regional language as the hero of her book. Traditionally, such figures were only allowed to feature as comic characters, faithful servants or villains, and their dialect acted as a signal to the reader to call up expectations of comedy, martyrdom or dirty deeds. They weren't supposed to be 'real people'.

Collect some examples of regionally accented characters from a specific type of text – for example, novels, TV drama, advertisements, comics (e.g. *Viz*). How far are the characters being presented as stereotypes, and how far as complex people with individual characteristics? If they are stereotyped, are certain accents and dialects associated with particular traits? What aspects of regional language are used to convey the idea of regional speech?

If the representation of working-class, regionally accented speakers has been traditionally as figures of comedy, servitude or crime, then that is doubly true of black characters who use a language variety such as Afro-Caribbean Creole (also called Patwa). This type of language has often been presented as a form of 'broken English', with the inference that the speaker is ill-educated and unintelligent, in need of instruction from, and the protection of, figures from white culture: generations of young readers until the 1960s, for example, grew up on comics which conveyed this message, while 'classics' such as *Robinson Crusoe* encode the same ideas.

Read through Text: *Robinson Crusoe* (1719), from the novel by Daniel Defoe.

Before the start of the passage, the narrator has shown Man Friday a boat he built some years previously, in an attempt to escape from the island. The passage then portrays a conversation between Robinson Crusoe and Man Friday, about the possibility of building another boat and going to Man Friday's own country.

What picture is given of Man Friday, and how does his language contribute to that picture?

Text: *Robinson Crusoe*

Upon the whole, I was by this time so fixed upon my design of going over with him to the continent, that I told him we would go and make one as big as that, and he should go home in it. He answered not one word, but looked very grave and sad. I asked him what was the matter with him? He asked me again, Why you angry mad with Friday? What me done? I asked him what he meant? I told him I was not angry with him at all. No angry? says he, repeating the words several times; Why send Friday home away to my nation? - Why, says I, Friday, did you not say you wished you were there? - Yes, yes, says he, wish be both there; no wish Friday there, no master there. In a word, he would not think of going there without me. I go there, Friday! says I; what shall I do there? he returned very quick upon me at this: You do great deal much good, says he; you teach wild mans be good, sober, tame mans; you tell them know God, pray God, and live new life. - Alas! Friday, says I, thou knowest not what thou sayest; I am but an ignorant man myself. - Yes, yes, says he, you teachee me good, you teachee them good. - No, no, Friday, says I, you shall go without me, leave me here to live by myself, as I did before. He looked confused again at that word; and running to one of the hatchets which he used to wear, he takes it up hastily, and gives it to me. What must I do with this? says I to him. You take kill

309

Friday, says he. What must I kill you for? said I again. He returns very quick, What you send Friday away for? Take kill Friday, no send Friday away. This he spoke so earnestly, that I saw tears stand in his eyes; in a word, I so plainly discovered the utmost affection in him to me, and a firm resolution in him, that I told him then, and often after, that I would never send him away from me, if he was willing to stay with me.

Commentary

The book is set in the South Seas, so in reality, Man Friday would have spoken a Polynesian language. However, there is no sense of this, as the focus of the narrative is all on Robinson Crusoe's experiences and perceptions rather than on Man Friday's life – the latter even has no name of his own, only the name given to him by his white 'master' (who first encountered him on a Friday). The book assumes the rightness of the white character imposing all the values of white society, including language, on the black character: Man Friday is expected to learn English but there is no suggestion of Robinson Crusoe learning any Polynesian; Man Friday is 'converted' to Christianity, rather than Crusoe learning any interesting new religious beliefs. In the end, the novel reflects the eighteenth-century culture which gave rise to it.

The point of this passage is to demonstrate two main ideas: the good character of Robinson Crusoe, and the devotion of Man Friday to his white companion. Crusoe's character is depicted as modest and humble via his quizzing of Man Friday, protesting as he does so that he is an unworthy moral leader; in turn, this provokes Man Friday to declare his admiration. Crusoe is therefore seen as morally superior.

Man Friday's language is not based on any real code, but is rather a constructed form which suggests a childlike speaker; at certain points, the fact that the narrator feels compelled to 'translate' Man Friday's expressions leads the reader to conclude that the speaker is unclear. This brings the narrator closer to the reader and moves Man Friday further away, encoding him as 'foreign' and 'alien'. Impressions of language therefore support the power relations within the story.

So far, the focus has been on the representation of the language of non-white speakers from a white point of view. The material that follows will shift its focus to the perspective of black speakers and writers.

Read through Text: 'Home Again', which is an extract from a story written by a Patwa speaker; the story is about being in the Caribbean and contrasting it with life in England. Patwa as a form of language is actually a very complex code, often involving the combination of European vocabulary with African grammatical structures.

Because Patwa is essentially a spoken variety, there is no standardised spelling system, so people who want to construct a written text have to devise a system that will be accessible. The spelling here was devised by the Afro-Caribbean Language Centre in Manchester, where this writer was part of a working group. (Note: the spelling of 'Patwa' is a recent change from the former 'Patois', which was thought to suggest a Eurocentric view.)

Compare the Patwa and Standard English versions, and try to trace some of the rules of Patwa.

Text: 'Home Again'

Jamaican Patwa or Creole	*Standard English*
Winter deh an Inglan but mi deh-ya inna de sun all day. And when mi memba how Oonu a shiver inna de col mi jus sip mi coconut waata an laugh.	It is winter in England but I am here in the sun all day. And when I remember how you are all shivering in the cold I just sip my coconut water and laugh.
Mi av one school frien a live inna de country still. So mi seh to miself, 'Mi a go look fi she.'	I have one school friend who is still living in the country. So I said to myself, 'I am going to visit her.'

Mi tek de bus fram toun.	I took the bus from town.
De bus pack wid people.	The bus was packed with people.
It so hat me staat fi sweat.	It was so hot I started to sweat.
At laas mi reach fi-mi stap.	At last I reached my stop.
Mi frien a wait deh.	My friend was waiting there.
She come meet mi.	She had come to meet me.
In no time wi reach de house.	In no time we reached the house.
It big an cool an nice.	It was big and cool and nice.
Mi ol frien-dem	My old friends were
glad fi see mi.	glad to see me.

Commentary

Verbs

The past tense is not marked in the verb itself, but is signalled via adverbs or simply the context of use; progressive forms ('was waiting', 'am going') are marked with 'a' in front of the verb; the verb 'to be' is often omitted altogether.

Personal pronouns

mi	wi
yu	oonu
she	dem
im	

(Possessive pronouns: add 'fi': fi-mi, fi-yu, etc.)

Prepositions

'Fi' is also used to mean both 'to' and 'for'.

Nouns

Plurals can be made by adding 'dem' – e.g. frien-dem.

While vocabulary is often similar to English, the pronunciation of words can make them sound unfamiliar when spoken. Important aspects of accent include the use of /t/ for /θ/ and /d/ for /ð/, and /ɑː/ for /ɔː/ and /ɒ/ ('water', 'because', 'stop').

Activity

Now translate the Standard English sentences below into Patwa. You will need some additional vocabulary, as follows:

picni-dem	children
gi	give
likkle	little
caaz	because
cyar	car
fambli	family
mus	must
dat time	in those days
spen time	stay (with)
maaga	thin
nyam	eat
wile	while

> 1   You (plural) came with her to see the children in those days.
> 2   His family gave us their car while we stayed with them.
> 3   He must eat, because he is so thin and little!
> (Answers on p. 315)

Activity

Rather than offering a white perspective on black experience, Text: 'The Fat Black Woman Goes Shopping' offers a black perspective on white society. Read the poem through, and discuss how the writer uses aspects of Patwa to construct the voice of the central character.

Text: 'The Fat Black Woman Goes Shopping'

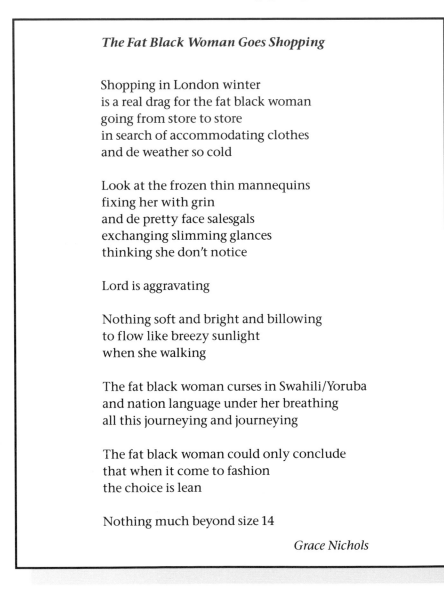

The Fat Black Woman Goes Shopping

Shopping in London winter
is a real drag for the fat black woman
going from store to store
in search of accommodating clothes
and de weather so cold

Look at the frozen thin mannequins
fixing her with grin
and de pretty face salesgals
exchanging slimming glances
thinking she don't notice

Lord is aggravating

Nothing soft and bright and billowing
to flow like breezy sunlight
when she walking

The fat black woman curses in Swahili/Yoruba
and nation language under her breathing
all this journeying and journeying

The fat black woman could only conclude
that when it come to fashion
the choice is lean

Nothing much beyond size 14

Grace Nichols

Commentary

Features of Patwa include the following:

◎ omission of articles – e.g. 'fixing her with grin'
◎ use of base form of the verb instead of the inflected form – e.g. 'when it *come* to fashion'
◎ omission of the verb to be – e.g. 'when she walking'.

The syntax is also contracted, so we find 'pretty face salesgals' and 'Lord is aggravating'.

Pronunciation is suggested in the use of 'de' for 'the', and in the spelling of 'sales*gals*'.

What the Patwa helps to do is to present us with the point of view of the fat black woman and, in the process, to construct a positive picture of her. Her natural environment of the warm Caribbean is suggested in 'breezy sunlight', and this is contrasted favourably with the cold London winter. Another favourable contrast is made between the 'frozen thin mannequins' and the fat, soft and warm black woman. The writer paints a seductive, sensuous picture of the kind of clothes the woman seeks but can't find: 'soft and bright and billowing'. There is a gentle humour in this poem, expressed in the way the woman tolerates the salesgirls and curses with a weary resignation that 'the choice is lean' in their meagre fashion world.

Nichols has created a sense of authentic talk, and this is crucial to the way the fat black woman seems real compared with her lifeless and colourless surroundings. The poem turns the idea of 'fat is bad, thin is beautiful' on its head, to present a positive view of size and gender as well as ethnicity.

Answer to activity

Translation of Standard English into Patwa (p. 313)

1   Oonu come wid she fi-see de picni-dem.
2   Im fambli gi wi fi-dem cyar wile we spen time wid dem.
3   Im mus nyam, caaz im so maaga an likkle!

index of terms

This is a form of combined glossary and index. Listed below are some of the main key terms used in the book, together with brief definitions for purposes of reference. The page references will normally take you to the first use of the term in the book where it will be shown in **bold**. In some cases, however, understanding of the term can be helped by exploring its uses in more than one place in the book and accordingly more than one page reference is given.

Not all terms used are glossed here as a limited number of terms in the book receive extensive discussion and explanation in particular units. This is also by no means a full index of linguistic terms so it should be used in conjunction with other books, dictionaries and encyclopaedias which are indicated in the Further Reading section.

clause 142

A structural unit which is part of a **sentence** either as a main clause which can stand alone and be equivalent to a sentence or as a subordinate or dependent clause. For example, 'The owner, who lives abroad, has written to all the neighbours' consists of a main clause 'The owner ... has written to all the neighbours' and a subordinate clause 'who lives abroad'.

cohesion 171, 188

The patterns of language created within a text, mainly within and across sentence boundaries and which collectively make up the organisation of larger units of the text such as paragraphs. Cohesion can be both lexical and grammatical. Lexical cohesion is established by means of chains of words of related meaning linking across sentences; grammatical cohesion is established mainly by grammatical words such as 'the', 'this', 'it' and so on.

conjunction 215

A general term which describes words which link sentences and clauses together, indicating temporal, spatial,logical and causal relationships. Words such as 'and', 'but', 'therefore', 'because' are conjunctions.

connotation 3, 99

The connotations of a word are the associations it creates. For example, the connotations of December, mainly within British and North American culture, would be of 'cold', 'dark nights' and 'Christmas parties'. Connotations are often either individual or cultural.

co-operative principle 279

Refers to the way in which most conversations are conducted in a coherent manner with participants acting towards one another as efficiently and collaboratively as possible.

deictic 152, 200

Deictics are words which point backwards, forwards and extratextually and which serve to situate a speaker or writer in relation what what is said. For example, in the sentence 'I'm going to get some wine from that shop over there' the main deictic words are 'that' and 'there'.

denotation 99

The literal, dictionary definition of a word.

derivational morpheme (see **morpheme**)

discourse 165, 297

A term used in linguistics to describe the rules and conventions underlying the use of language in extended stretches of text, spoken and written. (Such an academic study is referred to as 'discourse analysis'.) The term is also used as a convenient general term to refer to language in action and the patterns which characterise particular types of language in action; for example, the 'discourse' of advertising.

ellipsis 210

Ellipsis refers to the omission of part of a structure. It is normally used for reasons of economy and, in spoken discourse, can create a sense of informality. For example, in the sentence 'She went to the party and danced all night' the pronoun 'she' is ellipted from the second clause; in the dialogue

'You going to the party?'
'Might be'

the verb 'Are' and the pronoun 'I', respectively, are omitted with the ellipsis here creating a casual and informal tone.

endophoric/exophoric (see **reference**)

false start 284
A move, normally in conversation, in which a speaker starts to say something and then changes direction.

finite verb 142–3
A finite verb or verb phrase can occur on its own in a clause or sentence and is normally marked for tense and mood. A non-finite verb only occurs in a subordinate clause and normally lacks explicit reference to time or person. For example, 'Walking through the town, we came across an old pub' contains a non-finite verb 'walking' and a finite verb 'came'.

filler 254
Fillers are items which do not carry conventional meaning but which are inserted, usually in spoken discourse, to allow time to think, to create a pause and so on. Examples are items such as: 'erm', 'er', 'ah'.

foregrounding 174
Language is foregrounded when a particular form or structure is highlighted or draws attention

to itself in some way, for example by being placed in an unusual order or by being repeated several times.

formality 113, 179ff.
A level of language use which refers to a particular social context or situation. Formal language is used in social situations which are distant and more impersonal; informal language is used in social situations which are intimate and casual.

free morpheme (see **morpheme**)

genre 29
Another word for text-type. Examples of a genre are: narrative; report; argument.

generic 196
A term which is used to refer to a particular example of a general class or category. For example, the sentence 'bats can see in the dark' contains a generic noun 'bats'. Some generic nouns such as 'man' to refer to both men and women are sexist.

grapheme 11
The smallest unit in written language which is normally defined with reference to another unit with which it contrasts. For example, the letter 'a' can be upper-case or lower-case and can be pronounced differently in different words; for example, $a$dd/$a$le.

grammatical ambiguity (see **ambiguity**)

grammatical cohesion (see **cohesion**)

319

hedge(s) 284

Hedges are words and phrases which soften or weaken the force with which something is said. Examples of hedges are: 'kind of', 'sort of', 'by any chance', 'as it were', 'admittedly'.

homophone 59, 81

Words which have the same pronunciation but which differ in meaning; for example, 'threw/through'.

hypernym (see **hyponym**)

hyponym 101

Hyponymy is the relationship which exists between specific and general words. For example, 'rose' is a hyponym of the more general word 'flower'. General words such as 'flower', 'animal' and 'vehicle' are also sometimes called hypernyms.

iconic 3

A direct representation of something (contrast **symbolic**).

idiom 97

A sequence of words which functions as a single unit of meaning and which cannot normally be interpreted literally. For example, 'She is over the moon' contains the idiom 'over the moon' meaning 'happy'.

inflectional morpheme (see **morpheme**)

initialism 19

A feature of words in which whole words are abbreviated to initial letters. For example, 'incl.' (for 'including').

intertextuality 233

The way in which one text echoes or refers to another text. For example, an advertisement which stated 'To be in Florida in winter or not to be in Florida in winter' would contain an intertextual reference to a key speech in Shakespeare's *Hamlet*. (See also Unit 1.)

intransitive (see **transitive**)

lexeme 77

Lexeme or 'lexical item' is sometimes used in order to avoid difficulties of referring to 'words'. For example, the abstract 'lexeme' 'walk' underlies all the separate instances 'walks', 'walked', 'walking'; the **idiom** 'smell a rat' is also a lexeme in so far as it functions in the manner of a single word.

lexical ambiguity (see **ambiguity**)

lexical cohesion (see **cohesion**)

loan words 110

Words which are borrowed into one language from another. For example, 'siesta' from Spanish and 'sputnik' from Russian.

metaphor 72, 82ff.

A word or phrase which establishes a comparison or analogy between one object or idea and another. For example, 'I *demolished* his argument' contains a comparison between argument and war, also underlining the idea that arguments can be constructed like buildings.

modal verb 146

Modality is normally conveyed by means of modal verbs (also known as modal auxiliary verbs

contrasts with another closely related speech sound. For example, *d*in and *b*in are closely related in articulation but are distinguished by the contrasting phonemes *b* and *d*.

politeness principle 278
A principle of conversation in which speakers indicate respect for each other by adopting appropriate strategies to maintain polite and smooth-running interaction.

polysemy 78
A semantic process by which certain words have several meanings. For example, the word 'lap' is polysemous.

pronoun 135
Words which normally substitute for nouns and noun phrases. For example, 'I', 'you', 'it', 'they', 'their', 'some', 'any', 'this', 'myself'.

reference 189
The act of referring to something (often called a referent). Many words also allow reference to each other and establish links and patterns across a text. Different types of reference include: 'anaphoric' and 'cataphoric' reference. Anaphoric reference points backwards; for example, the grammatical word 'he' in the following sentence 'I saw the man. *He* was wearing . . .'; 'cataphoric reference' points forward; for example the word 'here' in the following sentence '*Here* is the nine o' clock news'. Reference within a text is generally referred to as 'endophoric' reference; reference to the world outside

the text is generally referred to 'exophoric' reference.

reinforcer 284
A 'word' such as 'yeah', 'mm' which can serve as a support to one speaker from another to continue in what they are saying.

reverse rhyme 62
The repetition of initial rather then final syllables; for example, *st*ar, *st*one.

semantic change 117
A change in a word's meaning over time. For example, in the English of Jane Austen's time the word 'injury' means emotional upset.

semantic field 88, 173–4
A group of words which are related in meaning, normally as a result of being connected with a particular context of use. For example, 'chop', 'sprinkle', 'salt', 'dice', 'wash', 'simmer', 'boil', 'herbs' are all connected with the semantic field of cookery.

semiotic 2
Human communication by means of signs and symbols.

sentence 143
A difficult term to define because the structure of sentences differs according to whether spoken or written language is used. Traditionally, a sentence has a subject and a main **verb**, though in literary texts a sentence can be a single word; in spoken English, however, structures such as 'over here', 'if you like', 'perhaps' can constitute a sentence. (See **clause**.)

speech act 250

A speech act refers to what is done when something is said (for example, warning, threatening, promising, requesting). 'I declare the meeting open' in this sense does what it says.

speech event 247

A use of language in a social context in which the speakers normally follow a set of agreed rules and conventions. For example, telling a joke, recounting a story, purchasing stamps in a post office are all speech events.

substitution 210

Substitution allows a speaker or writer to substitute one word or phrase for another in a text. 'Do' is normally used to substitute for verbs or verb phrases, whereas words like 'so' can be used to substitute for whole clauses. For example:

'Are you going to the party? I would do but I'm a bit tired.'

symbolic 3

Something is symbolic when it suggests associations rather than refers to something directly.

synonymy 78

Synonyms are words which have equivalent meanings. For example, 'cheap' and 'inexpensive'.

tag question 284

Tags are strings of words which are normally added to a declarative statement and which turn the statement into a question. For example, 'It's cold, *isn't it?*'

tense 133, 221

Tense is a very important grammatical category and is mainly associated with the **verb** in a sentence. English has two primary tenses, the present tense and the past tense. (The future is normally referred to by means of **modal** verbs such as 'will' and by adverbs or adverbial phrases such as 'tomorrow' or 'on Monday'.)

theme 225

The theme of a clause is normally the first complete word unit in a sentence, for example:

Mr Kipling makes exceedingly good cakes.

has the unit 'Mr Kipling' as its theme. If the structure of the sentence is altered to form:

Exceedingly good cakes Mr Kipling makes.

then the phrase 'Exceedingly good cakes' becomes the theme; indeed, in some definitions of theme the word 'exceedingly' alone is the theme and is marked because it does not normally appear in this position and is put to the front of the sentence for purposes of emphasis. The theme of the clause signals what the clause is going to be about, marking out a topic for our attention. The grammatical subject of the sentence is normally also the theme, as in '*Mr Kipling* makes exceedingly good cakes'.

transitive 162

Whether a verb is **transitive** or **intransitive** can be a significant feature of the meaning of a clause. A transitive

323

verb has an object which is in some way affected by the 'action' performed by the verb. For example:

The boy hit the ball.

contains a verb 'hit' in a transitive form; in the following sentence, however, the verbs 'struck' and 'elapsed' do not affect an object and are therefore intransitive:

The clock struck. An hour had elapsed.

Several verbs may be used transitively or intransitively (e.g., 'grow', 'call', 'write', 'read').

A verb is a major category of grammar. Verbs can be either main verbs or auxiliary verbs. For example in the sentence:

I do intend to go to the match.

'intend' is a main verb and 'do' is an auxiliary verb. Auxiliary verbs cannot normally stand on their own, whereas main verbs can (e.g., I intend to go to the match). Verbs also have other forms. Here, for example, 'to go' is an infinitive form of the verb 'go'.

Verbs can be inflected to show tense. For example:

She works hard (present tense).
She worked hard (past tense).

– and can also form present and past participles: working (present participle); worked (past participle). Participles can be used as modifiers:

The working day.
A worked example.

Voice is a grammatical feature which indicates whether a subject in a sentence is the agent of an action or is affected by the action. Voice can normally be either active or passive. For example:

The dog bit the man (active).
The man was bitten by the dog (passive).

In the passive sentence it is of course still the dog which bites and in this sense the dog remains the underlying subject of the sentence; but the man is given greater emphasis in the passive sentence. The passive voice also allows the 'by-phrase' to be omitted, thus deleting any reference to an agent. For example:

The man was bitten.

Such structures allow the responsibility for an action or event to be concealed. In a text the choice of active or passive forms is often connected to questions of **theme** and **cohesion.**

index of main texts

Academic writing

235

Advertisements

breakfast cereals   203-4
BT (British Telecom)   231, 300-1
BR (British Rail)   243-4
Christian Aid   150
Cognac (Hine)   35
Daewoo cars   234
estate agents   19
Gap (chain store)   220
Hewlett Packard printers   95
Leatherland   232
Ovaltine   205
personal stereos   24
Raleigh bikes   236
Reebok trainers   140
Subaru cars   213
Sting CT (herbicide)   176
Tampax sanitary towels   32-3
VW cars   178

Cartoons (and graphic novel)

46-7, 85-6, 299

Children's writing

12-15, 18, 21-2, 191, 227

Informational texts/ leaflets/appeals

Amnesty International   102
development plan (planning
      application)   186
Friends of the Earth   156
High Peak Borough Council   216
legal discourse (Town and Country
      Planning Act)   182
Milk Message (CWS)   136
Oxfam   145
public statement (development
      plans)   186
Severn Trent Water   147

Jokes

163-4, 293

Literary texts

Atwood, 'This is a Photograph of
      Me'   151-2
Beowulf (and translations)   111-12
Browning, 'Meeting at Night'   52
Carroll, *Alice in Wonderland*   192
Coleridge, 'Kubla Khan'   63
Defoe, *Robinson Crusoe*   309-10
Dickens, *Bleak House*   141-2
Eliot, *Silas Marner*   306-7
Forsyth, *The Shepherd*   227-8
Godber, *Lucky Sods*   285
Grafton, *K is for Killer*   222-3
Henley, 'Ballade Made in the Hot
      Weather'   64-5
Herbert, 'Easter Wings'   7

Menus

Newspapers and journalism

Oral narratives and dialogues

Signs, slogans and logos

Speeches and political rhetorics

further reading

Unit 1

Knowles, G. (1987) *Patterns of Spoken English* (Longman, Harlow).

Unit 2

Aitchison, J. (1994) *Words in the Mind,* 2nd edn (Blackwell,Oxford).

Carter, R. (1987) *Vocabulary: Applied linguistic perspectives* (Routledge, London).

McCarthy, M. (1990) *Vocabulary* (Oxford University Press, Oxford).

Unit 3

Carter, R. and Nash, W. (1990) *Seeing Through Language: A guide to styles of English writing* (Blackwell, Oxford).

Woods, E. (1994) *Introducing Grammar* (Penguin, Harmondsworth).

Unit 4

Bex, T. (1996) *Variety in Written English* (Routledge, London).

Nunan, D. (1994) *Introducing Discourse Analysis* (Penguin, Harmondsworth).

Unit 5

Carter, R. and McCarthy, M. (1997) *Exploring Spoken English* (Cambridge University Press, Cambridge).

Cook, G. (1990) *Discourse* (Oxford University Press, Oxford).

General books

Carter, R. (1995) *Keywords in Language and Literacy* (Routledge, London).

Crystal, D. (1991) *A Dictionary of Linguistics and Phonetics,* 3rd edn (Blackwell, Oxford).

Crystal, D. (1995) *The Encyclopaedia of the English Language* (Cambridge University Press, Cambridge).

Cook, G. (1992) *The Discourse of Advertising* (Routledge, London).

Durant, A. and Fabb, N. (1990) *Literary Studies in Action* (Routledge, London).

Freeborn, D., French, P. and Langford, D. (1993) *Varieties of English,* 2nd edn (Macmillan, Basingstoke).

Goddard, A. (1993) *Researching Language* (Framework Press, Manchester).

Hughes, R. (1996) *English in Speech and Writing* (Routledge, London).

Mills, S. (1995) *Feminist Stylistics* (Routledge, London).

Montgomery, M. (1995) *An Introduction to Language and Society,* 2nd edn (Routledge, London).

Short, M. (1996) *Exploring the Language of Poetry, Prose and Drama* (Longman, Harlow).

Simpson, P (1996) *Language through Literature* (Routledge, London).

Wright, T. (1994) *Investigating English* (Edward Arnold, London).

Widdowson, H.G. (1992) *Practical Stylistics* (Oxford University Press, Oxford).

Books for teachers

Bain, R., Taylor, M. and Fitzgerald, M. (1992) *Looking into Language* (Hodder & Stoughton, Sevenoaks).

Carter, R. (1997) *Investigating English Discourse: Language, literacy, literature* (Routledge, London).

Carter, R. and McRae, J. (eds) (1996) *Literature, Language and the Learner: Creative classroom practice* (Longman, Harlow).

Fairclough, N. (1988) *Language and Power* (Longman, Harlow).

McCarthy, M. (1991) *Discourse Analysis for Language Teachers* (Cambridge University Press, Cambridge).

McCarthy, M and Carter, R (1994) *Language as Discourse: Perspectives for Language Teaching* (Longman, Harlow).

McRae, J. (1991) *Literature with a Small 'l'* (Macmillan, Basingstoke).

Simpson, P. (1993) *Language, Ideology and Point of View* (Routledge, London).

Van Lier, L. (1995) *Introducing Language Awareness* (Penguin, Harmondsworth).

references

Burns, A., Joyce, H. and Gollin, S. (1995) *'I see what you mean'. Using Spoken Discourse in the Classroom: A handbook for teachers* (NCELTR, Macquarie University, Sydney).

Crystal, D. (1995) *The Cambridge Encyclopedia of the English Language* (Cambridge University Press, Cambridge).

Giddens, A. (1993) *Sociology* (Polity Press,Oxford).

Grice, P. (1975) 'Logic and conversation', in Cole, P and Morgan, J. (eds) *Syntax and Semantics, vol. 3: Speech acts* (Academic Press, New York), pp. 41-58.

Halliday, M.A.K. and Hasan, R. (1976) *Cohesion in English* (Longman,Harlow).

Kramer, C. (1977) 'Perceptions of male and female speech', *Language and Speech*, 20: 151-61.

Lakoff, R. (1975) *Language and Woman's Place* (Harper & Row, New York).

Labov, W. (1972) 'The transformation of experience in narrative syntax', in Labov, W. *Language in the Inner City* (University of Philadelphia Press, Philadelphia, PA), pp. 354-96.

Nunan, D. and Lockwood, J. (1991) *The Australian English Course* (Cambridge University Press, Cambridge/Sydney).

Sadker, M. and Sadker, D. (1985) 'Sexism in the schoolroom of the 80's', *Psychology Today* March: 54-7.

Searle, J. (1969) *Speech Acts: An essay in the philosophy of language* (Cambridge University Press, Cambridge).

Tannen, D. (1992) *You Just Don't Understand: Men and women in conversation* (Virago,London).

Wolfson, N. (1982) *CHP: The conversational historic present in American English narrative* (Foris Publications, Cinnaminson, NJ).